NARROWING TH

NARROWING THE FIELD

USING THE DOSAGE METHOD TO WIN AT NATIONAL HUNT RACING

2009 / 2010

BEN AITKEN

HIGH STAKES

First published in 2009 by High Stakes Publishing,
21 Great Ormond Street, London WC1N 3JB

www.highstakespublishing.com

A CIP catalogue record for this book is available from the British Library.

ISBN 978-1-84344-058-1

2 4 6 8 10 9 7 5 3 1

Printed and bound in Great Britain by Cpod, Trowbridge, Wiltshire

Love and thanks to my wife Lyndsey.
Without her dedicated love and support this book
would never have seen the light of day.

Forth and Suzy, your *support* has also been greatly appreciated!

For further analysis please visit:
www.narrowingthefield.blogspot.com

CONTENTS

Introduction

It is my belief that some thoroughbred race horses are just not built to win certain races. No matter what else may be in their favour, if they do not have the genetic make-up required for the rigours of a particular race they will struggle to succeed at the top level.

How did I reach this conclusion? Well..........

Being a horse racing fan and student of form for a number of years I, like most punters out there, was constantly searching for different angles to study races and improve my betting. I dedicated a vast quantity of my time to trawling through numerous racing books full of trends and statistics for British National Hunt racing, looking for an edge or an alternative angle. Although most of these books had decent principles and theories I also found that while every form of analysis had its strengths they also had their limitations. I still wanted something more, something different. It was whilst reading one of these racing books that I came across the term Dosage. The author did not go into any great detail on the subject but my antenna had started twitching. Was this the angle I had been looking for? Always keen to expand my racing knowledge, I started digging. The deeper I delved the more excited I became about the term Dosage. This was a method that relied upon breeding and blood lines, the fundamental pillar that horse racing is founded upon.

Dosage had been around since the early 20th century when French researcher Lt. Col. J. J. Vullier published a study on the subject. Lt. Col. J. J. Vullier's findings were subsequently modified by an Italian breeding expert, Dr Franco Varola, but it was not until the early 1980's that dosage in its current form was developed. This improved version of Dosage was conceived by American scientist Steven A. Roman, Ph.D. His new approach to Dosage was supported by solid statistical data and quickly caught on in

America. Steven A. Roman's analysis was primarily centred on the Kentucky Derby and later the other major stakes races in America.

After a lengthy study of Dosage, whereby the fundamentals of the theory were provided by Steven Roman's book; *Dosage: Pedigree and Performance*, I began asking myself some questions -

- Will Dosage ratings work when applied to British National Hunt Racing?
- Can you narrow down a field of National Hunt runners using Dosage ratings?
- Do horses within a certain Dosage range win certain races?

This book will provide the evidence that for the majority of races analysed the answer to these questions is yes.

This was the angle I was looking for. The Dosage ratings gave me an alternative angle with which to handicap a race, an edge that most punters were unfamiliar with.

This book offers you an in depth Dosage study of the last fifteen winners (where possible) of all the major British and Irish National Hunt races. It will inform you of the dosage range that a majority of winners fall within and indicate notable defeats suffered due to incorrect Dosage Profiles. Dosage demonstrates why War of Attrition won a Gold Cup but failed to even place in the previous years Arkle Chase and why Kasbah Bliss has failed on three occasions to win the World Hurdle. Put simply, they were not built to win those races; they did not have the correct genetic make up required.

I have always found that at the top level of racing, horses can be very evenly matched and even the smallest determining factor can have an influence on the outcome of a race. Dosage ratings can be this determining factor and has enabled me to separate horses that on the face of it looked equally matched. By applying the principles outlined in this book you too will be able to apply this alternative edge to your betting.

After reading the analysis set out in this book you should be able to study a field of runners and, based on the runner's dosage ratings, narrow the field to potential winners and horses that are likely to struggle under the race conditions. I personally use dosage as my starting point when handicapping a race then, once I have narrowed the field, I use more traditional forms of analysis such as going preference, trainer form and class form. I am confident the information offered up to you in this book will bring a new dimension to your betting approach and race analysis regardless of how you decided to use it.

Dosage Explained

What are Dosage ratings?

Dosage ratings are numerical figures which indicate the probable speed or stamina capabilities of a horse based on the appearance of influential sires in its bloodline. An influential sire has been determined not by its own achievements on the race track but the proven, consistent ability and success of its offspring. This is based on the theory that certain stallions can have a sustained significant influence on thoroughbred horses for a number of generations. Essentially, Dosage ratings are a horse's genetic make-up expressed in figures.

Dosage is expressed by three interrelated figures; the Dosage Profile, the Dosage Index and the Centre of Distribution, the latter two being the most important figures for analysis purposes. The Dosage Profile (DP) is a five numbered figure relating to specific categories which is the totals of all the points gained from influential sires. The Dosage Index (DI) is essentially the ratio of speed points to stamina points from the DP. The DI indicates a numerical figure which overall should give you an indication of whether a horse is genetically speed or stamina orientated. The Centre of Distribution (CD) is a figure between -2 and +2 which indicates the distance a horse could potentially be successful over. Overall these figures should enable you to calculate what a particular horse could achieve in a particular race.

What are Influential Sires?

A horse's Dosage rating comprises figures based upon where influential sires appear in its four generation pedigree. As briefly introduced, an influential sire is determined not by its own achievements but the proven, consistent ability and success of its offspring.

At this moment in time there are 210 influential sires listed by Dr Roman (main developer of the Dosage method), calculated using numerical analysis of their offspring's abilities. The sires on the list are referred to as Chefs-de-Race (Masters of the Breed).

Stallions that have had fleeting success with their progeny are not categorised as Chefs-de-Race. A sire has to have shown consistent success at the top levels over a number of progeny to be included on this list. For example, Montjeu has produced a number of Group 1 winners in recent years but to be potentially considered as a Chefs-de-Race in the future he is going to have to continue to produce Group 1 winners.

Chefs-de-Race Categories

All stallions on the Chefs-de-Race list are assigned to one or two of the following categories –

BRILLIANT – INTERMEDIATE – CLASSIC – SOLID – PROFESSIONAL

These represent Speed (Brilliant) through to Stamina (Professional).

A sire that has been placed in the Brilliant section is one that produces runners that shine at shorter distances. The appearance of this sire will improve the foal's Brilliant score.

A sire that has been placed in the Professional section is one that produces runners who should show their best form over the longer distances.

The following table shows example's of actual sires from the Chefs-de-Race list and the categories they have been assigned -

	Category	Chefs-de-Race
Speed	**BRILLIANT**	Peter Pan
↕	**INTERMEDIATE**	Indian Ridge
	CLASSIC	Roberto
	SOLID	Sea Bird II
Stamina	**PROFESSIONAL**	Ela-Mana-Mou

For the full list of current Chefs-de-Race stallions please see appendix A.

Depending in which generation of the horse's pedigree it appears, the stallion contributes a certain number of dosage points to its offspring.

- 1st generation (sire) = 16 points
- 2nd generation (grandsire) = 8 points
- 3rd generation (great-grandsire) = 4 points
- 4th generation (great-great grandsire) = 2 points

For example, Sadler's Wells in the 1st generation contributes more Dosage points than Sadler's Wells in the 2nd generation. This follows the long held theory that a sire's influence becomes reduced with each passing generation.

On occasions a stallion will be named in more than one category. Sadler's Wells is such a horse. His points have been distributed equally between Classic and Solid. For example, if he were to appear in a horse's pedigree in the 3rd generation (great-grand sire) he would be adding 4 points to the Dosage profile. Two of these points would contribute to the Classic score and the other 2 points would be added to the Solid score.

Please remember that to contribute Dosage points a stallion must be on the Chefs-de-Race list. If it is not on the list then no points will be contributed towards any offspring or future generations.

How is Dosage Calculated?

In order to better understand dosage figures, it is valuable to go through the actual procedure of doing the calculations. I would like to add however that you never need to manually work out a horse's dosage rating. The brilliance of the internet allows us to simply log onto www.pedigreequery.com (this is a free site) and search for the horse in question. This will bring up the horse's pedigree and its Dosage rating.

Even though Dosage figures are merely a mouse click away, seeing how the figures are generated provides a stronger knowledge of what these figures mean and how they relate to a particular thoroughbred. In my opinion it is worthwhile understanding how the dosage figures are achieved. To explain what the Dosage ratings mean we will use triple Champion Hurdle winner Istabraq as our example.

Dosage Profile	Total	Dosage Index	Centre of Distribution
11-9-26-10-0	56	1.43	0.38

Istabraq

What is the Dosage Profile?

Put simply, the Dosage Profile is the total number of points this horse has inherited from influential sires in each category from its past four generations. Istabraq has inherited 11 Brilliant, 9 Intermediate, 26 Classic, 10 Solid and 0 Professional points. This implies that Istabraq has more speed in his pedigree than stamina.

What is the Dosage Index?

Once we have the DP we can work out the DI. The DI is the ratio of speed points in its DP compared to stamina points. In the DP the Brilliant and Intermediate categories are classed as speed and the Solid and Professional categories are classed as stamina. The points in the Classic category are divided equally between speed and stamina.

To calculate a horse's Dosage Index the following equation is used.

(Speed)

$$\frac{\textbf{Brilliant + Intermediate + } \tfrac{1}{2}\textbf{ Classic}}{\textbf{Solid + Professional + } \tfrac{1}{2}\textbf{ Classic}}$$

(Stamina)

Along with the CD figure, which we will come to in a moment, the DI is an important figure when analysing and handicapping a race. Within this book the DI not only provides you with the distinction between a speedy and a stamina winner but also a numerical range within which the winner tends to fall. Horses with a DI above 1.00 have more speed than stamina and horses with a DI below 1.00 have more stamina than speed. For example, Denman has a relatively low DI of 0.18 and his Gold Cup win in 2008 demonstrated this as he pounded his opponents into submission with not a turn of pace but a constant gallop.

Below is DI expressed as a table with example horse's and their DI rating's -

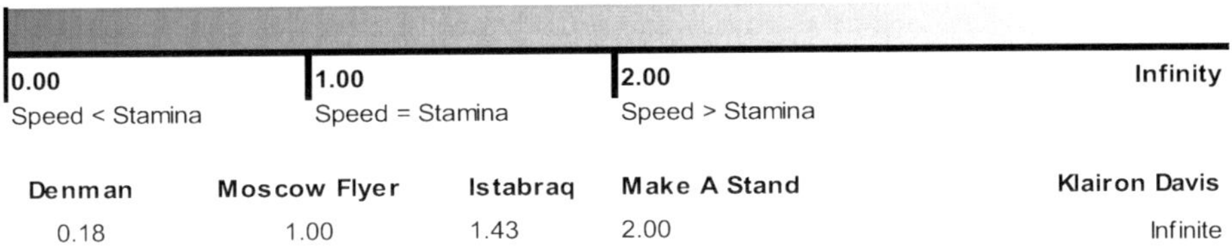

0.00	**1.00**	**2.00**	**Infinity**
Speed < Stamina	Speed = Stamina	Speed > Stamina	

Denman	**Moscow Flyer**	**Istabraq**	**Make A Stand**	**Klairon Davis**
0.18	1.00	1.43	2.00	Infinite

What is the Centre of Distribution?

The CD marks the balancing point of all the numbers in its DP and is always a number ranging from +2 to -2. Again the CD is worked out from the DP, to calculate a horse's CD the following equation is used.

$$\frac{((2 \times \text{Brilliant}) + \text{Intermediate}) - ((2 \times \text{Professional}) + \text{Solid})}{\text{Total DP Points}}$$

Theoretically the CD is an indicator of the distance a horse will be effective over. For example, in this book you will see that every Dosage strong winner of the King George VI chase in the past 13 runnings has had a CD between -0.22 and -1.11. Using the following table you can see this range corresponds accurately with the distance this race is run over; 3 miles. From my research I have found that not only does the CD affect the distance capabilities of a racehorse but different tracks and even different conditions call for varying CD ratings.

As with the DI I have included a table to help you better understand the CD scale -

	Brilliant	*Intermediate*	*Classic*	*Solid*	*Proffesional*
Approx Distance		2 Mile	2mile 4/5f	3 Mile +	
CD Scale	**2.00**	**1.00**	**0.00**	**-1.00**	**-2.00**

Example Horse's	
Call Equiname	1.50
Master Minded	0.50
Istabraq	0.38
Beef or Salmon	-0.75
Denman	-0.90

Unfortunately CD and distance are not always as directly related as this table above demonstrates, however this is a good indicator. Two horses with the same CD may be effective over varying trips such is the unpredictable nature of horse racing.

For a full explanation of how to calculate the Dosage rating of a horse please see Appendix B.

As mentioned previously, Dosage Ratings in their current form were developed by Dr Steven Roman who has a web-site (*http://www.chefs-de-race.com*) and a book (*Dosage: Pedigree and Performance*) both dedicated to the subject. In my book I have taken the principles of Dr Roman's findings and applied them to British National Hunt Racing, if you wish to investigate the finer details of Dosage I would thoroughly recommend both Dr Romans web-site and his publication.

Dosage Trends Table Page Explained

Example Page

(1)

Ryanair Chase -Cheltenham

11th March -cl1 g1 -2m5f -5yo+

(2)

Dosage Strength

★★★★★

(3) Year	(4) Horse	(5) DP	(6) tot	(7) DI	(8) CD	(9) Run sty	(10) Field Size	(11) Gng
2009	Imperial Commander	3-2-4-2-1	12	1.40	0.33	cp	10	gs
2008	Our Vic	2-0-9-5-0	16	0.68	-0.06	fr	9	gs
2007	Taranis	~~0-0-6-0-0~~	6	~~1.00~~	~~0.00~~	cp	9	gs
2006	Fondmort	2-0-2-4-0	8	0.60	0.00	cp	11	gd
2005	Thisthatandtother	1-2-13-0-0	16	1.46	0.25	cp	12	gd

(12) **DP**

4/5 had 8 pts or more in their Dosage Profile

4/5 had between 8 and 16 pts in their Dosage Profile

(13) **DI**

4/4 had a DI of between 0.60 and 1.46

Majority Range : 0.60 to 1.46 -100% of winners

(14) **CD**

4/4 had a CD of -0.06 and above

3/4 had a CD of 0.00 and above

(15) **Majority Range : -0.06 to 0.33 -100% of winners**

(16) **Average**

DI 1.04 / CD 0.13

(17) **Running Style**

fr-1 / cp-4 / hu-0 -No Hold up runner has taken the honours yet and only one horse has won from the front so it looks best to run close to pace if you want to win the Ryanair.

(18) **Summary**

Very early days yet but this grade 1 race is already starting to show a dosage bias. Stamina based horses have struggled in this race and it looks like the emphasis is very much on speed rather than stamina over this 2m5f trip. Given that horse's of Voy Por Ustedes and Monets Garden calibre were beaten in this race I excpect the trend of negative CD horses and horses with less than 8 dosage points struggling in this race to continue. Our Vic did win this race (2008) with a CD just on the negative side but he was also beaten in this race on the 4 other occasions it has been run. The majority ranges above are the best starting point when looking for future winners of this race.

(19) **Notable Defeats**

'09 Voy Por Ustedes -1-0-6-1-4 (12) / 0.50 / -0.58 -sp 4/5

'07 Monets Garden -0-0-0-2-0 (2) / 0.00 / -1.00 -sp 7/4

(20) **Dosage Fact**

The first 3 home in the 2005 & 2006 runnings all fell within the majority ranges identified above.

(1) *Race title and course race is due to be run followed by date, class and distance of race plus any age restrictions.* The reason only graded races and top handicaps have been chosen for analysis is due to the fact that at lower class levels, as with other types of form analysis, Dosage ratings can become un-reliable.
(2) *Race strength rated out of five.* This is the rating I have given the race depending on how strong I think the Dosage trends are for that race.
(3) *Year race was run.* The last fifteen runnings have been chosen because I feel if we go any further back than this the data can become out-dated as the thoroughbred is an ever evolving breed. If a meeting was cancelled and re-arranged at a different track then the results will not be considered for analysis. When race conditions have changed significantly; i.e. a handicap up to a non handicap graded race or a dramatic change in race distance; these results have also been excluded.
(4) *Name of winning horse.*
(5) *The Dosage Profile of the winning horse.*
(6) *Sum of the Dosage Points for that horse.*
(7) *Dosage Index of winning horse.* If the total Dosage points equal less than 8 then these figures have a strike through and are **not included** in analysis.
(8) *Centre of Distribution of winning horse.* If the total Dosage points equal less than 8 then these figures have a strike through and are **not included** in analysis.
(9) *Running style of winning horse in this specific race.* Dosage can have an effect on the running style of a horse. For example front runners, in general, have a speedier dosage rating.
fr = Front runner cp = Close to pace runner hu = Hold up runner
(10) *Number of runners that took part in that year's race.* This has been included to show that even in large field's dosage is effective.
(11) *Ground conditions on day of the race.* This has been included as the going can sometimes play a major role when it comes to Dosage performance.
(12) *Analysis of the Dosage Profile.* Eight points or more is what I would class as 'Dosage strong'; horses with less than 8 points do not have enough influential sires to be included in the analysis and are referred to as 'Dosage weak'.

(13) *Analysis of the Dosage Index.* In here you will see what ranges the winner's DI mostly fell below or above. Negatives trends are also identified here.
(14) *Analysis of the Centre of Distribution.* In this section you will see the ranges the winner's CD mostly fell below or above. Negatives trends are also identified here.
(15) *Majority range for DI and CD ratings.* These figures indicate the range where most of the winner's ratings fell within. This section is particularly helpful when looking at future races.
(16) *Average DI rating and CD rating of the previous winners.* The average is merely a guide and not something to be religiously stuck to.
(17) *Summary of what position the previous winners took up during the race.* This lets you see at a glance what running style is most suited to that particular race.
(18) *Summary of the race.*
(19) *High profile and short priced losers of previous renewals.* This segment highlights some well fancied horse's that had tried and failed to win that particular race. According to Dosage, these runners were simply not built to win this race. The section is arranged as follows – Year – Horse – Dosage figures – Starting price.
(20) *Dosage trivia or fact.* This is a snippet of interesting information relating to Dosage concerning that particular race.

The Dosage ratings for the horses included in the example can be found at www.pedigreequery.com as can the Dosage rating for any horse you may need, past or present.

An example of how to use the above information to handicap future races can be found in Appendix C.

Race Index

Race Analysis

Persian War Novices' Hurdle - Chepstow

24th October - cl1 g2 - 2m4f 110yds - 4yo+

Dosage Strength

★★

Year	Horse	DP	tot	DI	CD	Run sty	Field Size	Gng
2008	**Hells Bay**	**5- 1- 4- 6- 4**	**20**	**0.67**	**- 0.15**	hu	10	gd
2007	**Elusive Dream**	**12- 0- 24- 14- 4**	**54**	**0.80**	**0.04**	cp	8	gd
2006	**Kanpai**	**6- 1- 5- 0- 0**	**12**	**3.80**	**1.08**	cp	7	gs
2005	**Rimsky**	**4- 3- 9- 5- 1**	**22**	**1.10**	**0.18**	hu	7	sft
2004	**Knowhere**	**3- 3- 7- 0- 1**	**14**	**2.11**	**0.50**	cp	6	sft
2003	**Champagne Harry**	**7- 2- 6- 0- 1**	**16**	**3.00**	**0.88**	hu	6	gf
2002	**Supreme Prince**	**4- 2- 2- 4- 4**	**16**	**0.78**	**- 0.13**	cp	6	sft
2001	**One Knight**	~~0-0-0-0-0~~	**0**	~~inf~~	~~inf~~	cp	6	gs
2000	**Valley Henry**	**1- 4- 10- 3- 2**	**20**	**1.00**	**- 0.05**	hu	8	sft
1998	**Red Curate**	**1- 0- 7- 14- 2**	**24**	**0.23**	**- 0.67**	cp	11	gs
1997	**Boardroom Shuffle**	**3- 3- 6- 2- 0**	**14**	**1.80**	**0.50**	hu	8	sft
1996	**Jet Rules**	~~2-0-2-0-0~~	**4**	~~3.00~~	~~1.00~~	cp	5	sft
1995	**St Mellion Fairway**	**8- 6- 0- 0- 0**	**14**	**inf**	**1.57**	cp	6	hvy

DP

11/13 had 12 or more points in their Dosage Profile
10/13 had 14 or more points in their Dosage Profile

DI

10/11 had a DI of 0.67 and above
7/11 had a DI of 1.00 and above
0/11 had a DI between 1.11 and 1.79
Majority Range : 0.67 to 1.80 - 56% of winners

CD

10/11 had a CD of -0.15 and above
8/11 had a CD of -0.05 and above
0/11 had a CD between 0.19 and 0.49
Majority Range : - 0.15 to 0.50 - 64% of winners

Average

DI 1.53 / CD 0.34

Running Style

fr- 0 / cp- 8 / hu- 5 - Not a race you want to be setting the pace in as front runners have drawn a blank in the last 13 renewals. Close to pace runners hold the majority with 8 wins although held up runners are not far behind with 5.

Summary

The best starting point for handicapping future renewals of the Persian War Hurdle is to look for a horse with a CD of -0.15 and above. 10/11 winners fell into this category. Closer scrutiny does reveal that there were no winners in the 0.19 to 0.49 CD bracket although whether this is an aberration in the stats is hard to tell. What it suggests is that to win the Persian War Hurdle you want to be heavily speed orientated or holding a touch of stamina in your Dosage - horses that fall in-between fail to make the grade. This is proven by Pigeon Island in the 2007 running of the race. All in all this is a slightly muddling race for Dosage analysis and due to the aforementioned gapping in the stats the majority ranges mentioned above should be viewed with caution.

Notable Defeats

'07 Pigeon Island - 6-1-17-2-0 (26) / **1.48** / **0.42** - sp 7/2
'02 Risk Accessor - 3-3-7-0-15 (28) / **0.51** / - **0.75** - sp 5/2
'95 My Rossini - 0-0-3-0-11 (14) / **0.12** / - **1.57** - sp 2/1

Charlie Hall Chase - Wetherby

31st October - cl1 g2 - 3m 1f - 5yo+

Dosage Strength

★★★★

Year	Horse	DP	tot	DI	CD	Run sty	Field Size	Gng
2008	State of Play	2-0-11-2-5	20	0.60	-0.40	cp	6	gf
2007	Ollie Magern	0-1-2-0-5	8	0.33	-1.13	fr	7	gf
2006	Our Vic	2-0-9-5-0	16	0.68	-0.06	cp	10	sft
2005	Ollie Magern	0-1-2-0-5	8	0.33	-1.13	fr	8	sft
2004	Grey Abbey	2-1-4-4-1	12	0.71	-0.08	fr	6	gs
2003	Ballybough Rasher	0-0-0-8-4	12	0.00	-1.33	hu	6	gd
2002	Marlborough	3-3-4-0-0	10	4.00	0.90	hu	8	gs
2001	Sackville	2-1-5-2-2	12	0.85	-0.08	cp	9	gd
2000	See More Business	0-0-3-6-1	10	0.18	-0.80	cp	4	sft
1999	See More Business	0-0-3-6-1	10	0.18	-0.80	cp	6	gd
1998	Strath Royal	2-0-10-0-0	12	1.40	0.33	fr	5	gd
1997	One Man	~~1-0-4-1-0~~	6	~~1.00~~	~~0.17~~	hu	4	gf
1996	One Man	~~1-0-4-1-0~~	6	~~1.00~~	~~0.17~~	hu	4	gd
1995	Barton Bank	4-2-6-8-2	22	0.69	-0.09	cp	3	gf
1994	Young Hustler	6-0-10-0-0	16	2.20	0.75	fr	7	gd

DP

13/15 had between 8 and 22 points in their Dosage Profile

DI

11/13 had a DI of 1.40 and below
10/13 had a DI of 0.85 and below
9/13 had a DI of 0.71 and below
Majority Range : 0.00 to 0.85 - 77% of winners

CD

11/13 had a CD of 0.33 and below
10/13 had a CD of -0.06 and below
Majority Range : -1.33 to -0.06 - 77%of winners

Average

DI 0.93 / CD -0.30

Running Style

fr-5 / cp-6 / hu-4 - No advantage to any running style although hold up horses fair slightly worse than others.

Summary

A 3m 1f race run over Wetherby's galloping track and it pays to have stamina on your side. 9 of the last 10 winners had a CD of -0.06 or below and DI of 0.85 or below - only Marlborough fell out with this range. Of the 3 horses that had a CD figure on the plus side, 2 of them used their speed to steal the race from the front, preventing the stamina horses from landing a blow. The exceptional One Man was the only winner in the past 15 to have less than 8 points in his Dosage Profile - all other winners of this early season chase were Dosage strong.

Notable Defeats

'06 Iris's Gift - 5-0-2-1-0 (8) / **3.00** / **1.13 -** sp 8/1
'02 Lord Noelie - 3-3-6-2-0 (14) / **1.80** / **0.50 -** sp 3/1
'01 Legal Right - 9-6-21-1-3 (40) / **1.76** / **0.43** - sp 2/1
'01 Shotgun Willy - 3-1-10-0-0 (14) / **1.80** / **0.50** - sp 3/1
'99 Looks Like Trouble - 1-4-5-2-0 (12) / **1.67** / **0.33 -** sp 3/1

Dosage Fact

In the 1999 running only See More Business had a minus CD figure, the other runners all had a CD on the plus side. He won convincingly by 5 lengths.

West Yorkshire Hurdle- Wetherby

31st October - cl1 g2 - 3m1f - 4yo+

Dosage Strength

★★★★

Year	Horse	DP	tot	DI	CD	Run sty	Field Size	Gng
2008	Pettifour	4-1-3-4-4	16	0.68	-0.19	cp	8	gf
2007	Black Jack Ketchum	4-0-6-10-2	22	0.47	-0.27	hu	6	gf
2006	Redemption	8-3-17-0-0	28	2.29	0.68	cp	7	sft
2005	Inglis Drever	3-0-22-15-2	42	0.50	-0.31	cp	11	sft
2004	Telemoss	3-2-4-2-7	18	0.64	-0.44	hu	7	gs
2003	Gralmano	7-0-11-8-0	26	0.93	0.23	hu	8	gd
2002	Brother Joe	1-4-5-6-0	16	0.88	0.00	hu	7	gs
2001	Boss Doyle	2-0-6-0-2	10	1.00	0.00	fr	8	gd
2000	Boss Doyle	2-0-6-0-2	10	1.00	0.00	cp	7	sft
1999	Silver Wedge	3-3-16-0-0	22	1.75	0.41	cp	4	gd
1998	Marello	4-1-1-6-4	16	0.52	-0.31	hu	6	gd
1997	Pridwell	6-1-21-10-0	38	0.85	0.08	cp	2	gf
1996	Trainglot	7-3-8-0-0	18	3.50	0.94	cp	7	gd
1995	Cab On Target	4-3-5-0-6	18	1.12	-0.06	cp	4	gf
1994	Halkopous	9-4-3-0-0	16	9.67	1.38	hu	7	gd

DP

15/15 had 10 points or more in their Dosage Profile
13/15 had 16 points or more in their Dosage Profile

DI

12/15 had a DI of 1.75 and below
10/15 had a DI of 1.00 and below
0/15 had a DI of below 0.47
Majority Range : 0.47 to 1.12 - 73% of winners

CD

12/15 had a CD of 0.41 and below
10/15 had a CD of 0.08 and below
0/15 had a CD of below -0.44
Majority Range : -0.44 to 0.41 - 80% of winners

Average

DI 1.72 / CD 0.14

Running Style

fr-1 / cp-8 / hu-6 - Front running round Wetherby's hurdle track has proven too much for all bar Boss Doyle in 2001. Close to pace runners just hold sway over held up runners with 8 victories to 6.

Summary

A staying hurdle race but winners are not exclusively on the stamina heavy side. In fact one of the strongest Dosage pointers in this race is that no winner has had a DI below 0.47 or a CD below -0.44. The CD and DI figures also give strong majority ranges to work with. 11/15 winners had a DI between 0.47 and 1.12 and 12/15 winners had a CD between -0.44 and 0.41. The average Dosage ratings are warped slightly by the appearance of Halkopous on the winners roster and I expect the averages to fall to something closer to 1.00 and 0.00 once the '94 winner is removed for next years analysis. The strongest pointer of all in this race comes from the fact all 15 winners had 10 points or more in their Dosage profile. Looking closer we can see that 13/15 had 16 points or more highlighting the need for a Dosage strong contender in the West Yorkshire Hurdle.

Notable Defeats

'04 Crystal D'Ainay - **0-0-1-3-0 (4)** / 0.14 / -0.75 - sp 8/11
'03 Royal Emperor - **0-0-2-0-0 (2)** / 1.00 / 0.00 - sp 6/4
'01 Turnpole - 3-4-3-0-0 (10) / **5.67** / **1.00** - sp 7/4

Elite Hurdle - Wincanton

7th November - cl1 g2 - 2m - 4yo+

Dosage Strength

★★★★

Year	Horse	DP	tot	DI	CD	Run sty	Field Size	Gng
2008	Chomba Womba	4-0-4-2-0	10	1.50	0.60	cp	5	sft
2007	Kings Quay	3-0-11-6-0	20	0.74	0.00	hu	10	gd
2006	Crow Wood	3-1-9-2-1	16	1.13	0.19	fr	6	gd
2005	Royal Shakespeare	5-1-6-6-0	18	1.00	0.28	cp	9	gd
2004	Perouse	0-0-3-0-5	8	0.23	-1.25	fr	8	gd
2003	Well Chief	6-1-9-2-0	18	1.77	0.61	cp	4	gf
2002	Santenay	1-0-8-1-0	10	1.00	0.10	hu	6	gd
2001	Azertyuiop	2-0-2-8-2	14	0.27	-0.57	fr	4	gd
2000	Mister Morose	~~2-0-0-4-0~~	6	~~0.50~~	~~0.00~~	fr	7	gs
1999	Wahiba Sands	8-6-16-2-0	32	2.20	0.63	fr	4	gd
1998	Grey Shot	4-4-4-0-0	12	5.00	1.00	fr	4	gs
1997	Pridwell	6-1-21-10-0	38	0.85	0.08	cp	4	gd
1996	Dreams End	9-0-5-10-4	38	0.77	0.00	cp	8	gd
1995	Atours	17-22-11-8-0	58	3.30	0.83	cp	3	gf
1994	Valfinet	~~2-2-0-0-0~~	4	~~inf~~	~~1.50~~	fr	5	gd

DP

13/15 had 8 points or more in their Dosage Profile
10/15 had 12 points or more in their Dosage Profile

DI

11/13 had a DI of 0.74 and above
8/13 had a DI of 1.00 and above
2/13 had a DI above 2.20
Majority Range : 0.77 to 2.20 - 69% of winners

CD

11/13 had a CD of 0.00 and above
9/13 had a CD of 0.08 and above
2/13 had a CD above 0.63
Majority Range : 0.00 to 0.63 - 69% of winners

Average

DI 1.52 / CD 0.19

Running Style

fr-7 / cp-6 / hu-2 - Wincanton's flat-galloping track is no place for hold up runners as in this 2 mile hurdle only 2/15 have won from out the back. Front runners have a slightly better record than close to pace runners but both excel in this early season race.

Summary

The mix of good jumping ground and Wincanton's flat track give some strong angles to work with in the Elite hurdle. The CD figures give the strongest pointer with 11/13 having a rating of 0.00 and above. The 2 horses that fell below 0.00 - one being regular Dosage buster Azertyuiop - both front ran their way to victory. DI figures also give some strong pointers with 11/13 having a rating of 0.74 and above. Dosage strong animals should also be viewed favourably as 13/15 had 8 points or more in their profile.

Notable Defeats

'99 Chai-Yo - 1-1-8-6-2 (18) / **0.50** / **-0.39** - sp 3/1
'97 Mr Percy - 1-0-1-12-0 (14) / **0.12** / **-0.71** - sp 7/2
'94 Oh So Risky - 5-1-12-4-8 (30) / **0.67** / **-0.30** - sp 6/5

Dosage Fact

Both horses with a negative CD rating were trained by Paul Nicholls.

Badger Ales Trophy - Wincanton

7th November - cl1 Lst hcp - 3m1f - 5yo+

Dosage Strength

★★★★

Year	Horse	DP	tot	DI	CD	Run sty	Field Size	Gng
2008	Cornish Sett	5-1-6-6-0	18	1.00	0.28	hu	12	sft
2007	Abragante	4-1-9-4-0	18	1.12	0.28	hu	8	gd
2006	Parsons Legacy	4-5-10-0-1	20	2.33	0.55	cp	12	gd
2005	Iris Bleu	0-0-4-6-2	12	0.20	-0.83	hu	12	gd
2004	Royal Auclair	4-4-11-7-2	28	0.93	0.04	cp	10	gd
2003	Swansea Bay	2-2-7-0-1	12	1.67	0.33	hu	5	gf
2002	Swansea Bay	2-2-7-0-1	12	1.67	0.33	hu	12	gd
2001	Montifault	1-0-8-1-0	10	1.00	0.10	fr	8	gd
2000	Flaked Oats	3-0-3-0-2	8	1.29	0.25	fr	11	gs
1999	Flaked Oats	3-0-3-0-2	8	1.29	0.25	hu	9	gd
1998	Teeton Mill	0-0-4-4-2	10	0.25	-0.80	hu	7	gs
1997	Lively Knight	~~3-1-2-0-0~~	6	~~5.00~~	~~1.17~~	hu	9	gd
1996	Coome Hill	3-2-1-2-0	8	2.20	0.75	hu	9	gd
1995	Tug Of Peace	2-0-2-8-4	16	0.23	-0.75	cp	6	gf
1994	Lusty Light	5-3-8-0-2	18	2.00	0.50	cp	9	gd

DP

14/15 had 8 points or more in their Dosage Profile
13/15 had between 8 and 20 points in their Dosage Profile

DI

11/14 had a DI of 0.93 and above
10/14 had a DI of 1.00 and above
0/14 had a DI above 2.33
Majority Range : 0.93 to 2.00 - 64% of winners

CD

11/14 had a CD of 0.04 and above
9/14 had a CD of 0.25 and above
0/14 had a CD above 0.75
Majority Range : 0.04 to 0.55 - 71% of winners

Average

DI 1.23 / CD 0.09

Running Style

fr-2 / cp-4 / hu-9 - Although Wincanton is a flat-galloping track don't expect to many to take the race from the front in this 3m1f handicap chase. Hold up horses have the best strike rate with 9/15 winning from the back.

Summary

What is most striking here is the lack of stamina heavy winners in this staying handicap chase. 10/14 winners had a DI of 1.00 and above and 11/14 had a CD of 0.04 and above. Even closer examination shows that 9/14 winners had a CD of 0.25 and above. The fact that 12 of the last 15 runnings were run on ground that was good or good to firm may have a part to play in this along with the flat nature of the Wincanton's track. The good ground allows the speedier horses coming from off the pace to use their turn of foot which on soft winter ground would normally be blunted. Dosage totals point in the way of Dosage strong animals with only Lively Knight in '97 winning with a Dosage weak pedigree. If we compare the averages for this race (1.23 / 0.09) and the averages for the Charlie Hall Chase (0.93 / -0.30), which is run a week earlier over the same distance, we can see how different tracks call for alternatively bred thoroughbreds. Although the race distance is the same the tracks are laid out very differently, calling for varying Dosage ratings between the 2.

Notable Defeats

'08 Leading Attraction - **0-0-1-1-0 (2)** / 0.33 / -0.50 - sp 11/4
'05 Red Devil Robert - 3-3-6-0-0 (12) / **3.00** / **0.75** - sp 2/1
'04 Gunther McBride - 1-0-7-6-0 (14) / **0.47** / **-0.29** - sp 7/2
'02 Itsonlyme - 0-0-4-4-2 (10) / **0.25** / **-0.80** - sp 100/30
'01 Enrique - 2-0-17-5-12 (36) / **0.41** / **-0.69** - sp 7/2

James Nicholson Champion Chase - Down Royal

7th November - g1 - 3m - 4yo+

Dosage Strength

★★★★

Year	Horse	DP	tot	DI	CD	Run sty	Field Size	Gng
2008	Kauto Star	2-2-6-10-2	22	0.47	-0.36	cp	5	sft
2007	Taranis	~~0-0-6-0-0~~	6	~~1.00~~	~~0.00~~	fr	6	gd
2006	Beef Or Salmon	3-1-5-0-11	20	0.48	-0.75	cp	7	gs
2004	Beef Or Salmon	3-1-5-0-11	20	0.48	-0.75	cp	8	sft
2003	Glenelly Gale	4-3-5-0-6	18	1.12	-0.06	hu	4	frm
2002	More Than a Stroll	2-1-5-6-2	16	0.52	-0.31	hu	7	sft
2001	Foxchapel King	~~0-2-0-2-0~~	4	~~1.00~~	~~0.00~~	fr	7	gs
2000	Looks Like Trouble	1-4-5-2-0	12	1.67	0.33	fr	5	gd
1999	Florida Pearl	0-0-4-8-6	18	0.13	-1.11	cp	6	sft

DP

7/9 had 12 points or more in their Dosage Profile
6/9 had between 16 and 22 points in their Dosage Profile

DI

7/7 had a DI of 1.67 and below
6/7 had a DI of 1.12 and below
5/7 had a DI of 0.52 and below
Majority Range : 0.13 to 1.12 - 86% of winners

CD

7/7 had a CD of 0.33 and below
6/7 had a CD of -0.06 and below
5/7 had a CD of -0.31 and below
Majority Range : -1.11 to -0.06 - 86% of winners

Average

DI 0.70 / CD -0.43

Running Style

fr-3 / cp-4 / hu-2 - An even distribution of winning running styles for this grade 1 race with close to pace runners just holding a narrow advantage.

Summary

A relatively new race but still one that gives some decent Dosage pointers. Only the front running Looks Like Trouble had a CD on the plus side and he was also aided by good ground in the 2000 renewal. Every other winner had a CD of -0.06 and below with 5/7 having a CD of -0.31 and below. DI ratings also fall on the low side with 5/7 winners having a rating of 0.52 or below. With Down Royal being a galloping, undulating and testing track I expect the trend of stamina heavy winners to continue, especially since the chances of the ground riding good to soft or worse are fairly high. With regards to Dosage totals the 2 winners that had less than 8 points in their profile, Taranis and Foxchapel King, both front ran their way to victory.

Notable Defeats

'07 Justified - 3-6-6-0-1 (16) / **3.00** / **0.63** - sp 11/4
'04 Harbour Pilot - 5-2-7-0-0 (12) / **2.43** / **0.67** - sp 4/1
'03 Barrow Drive - 9-0-3-0-0 (12) / **7.00** / **1.50** - sp even

Haldon Gold Cup - Exeter

10th November - cl1 g2 Lmtd Hcp - 2m1f - 4yo+

Dosage Strength

★★★★

Year	Horse	DP	tot	DI	CD	Run sty	Field Size	Gng
2008	Ashley Brook	4-0-5-1-2	12	1.18	0.25	cp	9	gs
2007	Pablo Du Charmil	4-0-12-0-0	16	1.67	0.50	fr	5	gd
2006	Impek	0-0-8-0-0	8	1.00	0.00	fr	9	gd
2005	Monkerhostin	3-3-6-3-1	16	1.29	0.25	hu	11	gs
2004	Azertyuiop	2-0-2-8-2	14	0.27	-0.57	hu	7	gs
2003	Edredon Bleu	~~0-0-0-2-0~~	2	~~0.00~~	~~-1.00~~	fr	7	gd
2002	Edredon Bleu	~~0-0-0-2-0~~	2	~~0.00~~	~~-1.00~~	fr	6	gd
2001	Best Mate	1-1-10-5-1	18	0.64	-0.22	cp	4	gf
2000	Bellator	4-3-6-5-0	18	1.25	0.33	cp	6	sft
1999	Flagship Uberalles	6-1-7-4-0	18	1.40	0.50	cp	7	gs
1998	Lake kariba	9-2-4-6-1	22	1.44	0.55	cp	7	sft
1997	Viking Flagship	6-1-7-2-2	18	1.40	0.39	hu	6	gs
1996	Absalom's Lady	7-4-5-0-4	20	2.08	0.50	hu	6	gs
1995	Travado	4-3-11-0-0	18	2.27	0.61	cp	4	gf
1994	Travado	4-3-11-0-0	18	2.27	0.61	fr	6	gd

DP

13/15 had 8 points or more in their Dosage Profile
11/15 had 14 points or more in their Dosage Profile

DI

11/13 had a DI of 1.00 and above
9/13 had a DI of 1.25 and above
0/13 had a DI above 2.27
Majority Range : 1.00 to 2.27 - 85% of winners

CD

11/13 had a CD of 0.00 and above
10/13 had a CD of 0.25 and above
0/13 had a CD above 0.61
Majority Range : 0.25 to 0.61 - 77% of winners

Average

DI 1.40 / CD 0.28

Running Style

fr-5 / cp-6 / hu-4 - No real bias at play in this race although it may pay to be up with the pace or front running rather than being held up. Although close to pace runners have the best overall record they have only taken 1 of the last 7 renewals.

Summary

Speed, but not too much of it, is the name of the game in the Haldon Gold Cup. Only superstars Azertyuiop and Best Mate were able to win this race with a negative CD rating, a statistic that even superstar champion Kauto Star could not overcome. Every other winner had a CD on the plus side and a DI of 1.00 or above, suggesting speed is the key to this race. Looking a bit closer at the stats tells that no winner had a DI above 2.27 or CD above 0.61 so flat out speedsters such as Call Equiname struggled when tackling Exeter's undulations and uphill finish. DP totals point towards Dosage strong animals as only duel winner Edredon Bleu had less than 8 points in his Dosage Profile.

Notable Defeats

'08 Twist Magic - 1-0-11-8-2 (22) / **0.42** / **-0.45** - sp 9/4
'05 Kauto Star - 2-2-6-10-2 (22) / **0.47** / **-0.36** - sp 3/1
'00 Call Equiname - 14-4-2-0-0 (20) / **19.00** / **1.60** - sp 9/2

Dosage Fact

No Horse in the history of this race has won with a DI above 2.33 or a CD above 0.78.

Sharp Novices' Hurdle - Cheltenham

13th November - cl1 g2 - 2m - 4yo+

Dosage Strength

★★★★

Year	Horse	DP	tot	DI	CD	Run sty	Field Size	Gng
2008	Golan Way	4-0-9-4-1	18	0.89	0.11	fr	9	sft
2007	I'msingingtheblues	~~0-0-6-0-0~~	6	~~1.00~~	~~0.00~~	hu	9	gd
2006	Moon Over Miami	2-0-5-3-2	12	0.60	-0.25	hu	9	gd
2005	Boychuk	2-0-5-1-0	8	1.29	0.38	cp	10	gs
2004	Marcel	~~2-0-0-0-0~~	2	~~inf~~	~~2.00~~	hu	9	gd
2003	Self Defense	6-1-13-2-0	22	1.59	0.59	cp	7	gf
2002	Mutakarrim	9-1-14-6-0	30	1.31	0.43	hu	12	gd
2001	Fireball Macnamara	6-4-9-5-0	24	1.53	0.46	hu	7	gd
2000	Reiziger	2-4-16-0-2	24	1.40	0.17	hu	7	gs
1999	Silence Reigns	4-3-13-4-0	24	1.29	0.29	cp	7	gd
1998	Hoh Invader	5-1-7-4-1	18	1.12	0.28	cp	12	gd
1997	Circus Star	3-1-22-2-6	34	0.79	-0.21	hu	7	gd
1996	Kailash	7-3-2-4-0	16	2.20	0.81	fr	5	gf
1995	Mandys Mantino	2-0-0-4-2	8	0.33	-0.50	cp	12	gd
1994	Berude Not To	~~0-0-0-0-0~~	0	~~inf~~	~~inf~~	hu	8	sft

DP

12/15 had 8 points or more in their Dosage profile
9/15 had 16 points or more in their Dosage profile

DI

11/12 had a DI of 1.59 and below
9/12 had a DI of 1.31 and below
0/12 had a DI below 0.33
Majority Range : 0.60 to 1.59 - 83% of winners

CD

11/12 had a CD of -0.25 and above
9/12 had a CD of 0.11 and above
1/12 had a CD above 0.59
Majority Range : -0.25 to 0.59 - 83% of winners

Average

DI 1.20 / CD 0.21

Running Style

fr-2 / cp-5 / hu-8 - Hold up horses are the call in this novice hurdle with 8 winners. Close to pace runners win their fair share but front runners have struggled with only 2 winning.

Summary

Although this a 2 mile hurdle race winners should not be carrying vast amounts of speed in their Dosage. 11/12 winners had a DI of 1.59 and below with the only winner to have a higher rating, '96 winner Kailash, front running his way to victory. CD ratings show a slightly different picture as only one winner fell below -0.25 and 9/12 actually had a rating of 0.11 and above. This suggests a well balanced individual is best suited to the challenge of this novice race, preferably a horse that has a DI below 1.60 but a CD above 0.10. Although 3 winners have had less than 8 points in their Dosage Profile a majority of winners have been Dosage strong.

Notable Defeats

'08 American Trilogy - 2-2-7-0-1 (12) / **1.67** / 0.33 - sp 5/4
'07 Quaddick Lake - 0-0-4-2-2 (8) / **0.33** / **-0.75** - sp 11/4
'05 Buena Vista - 2-0-17-17-2 (38) / **0.38** / **-0.43** - sp 9/4
'98 Dance Suite - 7-5-14-0-0 (26) / **2.71** / **0.73** - sp 7/4

Juvenile Novices' Hurdle - Cheltenham

14th November - cl1 g2 - 2m - 3yo

Dosage Strength

★★★★

Year	Horse	DP	tot	DI	CD	Run sty	Field Size	Gng
2008	Simarian	2-3-5-6-0	16	0.88	0.06	cp	15	sft
2007	Franchoek	6-1-11-0-0	18	2.27	0.72	cp	9	gd
2006	Katchit	1-2-5-3-1	12	0.85	-0.08	hu	10	gs
2005	Fair Along	~~1-0-1-0-0~~	2	~~3.00~~	~~1.00~~	fr	13	gs
2004	Cerium	3-3-8-2-2	18	1.25	0.17	cp	10	gd
2003	Al Eile	5-4-14-0-5	28	1.33	0.14	hu	7	gd
2002	Don Fernando	8-6-18-0-6	38	1.55	0.26	hu	16	gs
2001	Greenhope	6-12-0-0-0	18	inf	1.33	fr	8	gd
2000	Montreal	1-0-5-4-0	10	0.54	-0.20	hu	8	gs
1999	High Stakes	7-5-11-0-1	24	2.69	0.71	hu	5	gd
1998	Katarino	0-0-7-1-0	8	0.78	-0.13	fr	9	gd
1997	The French Furze	13-7-13-5-0	38	2.30	0.74	fr	10	gd
1996	Noble Lord	4-4-4-0-0	12	5.00	1.00	fr	7	gd

DP

12/13 had 8 points or more in their Dosage Profile
10/13 had 12 points or more in their Dosage Profile

DI

12/12 had a DI of 0.54 and above
10/12 had a DI of 0.85 and above
8/12 had a DI of 1.25 and above
Majority Range : 0.78 to 2.30 - 67% of winners

CD

12/12 had a CD of -0.20 and above
9/12 had a CD of 0.06 and above
0/12 had a DI between 0.27 and 0.70
Majority Range : -0.20 to 0.26 - 58% of winners

Average

DI 1.77 / CD 0.39

Running Style

fr-5 / cp-3 / hu-5 - No advantage to any running style here with front runners and hold up horses sharing the honours. Close to pace runners have a good recent record, winning 3 of the last 5.

Summary

A 2 mile race that suits a speedy juvenile, with only 3 winners having a negative CD rating. None of the 15 winners had a CD below -0.20 or a DI below 0.54. Closer study reveals that 9/12 had a CD of 0.06 and above and 8/12 had a DI of 1.25 and above, highlighting the need for speed in this Grade 2 juvenile hurdle. There is an odd piece of 'gapping' in the CD stats where no winner had a rating between 0.27 and 0.70. The same applies to the DI stats where no winner fell between 1.56 and 2.26. It is hard to tell if this is a coincidence or whether horses that fall between these figures are at a disadvantage. Personally I would not rule a horse out if it fell in this range but it is something to look out for in future renewals. DP totals tell that it is best to concentrate on the Dosage strong as only course specialist Fair Along had less than 8 points in his profile.

Notable Defeats

'06 Freeze the Flame - 2-1-19-14-6 (42) / **0.42** / **-0.50** - sp 3/1
'01 Arellano - 5-1-12-8-6 (32) / **0.60** / **-0.28** - sp 5/2

Paddy Power Gold Cup Chase - Cheltenham

14th November - cl1 g3 hcp - 2m4f - 4yo+

Dosage Strength

★★★★

Year	Horse	DP	tot	DI	CD	Run sty	Field Size	Gng
2008	Imperial Commander	3-2-4-2-1	12	1.40	0.33	cp	19	sft
2007	L'Antartique	3-1-0-6-0	10	0.67	0.10	hu	20	gd
2006	Exotic Dancer	4-4-10-3-1	22	1.44	0.32	hu	16	gs
2005	Our Vic	2-0-9-5-0	16	0.68	-0.06	cp	18	gs
2004	Celestial Gold	~~1-1-0-2-0~~	4	~~1.00~~	~~0.25~~	hu	14	gd
2003	Fondmort	2-0-2-4-0	8	0.60	0.00	hu	9	gd
2002	Cyfor Malta	2-0-10-6-2	20	0.54	-0.30	cp	15	gs
2001	Shooting Light	1-0-7-12-6	26	0.21	-0.85	hu	14	gd
2000	Lady Cricket	4-4-1-1-2	12	2.43	0.58	hu	15	gs
1999	The Outback Way	2-2-8-10-0	22	0.57	-0.18	cp	14	gd
1998	Cyfor Malta	2-0-10-6-2	20	0.54	-0.30	cp	12	gd
1997	Senor El Betrutti	~~0-0-0-0-0~~	0	~~inf~~	~~inf~~	cp	9	gd
1996	Challenger Du Luc	1-0-6-4-1	12	0.50	-0.33	hu	12	gf
1995	Dublin Flyer	0-0-2-8-6	16	0.07	-1.25	fr	12	gd
1994	Bradbury Star	2-3-7-4-4	20	0.74	-0.25	hu	14	gs

DP

13/15 had 8 points or more in their Dosage Profile
12/15 had between 8 and 20 points in their Dosage profile

DI

12/13 had a DI of 1.44 and below
10/13 had a DI of 0.74 and below
9/13 had a DI of 0.68 and below
Majority Range : 0.21 to 0.74 - 69% of winners

CD

12/13 had a CD of 0.33 and below
10/13 had a CD of 0.10 and below
8/13 had a CD of -0.06 and below
Majority Range : -0.33 to 0.33 - 77% of winners

Average

DI 0.80 / CD -0.17

Running Style

fr-1 / cp-6 / hu-8 - Front runners have a tough time around here with only Dublin Flyer managing to use his masses of stamina to take the race from the front. Hold up runners hold a small advantage over close to pace runners.

Summary

Speed merchants need not apply for the Paddy Power Gold Cup. This is a race that is dominated by horses who favour stamina rather than speed in their Dosage. 10/13 had a DI of 0.74 and below and 9/13 had a CD of 0.00 and below. Admittedly 2 of the last 3 winners had figures above this but both of the high class pair, Imperial Commander and Exotic Dancer, had figures of DI 1.44 and below and CD 0.33 and below - not figures that would class them as speed heavy. Track characteristics rather than ground conditions are to answer for here. Although the ground has only been worse than good to soft on 1 occasion the undulating-galloping nature of Prestbury Park makes it difficult for any speed orientated animal to last home in this competitive handicap. Two Dosage weak animals have gone on to be victorious in the past 15, however the majority call is to side with the Dosage strong.

Notable Defeats

'03 Poliantas - **0-0-0-0-0 (0)** / inf / inf - sp 7/2
'02 Chicuelo - **0-0-4-0-0 (4)** / 1.00 / 0.00 - sp 2/1
'99 Call Equiname - 14-4-2-0-0 (20) / **19.00** / **1.60** - sp 3/1
'97 Sparky Gale - 3-3-6-0-0 (12) / **3.00** / **0.75** - sp 15/8

Dosage Fact

The last winner to have a Dosage rating higher than Lady Cricket's was 1989 winner Joint Sovereignty. His Dosage rating was an extremely speedy 15-0-1-0-0 / 31.00 / 1.80.

Trophy Handicap Chase - Cheltenham

14th November - cl1 g3 hcp - 3m3f - 4yo+

Dosage Strength

Year	Horse	DP	tot	DI	CD	Run sty	Field Size	Gng
2008	Joe Lively	3-3-5-0-1	12	2.43	0.58	fr	10	sft
2007	Sir Rembrandt	10-6-0-2-0	18	8.00	1.33	cp	10	gd
2006	My Will	~~0-0-1-1-0~~	2	~~0.33~~	~~-1.00~~	cp	12	gs
2005	Innox	0-0-6-4-0	10	0.43	-0.40	cp	16	gs
2004	Stormez	3-3-8-1-1	16	1.67	0.38	hu	11	gd
2003	Shardam	2-0-7-1-0	10	1.22	0.30	fr	8	gd
2002	Stormez	3-3-8-1-1	16	1.67	0.38	cp	10	gs
2001	Hati Roy	0-1-4-1-4	10	0.43	-0.80	cp	10	gd
2000	Foxchapel King	~~0-2-0-2-0~~	4	~~1.00~~	~~0.00~~	hu	13	gs
1999	Hanakham	2-0-6-0-6	14	0.56	-0.57	hu	5	gd
1998	Tennesse Twist	1-0-7-2-4	14	0.47	-0.57	cp	5	gd
1997	Banjo	1-0-7-4-4	16	0.39	-0.63	fr	6	gd
1996	Evangelica	8-3-20-5-4	40	1.11	0.15	hu	4	gf
1995	Willsford	2-2-0-0-18	22	0.22	-1.36	fr	8	gd
1994	Gold Cap	2-2-4-2-0	10	1.50	0.40	fr	6	gs

DP

13/15 had 10 points or more in their Dosage Profile
11/15 had between 10 and 18 points in their Dosage Profile

DI

11/13 had a DI of 1.67 and below
8/13 had a DI of 1.22 and below
Majority Range : 0.39 to 1.67 - 77% of winners

CD

11/13 had a CD of 0.40 and below
7/13 had a CD of 0.15 and below
Majority Range : -0.63 to 0.40 - 69% of winners

Average

DI 1.55 / CD -0.06

Running Style

fr-5 / cp-6 / hu-4 - No obvious bias in this long distance chase although close to pace runners just shade it with 6 wins. Hold up horses have only won 1 of the last 8 renewals.

Summary

The last 2 winners of this long distance chase defy the trend of speedy Dosage runners struggling in this race. The Dosage ratings do not exclusively consist of stamina heavy horses however I would still look to strike a negative against horses with a DI rating above 1.67 and a CD rating above 0.40, Joe Lively and Sir Rembrandt being the only 2 winners to fall above this. Dosage Profiles throw up an interesting statistic in that every winner had at least one point in either the Solid or professional section of their profile. This shows that even the smallest influence of stamina is needed to succeed in this marathon chase.

Notable Defeats

'08 Opera Mundi - **0-0-3-3-0 (6)** / 0.33 / -0.50 - sp 7/2
'07 Bob Bob Bobbin - 4-3-15-**0-0** (22) / **1.93** / **0.50** - sp 3/1
'06 Idle Talk - 8-4-8-**0-0** (20) / **4.00** / **1.00** - sp 9/2
'04 Royal Emperor - **0-0-2-0-0 (2)** / 1.00 / 0.00 - sp 5/1
'03 Carbury Cross - 10-6-0-0-2 (18) / **8.00** / **1.22** - sp 7/2

Greatwood Handicap Hurdle - Cheltenham

15th November - cl1 g3 hcp - 2m - 4yo+

Dosage Strength

★★★★

Year	Horse	DP	tot	DI	CD	Run sty	Field Size	Gng
2008	Numide	3-5-7-1-0	16	2.56	0.63	hu	12	sft
2007	Sizing Europe	2-2-6-0-0	10	2.33	0.60	cp	19	sft
2006	Detroit City	11-3-14-0-0	28	3.00	0.89	fr	9	gs
2005	Lingo	3-4-11-6-0	24	1.09	0.17	hu	19	gs
2004	Accordion Etoile	5-2-8-4-1	20	1.22	0.30	hu	9	gd
2003	Rigmarole	10-5-23-0-0	38	2.30	0.66	hu	10	gd
2002	Rooster Booster	6-6-6-4-2	24	1.67	0.42	hu	11	gs
2001	Westender	2-0-17-3-2	34	0.45	-0.38	cp	13	gd
2000	Hulysse Royal	4-3-10-7-0	24	1.00	0.17	cp	12	gs
1999	Rodock	3-5-9-0-1	18	2.27	0.50	hu	13	gd
1998	Grey Shot	4-4-4-0-0	12	5.00	1.00	fr	16	gs
1997	Mr Percy	1-0-1-12-0	14	0.12	-0.71	cp	17	gd
1996	Space Trucker	4-2-10-8-0	24	0.85	0.08	hu	9	gf
1995	Lonesome Train	11-9-8-0-0	28	6.00	1.11	cp	15	gd
1994	Atours	17-22-11-8-0	58	3.30	0.83	hu	10	gs

DP

15/15 had 10 points or more in their Dosage Profile
13/15 had 14 points or more in their Dosage Profile

DI

12/15 had a DI of 1.00 and above
9/15 had a DI of 1.67 and above
2/15 had a DI below 0.85
Majority Range : 1.00 to 6.00 - 80% of winners

CD

13/15 had a CD of 0.08 and above
10/15 had a CD of 0.30 and above
1/15 had a CD of below -0.38
Majority Range : 0.08 to 1.11 - 87% of winners

Average

DI 2.21 / CD 0.42

Running Style

fr-2 / cp-5 / hu-8 - It pays to be held up or close to the pace in the Greatwood. If the winner is going to front run they will need the required speedy dosage to pull it off. The 2 horses that front ran their way to victory here (Detroit City & Grey Shot) were 2nd and 3rd fastest of the past 15 winners based on dosage ratings.

Summary

A race where it helps to be dosage strong and be blessed with a decent amount of speed in your dosage. All 15 winners had 10 or more points in their DP and all bar 2 had a CD on the plus side. In the past eleven years only Westender has had a DI below 1.00 and a CD below 0.17 proving speed is definitely becoming the winners main asset. To highlight this speed trend even more the last 3 renewals have seen all 3 winners with DI's above 2.30 and CD's above 0.60. Although seen as a good trial for the Champion Hurdle in March only Rooster Booster has actually followed up in the past 15 years, with most winners of the Greatwood proving to have too much speed in their dosage for the big one.

Notable Defeats

'08 Rippling Ring - 4-0-15-7-0 (26) / **0.79** / **0.04** - sp 15/2
'07 Lead On - 4-2-2-4-10 (22) / **0.47** / **-0.64** - sp 4/1
'04 Perouse - 0-0-3-0-5 (8) / **0.23** / **-1.25** - sp 5/1
'03 Hasty Prince - 3-1-6-2-10 (22) / **0.47** / **-0.68** - sp 11/10
'99 She's Our Mare - 3-2-4-0-13 (22) / **0.47** / **-0.82** - sp 11/4

November Novices' Chase - Cheltenham

15th November - cl1 g2 - 2m - 4yo+

Dosage Strength

★★★★

Year	Horse	DP	tot	DI	CD	Run sty	Field Size	Gng
2008	Tatenen	3-1-7-1-0	12	1.67	0.50	fr	4	sft
2007	Moon Over Miami	2-0-5-3-2	12	0.60	-0.25	hu	8	sft
2006	Fair Along	~~1-0-1-0-0~~	2	~~3.00~~	~~1.00~~	fr	6	gs
2005	Accordion Etoile	5-2-8-4-1	20	1.22	0.30	hu	10	gs
2004	Fundamentalist	4-2-2-4-4	16	0.78	-0.13	cp	5	gd
2003	Thisthatandtother	1-2-13-0-0	16	1.46	0.25	hu	5	gd
2002	Azertyuiop	2-0-2-8-2	14	0.27	-0.57	cp	6	gs
2001	Seebald	8-3-12-7-0	30	1.31	0.40	hu	7	gd
2000	Best Mate	1-1-10-5-1	18	0.64	-0.22	hu	6	gs
1999	Fadalko	2-0-5-5-0	12	0.60	-0.08	fr	5	gd
1998	Mister Morose	~~2-0-0-4-0~~	6	~~0.50~~	~~0.00~~	cp	5	gs
1997	Queen of Spades	3-3-6-0-0	12	3.00	0.75	cp	5	gd
1996	Celibate	8-1-11-2-4	26	1.26	0.27	cp	4	gd
1995	Captain Khedive	9-0-7-0-2	18	2.27	0.78	hu	5	gs
1994	Martins Lamp	1-2-10-2-1	16	1.00	0.00	fr	5	sft

DP

13/15 had 12 points or more in their Dosage profile
11/15 had between 12 and 18 points in their Dosage profile

DI

11/13 had a DI of 1.67 and below
10/13 had a DI of 1.46 and below
1/13 had a DI below 0.60
Majority Range : 0.60 to 1.67 - 77% of winners

CD

12/13 had a CD of -0.25 and above
9/13 had a CD of -0.08 and above
Majority Range : -0.25 to 0.50 - 77% of winners

Average

DI 1.24 / CD 0.15

Running Style

fr-4 / cp-5 / hu-6 - Not much in it as far as running styles go although hold up horses just get the nod with 6 victories. Close to pace runners have only won 1 of the last 6 renewals.

Summary

Not a race for the super fast as only 2 winners have had a DI rating above 1.67 and the last one of those (Queen of Spades) was in 1997. The majority ranges highlighted give some strong angles to work with. 10/13 fell within the DI range of 0.60 and 1.67 - only future Queen Mother Chase winner Azertyuiop fell below this. 10/13 fell within the CD range of -0.25 and 0.50, with once again only Azertyuiop falling below this. DP totals tell us that it is the Dosage strong that come out on top a majority of the time with 13/15 winners having 12 points or more in their profile. Dosage Profiles show that every winner had at least 2 points in total in the Brilliant and/or Intermediate section of their profile. Generally 2 miles around Cheltenham for a novice chaser can be a relatively daunting prospect at this early stage of the season and I suspect this is the reason we have not seen a huge amount of speedy chasers taking the top spot.

Notable Defeats

'07 Papini - 2-1-14-6-5 (28) / **0.56** / **-0.39** - sp 3-1
'04 My Will - **0-0-1-1-0 (2)** / 0.33 / -0.50 - sp 13/8
'02 Golden Alpha - 6-4-5-1-0 (16) / **3.57** / **0.94** - sp 3/1
'01 Armaturk - 2-0-6-4-2 (14) / **0.56** / **-0.29** - sp 2/1
'98 Desert Mountain - 9-5-18-0-0 (32) / **2.56** / **0.72** - sp 11/4

Maplewood (Morgiana) Hurdle - Punchestown

15th November - g1 - 2m - 4yo+

Dosage Strength

★★★★

Year	Horse	DP	tot	DI	CD	Run sty	Field Size	Gng
2008	Hardy Eustace	4-2-6-0-2	14	1.80	0.43	fr	4	hvy
2007	Jazz Messenger	4-0-2-1-1	8	1.67	0.63	cp	7	sft
2006	Iktitaf	12-4-10-0-0	26	4.20	1.08	hu	4	sft
2005	Brave Inca	0-1-7-9-9	26	0.21	-1.00	fr	5	sft
2004	Harchibald	5-4-13-2-0	24	1.82	0.50	hu	5	gs
2003	Back In Front	3-3-14-4-2	26	1.00	0.04	cp	9	gs
2001	Limestone Lad	3-3-2-2-2	12	1.40	0.25	fr	6	sft
2000	Moscow Flyer	3-1-6-4-0	14	1.00	0.21	fr	5	sft
1999	Limestone Lad	3-3-2-2-2	12	1.40	0.25	fr	4	gs
1998	Nomadic	6-2-2-0-0	10	9.00	1.40	hu	6	hvy
1996	Cockney Lad	6-0-0-0-2	8	3.00	1.00	cp	6	sft
1995	Beakstown	2-0-2-0-4	8	0.60	-0.50	hu	4	gd
1994	Danoli	2-2-12-0-4	20	1.00	-0.10	fr	4	gs

DP

13/13 had 8 points or more in their Dosage Profile
9/13 had 12 points or more in their Dosage Profile

DI

11/13 had a DI of 1.00 and above
8/13 had a DI of 1.40 and above
Majority Range : 0.60 to 1.80 - 69% of winners

CD

11/13 had a CD of -0.10 and above
10/13 had a CD of 0.04 and above
9/13 had a CD of 0.21 and above
Majority Range : -0.10 to 0.63 - 62% of winners

Average

DI 2.16 / CD 0.32

Running Style

fr-6 / cp-3 / hu-4 - It pays to take the race by the scruff of the neck in the Maplewood Hurdle with 6/13 winning from the front. Hold up and close to pace runners do, however, win their fair share.

Summary

A good starting point in the Maplewood Hurdle is the DP totals, with all 13 winners having 8 points or more in their profile, a top class race for stoutly bred individuals. Despite 12/13 renewals being run on ground that was good to soft or worse the winners still had DI and CD ratings heading towards the speed side. 11/13 winners had a DI of 1.00 and above and 9/13 winners had a CD of 0.21 and above. Three winners of this race could also be classed as super fast as Iktitaf, Nomadic & Cockney Lad all had a CD of 1.00 or above and a DI of 3.00 and above. Unless another Brave Inca comes along in the near future I would be looking to be against horses with a DI below 1.00 and CD rating on the minus side.

Notable Defeats

'08 Jered - 0-1-3-4-2 (10) / **0.33** / **-0.70** - sp 4/5
'07 Ebaziyan - 4-1-10-6-3 (24) / **0.71** / **-0.13** - sp 5/1
'03 Scottish Memories - 3-0-3-4-2 (12) / **0.60** / **-0.17** - sp 7/2
'01 Youlneverwalkalone - 3-2-4-2-7 (18) / **0.64** / **-0.44** - sp 9/4

Amlin Lmtd Intermediate Handicap Chase - Ascot

21st November - cl1 g2 - 2m3f - 4yo+

Dosage Strength

★★★★★

Year	Horse	DP	tot	DI	CD	Run sty	Field Size	Gng
2008	My Petra	2-0-4-1-1	8	1.00	0.13	cp	6	gd
2007	Howle Hill	3-0-5-2-0	10	1.22	0.40	hu	8	gd
2006	Cerium	3-3-8-2-2	18	1.25	0.17	cp	9	sft
2003	Iris Royal	4-3-12-7-0	26	1.00	0.15	fr	5	sft
2001	Wahiba Sands	8-6-16-2-0	32	2.20	0.63	hu	4	gd
2000	Upgrade	9-1-10-2-0	22	2.14	0.77	fr	4	sft
1999	Nordance Prince	4-6-11-1-2	24	1.82	0.38	cp	11	gd
1998	Red Marauder	~~5-0-1-0-0~~	6	~~11.00~~	~~1.67~~	cp	11	gd
1997	Simply Dashing	6-3-4-5-0	18	1.57	0.56	hu	11	gs
1996	Strong Promise	4-5-5-2-0	16	2.56	0.69	cp	8	gf
1995	Sound Man	4-0-2-4-4	14	0.56	-0.29	cp	5	gd
1994	Raymylette	2-2-4-4-0	12	1.00	0.17	fr	11	gd

DP

11/12 had 8 points or more in their Dosage Profile
9/12 had 12 points or more in their Dosage Profile

DI

11/11 had a DI of 0.56 and above
10/11 had a DI of 1.00 and above
0/11 had a DI above 2.56
Majority Range : 1.00 to 2.20 - 82% of winners

CD

11/11 had a CD of -0.29 and above
10/11 had a CD of 0.13 and above
0/11 had a CD above 0.77
Majority Range : 0.13 to 0.69 - 82% of winners

Average

DI 1.48 / CD 0.34

Running Style

fr-3 / cp-6 / hu-3 - Its best to sit close to the pace in this intermediate handicap chase, similar to 6/12 previous winners. Front runners and hold up horse share 3 winners a piece.

Summary

A strong Dosage race and one that is well suited to the slightly faster thoroughbred. Any horse with a negative CD rating and a DI below 1.00 is going to have its work cut out as only '95 winner Sound Man has been victorious with these kind of credentials. Even the mighty Best Mate could not overcome this robust statistic. CD ratings give a strong pointer with 10/11 having a rating of 0.13 and above. The DI ranges are equally as strong with 10/11 having a rating of 1.00 or above. A statistic to be wary of is that no winner had a DI above 2.56 or a CD above 0.77, horses with vast quantities of speed are likely to be found out here. DP totals paint another strong picture as 11/12 had 8 points or more, only future Grand National winner Red Marauder had less.

Notable Defeats

'06 Chilling Place - 3-1-6-10-0 (20) / **0.54** / **-0.15** - sp 4/1
'03 Farmer Jack - 3-1-10-3-5 (22) / **0.69** / **-0.27** - sp 3/1
'01 Best Mate - 1-1-10-5-1 (18) / **0.64** / **-0.22** - sp 8/13
'97 Or Royal - **0-0-1-0-1 (2)** / 0.33 / -1.00 - sp 11/4

Ascot Hurdle - Ascot

21st November - cl1 g2 - 2m3f - 4yo+

Dosage Strength

★★★★

Year	Horse	DP	tot	DI	CD	Run sty	Field Size	Gng
2008	Chomba Womba	4-0-4-2-0	10	1.50	0.60	hu	8	gd
2007	Hardy Eustace	4-2-6-0-2	14	1.80	0.43	cp	8	gd
2006	Hardy Eustace	4-2-6-0-2	14	1.80	0.43	cp	7	sft
2003	Mr Cool	1-0-9-2-0	12	0.85	0.00	fr	4	gd
2002	Baracouda	2-3-8-1-2	16	1.29	0.13	hu	4	hvy
2001	Baracouda	2-3-8-1-2	16	1.29	0.13	hu	5	gd
2000	Kates Charm	0-0-5-5-2	12	0.26	-0.75	cp	5	sft
1999	Wahiba Sands	8-6-16-2-0	32	2.20	0.63	hu	6	gd
1998	Juyush	7-6-19-0-0	32	2.37	0.63	hu	7	gs
1997	Pridwell	6-1-21-10-0	38	0.85	0.08	hu	6	sft
1996	Muse	8-6-6-0-4	24	2.43	0.58	fr	3	gf
1995	Large Action	2-0-14-0-4	20	0.82	-0.20	fr	5	gd
1994	Oh So Risky	5-1-12-4-8	30	0.67	-0.30	hu	4	gd

DP

13/13 had 10 points or more in their Dosage Profile
10/13 had 14 points or more in their Dosage Profile

DI

11/13 had a DI of 0.82 and above
8/13 had a DI of 1.29 and above
0/13 had a DI above 2.43
Majority Range : 0.67 to 1.80 - 69% of winners

CD

12/13 had a CD of -0.30 and above
10/13 had a CD of 0.00 and above
0/13 had a CD above 0.63
Majority Range : 0.00 to 0.63 - 77% of winners

Average

DI 1.29 / CD 0.18

Running Style

fr-3 / cp-3 / hu-7 - Hold up horses are the call in the Ascot Hurdle with 54% of winners coming from out the back. Front runners and close to pace runners have supplied 3 winners each.

Summary

Stamina based winners are few and far between in this Grade 2 contest. Only 3/13 have had a CD below 0.00, the last being Kates Charm in 2000. There is a top limit to the CD rating however as no winner has succeeded with a rating above 0.63, horses in this range possibly finding the Ascot undulations and testing nature not to their liking over this distance. DI ratings also supply strong trends with 11/13 having a DI of 0.82 and above. As with the CD ratings the DI's also have an upper limit with no winner having a DI above 2.43. DP totals provide more strong trends as all 13 winners had 10 points or more in their Dosage Profile, making this a race for the Dosage strong.

Notable Defeats

'06 Mighty Man - 7-2-6-0-1 (16) / **3.00** / **0.88** - sp 15/8
'02 Landing Light - 3-3-19-13-10 (48) / **0.48** / **-0.50** - sp 4/1
'00 Celtic Native - 3-0-5-0-0 (8) / 2.20 / **0.75** - sp 6/4
'95 Atours - 17-22-11-8-0 (58) / **3.30** / **0.83** - sp 100/30

Dosage Fact

12 of the last 13 runners-up also had 8 points or more in their Dosage Profile. Champion hurdle winner Hors La Loi III being the exception.

Becher Chase - Aintree

22nd November - cl1 Lst hcp - 3m2f - 5yo+

Dosage Strength

Year	Horse	DP	tot	DI	CD	Run sty	Field Size	Gng
2008	Black Apalachi	2-0-8-4-0	14	0.75	0.00	fr	13	hvy
2007	Mr Pointment	2-0-7-4-5	18	0.44	-0.56	fr	19	gs
2006	Eurotrek	2-0-8-10-2	22	0.38	-0.45	cp	21	gd
2005	Garvivonnian	~~1-0-1-0-0~~	2	~~3.00~~	~~1.00~~	cp	19	gs
2004	Silver Birch	2-0-4-8-6	20	0.25	-0.80	fr	14	sft
2003	Clan Royal	0-0-2-10-2	14	0.08	-1.00	hu	15	gd
2002	Ardent Scout	0-0-3-0-15	18	0.09	-1.67	cp	15	gs
2001	Amberleigh House	5-1-8-2-4	20	1.00	0.05	hu	15	sft
2000	Young Kenny	1-0-8-0-11	20	0.33	-1.00	cp	11	sft
1999	Feels Like Gold	4-0-2-4-0	10	1.00	0.40	cp	12	gd
1998	Earth Summit	3-0-11-2-0	16	1.13	0.25	cp	8	gs
1997	Samlee	0-1-6-9-4	20	0.25	-0.80	cp	11	gs
1996	Into The Red	4-0-10-0-0	14	1.80	0.57	hu	8	gd
1995	Young Hustler	6-0-10-0-0	16	2.20	0.75	fr	10	gf
1994	Into The Red	4-0-10-0-0	14	1.80	0.57	cp	9	gd

DP

14/15 had 10 points or more in their Dosage Profile
13/15 had between 14 and 22 points in their Dosage Profile

DI

13/14 had a DI of 1.80 and below
11/14 had a DI of 1.13 and below
8/14 had a DI of 0.75 and below
Majority Range : 0.25 to 1.13 - 64% of winners

CD

11/14 had a CD of 0.40 and below
9/14 had a CD of 0.05 and below
Majority Range : -1.00 to 0.25 - 64% of winners

Average

DI 0.82 / CD -0.26

Running Style

fr-4 / cp-8 / hu-3 - Hold up runners fair the worst in this Listed handicap run over the National fences. With plenty of incidents likely to happen in front of them it can be difficult for held up runners to get into the race. Close to pace runners are the majority call with 8 victories.

Summary

Unsurprisingly the Becher chase has a slight bias towards stamina based Dosage ratings. The large fences and galloping track combining to make this handicap a rigorous challenge. 11/14 had a DI of 1.13 or below and 9/14 had a CD of 0.05 and below. More interestingly, the 3 horses that had a DI above 1.13 won the '94, '95 and '96 renewals. This means that every Dosage strong winner of the past 12 years had a DI of 1.13 and below. This coincides with the rise in field sizes, making the race a more true run affair than it had been in the '94 - '96 period. If the field sizes keep to the 12+ mark I would expect the more stamina based horses to keep winning. DP totals point towards the Dosage strong with only Garvivonnian, the 2005 winner, having less than 8 points in his profile.

Notable Defeats

'05 Forest Gunner - 9-0-1-0-0 (10) / **19.00** / **1.80** - sp 11/2
'98 Cavalero - **0-0-0-0-6 (6)** / 0.00 / -2.00 - sp 5/2
'94 Indian Tonic - **0-2-0-2-0 (4)** / 1.00 / 0.00 - sp 2/1

Worcester Novices' Chase - Newbury

26th - 28th November - cl1 g2 - 3m - 4yo+

Dosage Strength

Year	Horse	DP	tot	DI	CD	Run sty	Field Size	Gng
2008	Gone To Lunch	5-0-9-4-4	22	0.76	-0.09	cp	6	gs
2007	Joe Lively	3-3-5-0-1	12	2.43	0.58	cp	4	sft
2006	Boychuk	2-0-5-1-0	8	1.29	0.38	cp	5	gs
2005	Darkness	5-2-7-4-0	18	1.40	0.44	cp	7	gd
2004	Cornish Rebel	1-1-10-5-1	18	0.64	-0.22	hu	5	gd
2003	Ballycassidy	2-1-6-1-0	10	1.50	0.40	hu	6	gs
2002	Lucky Bay	0-0-2-8-6	16	0.07	-1.25	cp	6	sft
2001	Valley Henry	1-4-10-3-2	20	1.00	-0.05	hu	7	gd
2000	Shotgun Willy	3-1-10-0-0	14	1.80	0.50	cp	6	gs

DP

9/9 had 8 points or more in their Dosage Profile
7/9 had between 12 and 22 points in their Dosage profile

DI

8/9 had a DI of 1.80 and below
7/9 had a DI of 1.50 and below
Majority Range : 0.64 to 1.80 - 78% of winners

CD

8/9 had a CD of -0.22 and above
7/9 had a CD of -0.09 and above
Majority Range : -0.22 to 0.58 - 89% of winners

Average

DI 1.21 / CD 0.08

Running Style

fr-0 / cp-6 / hu-3 - Despite the small fields it still proves hard to win from the front as 0/9 renewals have gone to front runners. Close to pace runners have taken the most renewals.

Summary

A 3 mile trip but not one for the stamina heavy, any horse holding a major stock of stamina is likely to struggle in this graded novices' chase. 8/9 had a CD of -0.22 and above and a DI of 0.64 and above. Further still, 7/9 had a CD of -0.09 and above. The only stamina heavy winner, Lucky Bay, had conditions on his side in the 2002 renewal with the soft ground playing to the strengths of his stamina based Dosage. On the flip side it is also not prudent for a horse to hold vast amounts of speed in its Dosage as only the tough battler Joe Lively had a DI above 1.80. DP totals point in the direction of Dosage strong runners as all 9 winners had 8 points or more in their Profile.

Notable Defeats

'05 Iris's Gift - 5-0-2-1-0 (8) / **3.00** / **1.13** - sp 4/7
'03 Celestial Gold - **1-1-0-2-0 (4)** / 1.00 / 0.25 - sp 7/2
'02 One Knight - **0-0-0-0-0 (0)** / inf / inf - sp 11/8
'00 Bindaree - 1-1-3-4-1 (10) / **0.54** / **-0.30** - sp 2/1

Dosage Fact

The previous 5 runnings of this race (which were held at Worcester) were all won by horses with Dosage Ratings that fell out with the above parameters.

Long Distance Hurdle - Newbury

28th November - cl1 g2 - 3m - 4yo+

Dosage Strength

Year	Horse	DP	tot	DI	CD	Run sty	Field Size	Gng
2008	Duc De Regniere	~~1-0-2-0-1~~	4	~~1.00~~	~~0.00~~	hu	9	gs
2007	Inglis Drever	3-0-22-15-2	42	0.50	-0.31	hu	7	sft
2006	Inglis Drever	3-0-22-15-2	42	0.50	-0.31	hu	5	sft
2005	Inglis Drever	3-0-22-15-2	42	0.50	-0.31	cp	6	gd
2004	Baracouda	2-3-8-1-2	16	1.29	0.13	hu	6	gd
2003	Baracouda	2-3-8-1-2	16	1.29	0.13	cp	8	gs
2002	Bacchanal	4-7-16-1-0	28	2.11	0.50	fr	8	sft
2001	Historic	11-1-28-8-0	44	1.20	0.34	fr	8	sft
2000	Deano's Beeno	5-1-6-10-6	28	0.47	-0.39	cp	8	sft
1999	Deano's Beeno	5-1-6-10-6	28	0.47	-0.39	fr	9	gs
1998	Princeful	2-0-6-4-2	14	0.56	-0.29	cp	6	sft
1997	Go-Informal	4-1-3-0-0	8	4.33	1.13	cp	8	sft
1996	What A Question	3-0-14-1-4	22	0.83	-0.14	hu	11	gd
1995	Conquering Leader	4-1-3-4-6	18	0.57	-0.39	hu	7	sft
1994	Hebridean	4-0-4-4-2	14	0.75	0.00	hu	6	gs

DP

14/15 had 8 points or more in their Dosage Profile
11/15 had 16 points or more in their Dosage profile

DI

12/14 had a DI of 1.29 and below
9/14 had a DI of 0.83 and below
0/14 had a DI below 0.47
Majority Range : 0.47 to 1.29 - 86% of winners

CD

12/14 had a CD of 0.34 and below
9/14 had a CD of 0.00 and below
0/14 had a CD below -0.39
Majority Range : -0.39 to 0.13 - 79% of winners

Average

DI 1.10 / CD -0.02

Running Style

fr-3 / cp-5 / hu-7 - It pays to attack from behind in the Long Distance Hurdle with 7 winners stalking the field during the race. Close to pace winners have also won their fair share with 5 victories.

Summary

A strong Dosage race with very workable Dosage ranges to go to war with. On the face of it 3 miles around Newbury's galloping expanses on winter ground should suit stamina heavy horses. This however is not the case. The lowest winning CD rating was -0.39 and the lowest DI rating was 0.47 - every other winners Dosage fell above this. This is not to say the Long Distance Hurdle is for speedsters, however, as only 3 winners had a CD of above 0.13 and only 2 winners had a DI of above 1.29. As far as DP totals go this is a race to concentrate on the Dosage strong as only last years winner Duc De Regniere had less than 8 points in his total. Current World Hurdle Champion Big Bucks has Dosage figures of DI 0.43 and CD -0.50 and it would be interesting to see, if lining up in this years renewal, if he were able to overcome the race Dosage figures.

Notable Defeats

'08 Blazing Bailey - 3-0-16-2-9 (30) / 0.58 / **-0.47** - sp 3-1
'06 Irish Wolf - 2-3-15-0-0 (20) / **1.67** / **0.35** - sp 7/2
'04 Crystal D'Ainay - **0-0-1-3-0 (4)** / 0.14 / -0.75 - sp 5-1
'01 First Gold - 2-0-0-4-2 (8) / **0.33** / **-0.50** - sp 4/5

Dosage Fact

The only winner to have had Dosage figures lower than identified above was 1992 winner Tyrone Bridge and he actually finished 2nd but was placed 1st after a stewards enquiry.

Hennessey Gold Cup - Newbury

28th November - cl1 g3 hcp - 3m2f - 4yo+

Dosage Strength

Year	Horse	DP	tot	DI	CD	Run sty	Field Size	Gng
2008	Madison Du Berlais	~~0-0-3-1-0~~	4	~~0.60~~	~~-0.25~~	cp	15	gs
2007	Denman	0-1-1-6-2	10	0.18	-0.90	cp	18	sft
2006	State Of Play	2-0-11-2-5	20	0.60	-0.40	cp	16	sft
2005	Trabolgan	3-0-1-4-0	8	0.78	0.25	cp	19	gd
2004	Celestial Gold	~~1-1-0-2-0~~	4	~~1.00~~	~~0.25~~	hu	14	gd
2003	Strong Flow	2-1-11-0-0	14	1.55	0.36	hu	21	gs
2002	Be My Royal (dsq)	3-0-7-0-0	10	1.86	0.60	cp	25	gs
2001	Whats up Boys	6-1-3-4-4	18	0.89	0.06	cp	14	sft
2000	Kings Road	~~2-0-0-4-0~~	6	~~0.50~~	~~0.00~~	cp	17	hvy
1999	Ever Blessed	2-1-4-1-4	12	0.71	-0.33	hu	13	gs
1998	Teeton Mill	0-0-4-4-2	10	0.25	-0.80	cp	16	sft
1997	Suny Bay	~~2-0-2-0-0~~	4	~~3.00~~	~~1.00~~	fr	14	gs
1996	Coome Hill	3-2-1-2-0	8	2.20	0.75	fr	11	gd
1995	Couldn't Be Better	~~2-0-2-2-0~~	6	~~1.00~~	~~0.33~~	cp	11	sft
1994	One Man	~~1-0-4-1-0~~	6	~~1.00~~	~~0.17~~	cp	16	gs

DP

9/15 had 8 points or more in their Dosage Profile
9/15 had between 8 and 20 points in their Dosage Profile

DI

9/9 had a DI of 2.20 and below
6/9 had a DI of 0.89 and below
Majority Range : 0.18 to 0.89 - 67% of winners

CD

7/9 had a CD of 0.36 and below
5/9 had a CD of 0.06 and below
0/9 had a CD below -0.90
Majority Range : -0.40 to 0.60 - 67% of winners

Average

DI 1.00 / CD -0.05

Running Style

fr-2 / cp-10 / hu-3 - Close to the pace is definitely the position the winner wants to be in the Hennessey Gold Cup. 10 of the last 15 have taken this running position during the race. Coome Hill, who was one of the 2 front running winners, also had the speediest Dosage rating of any winner.

Summary

Disappointingly this is not a great race for Dosage analysis due to 6 winners having less than 8 points in their Dosage Profile. From the figures we have left to analyse the suggestion is that it may be prudent to stick to runners with a profile leaning towards stamina - 6/9 had a DI of 0.89 and below and a CD of 0.25 and below. Until we see more Dosage strong animals winning the Hennessey it may be best to treat Dosage analysis of the race with a degree of caution.

Notable Defeats

'06 Idle Talk - 8-4-8-0-0 (20) / **4.00** / **1.00** - sp 8/1
'04 Ollie Magern - 0-1-2-0-5 (8) / 0.33 / **-1.13** - sp 13/2
'01 Ad Hoc - 3-3-4-0-0 (10) / **4.00** / **0.90** - sp 5/1

Dosage Fact

3 of the first 5 home in the 2008 renewal had less than 8 points in their Dosage Profile - Madison Du Berlais, Air Force One and My Will.

Fighting Fifth Hurdle - Newcastle

28th November - cl1 g1 - 2m - 4yo+

Dosage Strength

★★★★★

Year	Horse	DP	tot	DI	CD	Run sty	Field Size	Gng
2007	Harchibald	5-4-13-2-0	24	1.82	0.50	hu	8	gs
2006	Straw Bear	5-1-6-4-4	20	0.82	-0.05	cp	9	gs
2005	Arcalis	2-2-16-0-0	20	1.50	0.30	hu	9	sft
2004	Harchibald	5-4-13-2-0	24	1.82	0.50	hu	8	gd
2003	The French Furze	13-7-13-5-0	38	2.30	0.74	hu	8	gd
2002	Intersky Falcon	5-1-16-0-0	22	1.75	0.50	cp	6	gs
2001	Landing Light	3-3-19-13-10	48	0.48	-0.50	cp	5	gs
2000	Barton	4-3-8-5-0	20	1.22	0.30	cp	6	sft
1999	Dato Star	5-1-7-4-1	18	1.72	0.28	fr	9	gd
1998	Dato Star	5-1-7-4-1	18	1.72	0.28	cp	6	gs
1997	Star Rage	6-1-9-0-2	18	1.77	0.50	cp	8	gd
1996	Space Trucker	4-2-10-8-0	24	0.85	0.08	hu	8	gd
1995	Padre Mio	3-1-16-0-4	24	1.00	-0.04	hu	7	gd
1994	Batabanoo	2-3-5-10-6	26	0.41	-0.58	hu	4	gd

DP

14/14 had 18 points or more in their Dosage Profile
11/14 had 20 points or more in their Dosage Profile

DI

12/14 had a DI of 0.82 and above
9/14 had a DI of 1.22 and above
1/14 had a DI above 1.82
Majority Range : 0.82 to 1.82 - 79% of winners

CD

12/14 had a CD of -0.05 and above
9/14 had a CD of 0.28 and above
1/14 had a CD above 0.50
Majority Range : -0.05 to 0.50 - 79% of winners

Average

DI 1.37 / CD 0.20

Running Style

fr-1 / cp-6 / hu-7 - The galloping-testing nature of Gosforth Park makes it difficult for front runners with only dual winner Dato Star succeeding from the front. Hold up horses just shade it from close to pace runners.

Summary

Despite Newcastle's testing track this race still favours slightly speedier bred animals. 12/14 winners had a CD of -0.05 and above, a stat that future Cheltenham winners Katchit and Inglis Drever both failed to overcome. Narrowing the stats further we see that 9/14 had a CD of 0.28 and above although only one winner, race specialist The French Furze, had a CD above 0.50. This gives strong majority ranges to work with when handicapping future renewals. DI ratings also follow the same path with 12/14 having a DI of 0.82 and above and 9/14 having a DI of 1.22 and above. Once more The French Furze is slightly faster than your average winner being the only horse to have a DI above 1.82. DP totals harden the Dosage strength of this race even more with 14/14 having 18 points or more in their profile, this was another negative against Katchit in the 2007 renewal.

Notable Defeats

'07 Katchit - **1-2-5-3-1 (12)** / 0.85 / **-0.08** - sp 5/4
'04 Inglis Drever - 3-0-22-15-2 (42) / **0.50** / **-0.31** - sp 9/4
'03 Westender - 2-0-17-13-2 (34) / **0.45** / **-0.38** - sp 7/2
'95 Chief Minister - 10-0-20-12-4 (46) / **0.77** / 0.00 - sp 15/8

Dosage Fact

3 of the above (Inglis Drever, Westender and Chief Minister) were all sired by Chef-de-Race Rainbow Quest.

Hattons Grace Hurdle - Fairyhouse

29th November - g1 - 2m4f - 4yo+

Dosage Strength

★★★★

Year	Horse	DP	tot	DI	CD	Run sty	Field Size	Gng
2008	Catch Me	3-3-3-0-1	10	3.00	0.70	hu	8	sft
2007	Aitmatov	1-0-9-3-5	18	0.44	-0.61	cp	8	hvy
2006	Brave Inca	0-1-7-9-9	26	0.21	-1.00	cp	5	hvy
2005	Solerina	3-1-8-2-0	14	1.33	0.36	fr	5	sft
2004	Solerina	3-1-8-2-0	14	1.33	0.36	fr	5	sft
2003	Solerina	3-1-8-2-0	14	1.33	0.36	fr	10	sft
2002	Limestone Lad	3-3-2-2-2	12	1.40	0.25	fr	5	sft
2001	Limestone Lad	3-3-2-2-2	12	1.40	0.25	fr	7	gs
2000	Youlneverwalkalone	3-2-4-2-7	18	0.64	-0.44	hu	7	gs
1999	Limestone Lad	3-3-2-2-2	12	1.40	0.25	fr	5	sft
1998	Istabraq	11-9-26-10-0	56	1.43	0.38	cp	6	gs
1997	Istabraq	11-9-26-10-0	56	1.43	0.38	fr	5	gs
1996	Large Action	2-0-14-0-4	20	0.82	-0.20	cp	8	gs
1995	Dorans Pride	~~2-0-2-0-2~~	6	~~1.00~~	~~0.00~~	fr	3	gs
1994	Danoli	2-2-14-0-4	20	1.00	-0.10	cp	7	gs

DP

14/15 had 10 points or more in their Dosage Profile
13/15 had 12 points or more in their Dosage Profile

DI

13/14 had a DI of 1.43 and below
8/14 had a DI of 1.33 and below
Majority Range : 0.44 to 1.43 - 86% of winners

CD

13/14 had a CD of 0.38 and below
8/14 had a CD of 0.25 and below
1/14 had a CD below -0.61
Majority Range : -0.20 to 0.38 - 71% of winners

Average

DI 1.23 / CD 0.07

Running Style

fr-8 / cp-5 / hu-2 - Despite Catch Me winning from out the back in last years renewal, hold up horses have struggled to win the Hattons Grace. Front runners have the best record but 6 of the 8 victories were gained by Limestone Lad and Solerina with 3 wins each.

Summary

This is not a race for a speedy sort as only last years winner Catch Me had a DI above 1.43 and a CD above 0.38. 13/14 had a DI of 1.43 and below and a CD of 0.38 and below, even top class horses such as Hardy Eustace and Asian Maze have found these powerful stats impossible to overcome. Ground conditions may have a part to play in keeping the Dosage ratings to the low end as every renewal was run on ground that was either good to soft or worse. DP totals show that it is the Dosage strong that should be concentrated upon as only Dorans Pride has managed to win with less than 10 points in his profile. Since the dominance of Solerina and Limestone Lad ended we have seen 2 stamina based winners and 1 speed based winner. With the testing nature of the track and usual soft ground I expect we may see more horses with lower CD ratings starting to win, however any front running horses lining up with a Dosage similar to the triple winners profile should be feared.

Notable Defeats

'08 Hardy Eustace - 4-2-6-0-2 (14) / **1.80** / **0.43** - sp 4/1
'06 Asian Maze - 3-2-1-2-0 (8) / **2.20** / **0.75** - sp 4/7
'01 Ned Kelly - 5-0-7-0-0 (12) / **2.43** / **0.83** - sp 2/1
'97 Cockney Lad - 6-0-0-0-2 (8) / **3.00** / **1.00** - sp 11/4

Royal Bond Novices' Hurdle - Fairyhouse

29th November - g1 - 2m - 4yo+

Dosage Strength

★★★

Year	Horse	DP	tot	DI	CD	Run sty	Field Size	Gng
2008	Hurricane Fly	2-1-9-4-0	16	0.88	0.06	cp	8	sft
2007	Muirhead	3-3-5-0-1	12	2.43	0.58	hu	10	hvy
2006	Hide The Evidence	3-3-3-0-1	10	3.00	0.70	hu	9	hvy
2005	Iktitaf	12-4-10-0-0	26	4.20	1.08	hu	8	sft
2004	Wild Passion	2-0-0-1-5	8	0.33	-0.88	hu	9	sft
2003	Newmill	~~0-0-4-2-0~~	6	~~0.50~~	~~-0.33~~	fr	12	sft
2002	Hardy Eustace	4-2-6-0-2	14	1.80	0.43	cp	10	sft
2001	Like-A-Butterfly	3-2-4-0-7	16	0.78	-0.38	cp	5	gs
2000	Liss A Paoraigh	5-2-6-0-1	14	2.50	0.71	cp	8	gs
1999	Moscow Flyer	3-1-6-4-0	14	1.00	0.21	fr	4	sft
1998	Alexander Banquet	0-1-6-7-0	14	0.40	-0.43	cp	8	gs
1997	Feathered Leader	6-1-3-4-4	18	0.89	0.06	cp	9	gs
1996	Istabraq	11-9-26-10-0	56	1.43	0.38	cp	7	gs
1995	That's My Man	2-2-4-0-0	8	3.00	0.75	fr	6	gs
1994	Gambolling Doc	5-3-0-0-0	8	inf	1.63	hu	8	gs

DP

14/15 had 8 points or more in their Dosage Profile
10/15 had 12 points or more in their Dosage Profile

DI

12/14 had a DI of 0.78 and above
9/14 had a DI of 1.00 and above
Majority Range : 0.89 to 3.00 - 64% of winners

CD

11/14 had a CD of 0.06 and above
9/14 had a CD of 0.21 and above
1/14 had a CD below -0.43
Majority Range : 0.06 to 0.75 - 64% of winners

Average

DI 1.74 / CD 0.35

Running Style

fr-3 / cp-7 / hu-5 - Close to pace runners hold a slender advantage over held up runners although 4 of the last 5 winners were held up out the back during the race.

Summary

A race for the speedier novice with only 3 winners having a CD on the minus side. The other 11 all had a CD of 0.06 and above, narrowing the ratings further, 9/14 had a CD of 0.21 and above. DI ratings also highlight the lack of stamina winners as 12/14 had a DI of 0.78 and above, narrowing it further with 9/14 having a DI of 1.00 and above. Recent years have seen 3 exceptionally speedy bred novices take this with Iktitaf, Hide the Evidence and Muirhead all having a DI of 2.43 and above and a CD of 0.58 and above. DP totals give a strong indicator as only future Champion Chase hero Newmill won the race with less than 8 points in his profile.

Notable Defeats

'06 Blazing Sky - 0-0-5-3-0 (8) / **0.45** / **-0.38** - sp 4/1
'01 Golden Row - **0-0-1-0-1 (2)** / 0.33 / -1.00 - sp 9/4
'00 Quadco - 3-0-8-0-11 (22) / **0.47** / **-0.73** - sp 6/4
'99 Stage Affair - 3-2-18-7-4 (34) / **0.70** / **-0.21** - sp 4/11

Drinmore Novices' Chase - Fairyhouse

29th November - g1 - 2m4f - 5yo+

Dosage Strength

Year	Horse	DP	tot	DI	CD	Run sty	Field Size	Gng
2008	Trafford Lad	2-1-16-2-1	22	1.00	0.05	cp	8	sft
2007	Sky's The Limit	1-1-6-2-0	10	1.00	0.10	hu	8	hvy
2006	Cailin Alainn	1-9-6-2-0	18	2.60	0.50	cp	10	hvy
2005	Kill Devil Hill	3-3-2-0-0	8	7.00	1.13	cp	6	hvy
2004	Watson Lake	4-1-5-0-0	10	3.00	0.90	fr	5	sft
2003	Nil Desperandum	0-0-7-7-0	14	0.33	-0.50	cp	10	sft
2002	Le Coudray	1-0-8-4-5	18	0.38	-0.67	cp	9	sft
2001	Harbour Pilot	3-2-7-0-0	12	2.43	0.67	cp	6	gs
2000	Sackville	2-1-5-2-2	12	0.85	-0.08	cp	5	gs
1999	Alexander Banquet	0-1-6-7-0	14	0.40	-0.43	cp	8	sft
1998	Promalee	4-4-2-2-0	12	3.00	0.83	cp	9	gs
1997	Private Peace	~~0-0-0-2-0~~	2	~~0.00~~	~~-1.00~~	cp	9	gs
1996	Dorans Pride	~~2-0-2-0-2~~	6	~~1.00~~	~~0.00~~	cp	8	gs
1995	Johnny Setaside	~~2-2-2-0-0~~	6	~~5.00~~	~~1.00~~	cp	9	gs
1994	Sound Man	4-0-2-4-4	14	0.56	-0.29	fr	7	gs

DP

12/15 had 8 points or more in their Dosage Profile
11/15 had between 10 and 22 points in their Dosage Profile

DI

9/12 had a DI of 0.56 and above
7/12 had a DI of 1.00 and above
0/12 had a DI between 1.01 and 2.42
Majority Range : 0.85 to 3.00 - 58% of winners

CD

10/12 had a CD of -0.43 and above
8/12 had a CD of -0.08 and above
0/12 had a CD between 0.11 and 0.49
0/12 had a CD of below -0.67
Majority Range : -0.43 to 0.67 - 58% of winners

Average

DI 1.88 / CD 0.18

Running Style

fr-2 / cp-12 / hu-1 - Close to pace runners steal the show in the Drinmore. A massive 80% of winners have raced close to the pace in the past 15 runnings. Sky's the limit is the only winner to have been held up.

Summary

Not many strong pointers with regards to Dosage in the Drinmore Novices' Chase. Winners show a slight bias towards speed and the last 5 winners had a DI of 1.00 and above and a CD of 0.05 and above. 0/12 have had a CD below -0.67 so any runner with mass quantities of stamina in their Dosage is likely to struggle. The strongest pointer available may come from the fact that 0/12 had a DI between 1.01 and 2.42 or a CD between 0.11 and 0.49. This suggests that to win the Drinmore it is best to have either stamina tendencies or speed tendencies but not a mix of both. Last years Arkle Chase winner Forpadydeplasterer falls into this category and he failed to overcome this statistic when finishing 2nd.

Notable Defeats

'08 Forpadydeplasterer - 5-1-8-4-0 (18) / **1.25** / **0.39** - sp 7/2
'03 Pizzaro - 1-1-1-5-2 (10) / **0.33** / **-0.60** - sp 7/4
'01 Macs Gildoran - 3-0-5-0-2 (10) / **1.22** / **0.20** - sp 11/10

Winter Novices' Hurdle - Sandown

4th December - cl1 g2 - 2m4f - 4yo+

Dosage Strength

Year	Horse	DP	tot	DI	CD	Run sty	Field Size	Gng
2008	Junior	5-1-18-7-1	32	0.88	0.06	hu	7	sft
2007	Lightning Strike	8-3-11-0-0	22	3.00	0.86	cp	6	hvy
2006	Labelthou	~~2-0-2-0-0~~	2	~~3.00~~	~~1.00~~	fr	5	sft
2005	Neptune Collonges	~~0-0-0-2-0~~	2	~~0.00~~	~~-1.00~~	cp	4	hvy
2004	Ladalko	~~0-0-1-1-0~~	2	~~0.33~~	~~-0.50~~	hu	7	gs
2003	Inglis Drever	3-0-22-15-2	42	0.50	-0.31	hu	7	gs
2002	Coolnagorna	3-11-4-0-0	18	8.00	0.94	fr	7	sft
2001	Rouble	3-1-7-4-3	18	0.71	-0.17	cp	5	sft
1999	Whats Up Boys	6-1-3-4-4	18	0.89	0.06	cp	7	gs
1998	Barton	4-3-8-5-0	20	1.22	0.30	hu	7	gd
1997	Song Of Sword	6-2-11-6-5	30	0.82	-0.07	fr	9	gs
1996	Yahmi	7-8-7-1-1	24	3.36	0.79	hu	6	gd
1995	See More Business	0-0-3-6-1	10	0.18	-0.80	cp	5	gd
1994	Roberty Lea	7-3-15-2-1	28	1.67	0.46	hu	8	gd

DP

11/14 had 10 points or more in their Dosage Profile
10/14 had 18 points or more in their Dosage Profile

DI

10/11 had a DI of 0.50 and above
8/11 had a DI of 0.82 and above
Majority Range : 0.50 to 1.67 - 64% of winners

CD

10/11 had a CD of -0.31 and above
9/11 had a CD of -0.17 and above
7/11 had a CD of 0.06 and above
Majority Range : -0.31 to 0.46 - 64% of winners

Average

DI 1.93 / CD 0.19

Running Style

fr-3 / cp-5 / hu-6 - Hold up horses just come out on top from close to pace runners in the Winter Novices' Hurdle.

Summary

Stamina heavy horses struggle in the Winter Novices' Hurdle. Apart from the stamina laden See More Business every winner had a CD of -0.31 and above and a DI of 0.50 and above. Although the majority call is to side with Dosage strong runners, 3 Dosage weak horses have won this race in the past 5 years and it would be foolish to ignore these types when handicapping this novice hurdle in future. Apart from the stamina strong See More Business every winner had at least 3 points in the Brilliant section of their Dosage profile.

Notable Defeats

'04 No Refuge - 5-0-13-2-8 (28) / **0.70** / **-0.29** - sp 5/2
'03 Control Man - 0-0-5-7-0 (12) / **0.26** / **-0.58** - sp 5/2
'97 Noisy Miner - 2-2-6-8-0 (18) / **0.64** / **-0.11** - sp 7/4

Henry VIII Novices' Chase - Sandown

5th December - cl1 g2 - 2m - 4yo+

Dosage Strength

★★★★

Year	Horse	DP	tot	DI	CD	Run sty	Field Size	Gng
2008	Araldur	~~0-3-3-0-0~~	6	~~3.00~~	~~0.50~~	cp	5	gs
2007	Marodima	~~0-0-4-2-0~~	6	~~0.50~~	~~-0.33~~	fr	5	sft
2006	Fair Along	~~1-0-1-0-0~~	2	~~3.00~~	~~1.00~~	fr	5	sft
2005	Racing Demon	2-0-6-4-0	12	0.71	0.00	hu	7	sft
2004	Contraband	2-4-18-2-0	26	1.36	0.23	cp	5	gs
2003	Thisthatandtother	1-2-13-0-0	16	1.46	0.25	cp	7	gd
2002	Impek	0-0-8-0-0	8	1.00	0.00	cp	3	sft
2001	Fondmort	2-0-2-4-0	8	0.60	0.00	hu	8	gs
1999	Decoupage	2-1-6-9-14	32	0.23	-1.00	hu	7	gd
1998	Dines	1-1-6-0-0	8	1.67	0.38	fr	5	gd
1997	Direct Route	3-3-4-2-0	12	2.00	0.58	hu	7	gd
1996	Mulligan	5-7-4-0-2	18	3.50	0.72	fr	3	gd
1995	Certainly Strong	3-3-4-4-2	16	1.00	0.06	cp	6	gd
1994	Sound Reveille	0-2-4-10-6	22	0.22	-0.91	fr	4	gd

DP

11/14 had 8 points or more in their Dosage Profile
8/14 had 12 points or more in their Dosage Profile

DI

10/11 had a DI of 2.00 and below
9/11 had a DI of 1.67 and below
8/11 had a DI of 1.46 and below
Majority Range : 0.60 to 2.00 - 73% of winners

CD

9/11 had a CD of 0.00 and above
6/11 had a CD of 0.06 and above
1/11 had a CD above 0.58
Majority Range : 0.00 to 0.58 - 73% of winners

Average

DI 1.25 / CD 0.03

Running Style

fr-5 / cp-5 / hu-4 - No preference to any running style in this Grade 2 novices' chase. Hold up runners have only won 1 of the last 7 renewals.

Summary

The strongest statistic available in this novice chase comes from the CD stats. Horses with a Dosage leaning towards the stamina side are going to struggle as 9/11 winners had a CD of 0.00 and above. Only one horse has won with a CD above 0.58, '96 winner Mulligan, so be wary of backing horses with a vast amount of speed in their Dosage. The same applies to DI ratings, Mulligan was the only horse with a DI above 2.00, so it is best to concentrate on runners with a lower DI than this. The majority ratings mentioned in the analysis give a strong indication of what to look for in a Henry VIII winner. Until the last 3 seasons every winner had 8 or more points in their DP total. Whether the trend of Dosage weak winners is likely to continue is impossible to tell ,however, it is something to keep an eye on.

Notable Defeats

'07 Moon Over Miami - 2-0-5-3-2 (12) / **0.60** / **-0.25** - sp 9/4
'06 My Way De Solzen - 1-2-9-3-5 (20) / **0.60** / **-0.45** - sp 4/7
'99 Fadalko - 2-0-5-5-0 - 2-0-5-5-0 (12) / **0.60** / **-0.08** - sp 13/8
'98 Mountain Storm - 5-3-6-0-0 (14) / **3.67** / **0.93** - sp 9/4

Listed Handicap Hurdle - Sandown

5th December - cl1 Lst - 2m - 4yo+

Dosage Strength

★★★★

Year	Horse	DP	tot	DI	CD	Run sty	Field Size	Gng
2008	Sunnyhillboy	3-0-7-4-0	14	0.87	0.14	hu	12	sft
2007	Ring The Boss	3-0-6-2-5	16	0.60	-0.38	fr	13	hvy
2006	Overstrand	3-4-18-17-2	44	0.57	-0.25	hu	17	hvy
2005	Verasi	10-3-8-2-1	24	2.43	0.79	hu	19	hvy
2004	Monte Cinto	3-0-5-0-6	14	0.65	-0.43	hu	21	gs
2003	Overstrand	3-4-18-17-2	44	0.57	-0.25	hu	14	gs
2002	Spirit Leader	6-3-3-4-4	20	1.11	0.15	hu	12	sft
2001	Rob Leach	4-3-22-5-0	34	1.13	0.18	cp	11	sft
1999	Copeland	3-0-9-4-0	16	0.88	0.13	cp	12	gs
1998	Polar Prospect	5-3-16-0-0	24	2.00	0.54	hu	13	gd
1997	Major Jamie	6-0-4-2-2	14	1.33	0.43	cp	21	gs
1996	Make A Stand	6-0-4-0-2	12	2.00	0.67	fr	15	gd
1995	Chiefs Song	3-1-4-0-6	14	0.75	-0.36	cp	21	gd
1994	Relkeel	0-2-3-10-1	16	0.28	-0.63	hu	7	gs

DP

14/14 had 12 points or more in their Dosage Profile
9/14 had 16 points or more in their Dosage profile

DI

13/14 had a DI of 2.00 and below
11/14 had a DI of 1.33 and below
10/14 had a DI of 1.13 and below
Majority Range : 0.57 to 1.33 - 71% of winners

CD

12/14 had a CD of 0.54 and below
10/14 had a CD of 0.18 and below
1/14 had a CD below -0.43
Majority Range : -0.43 to 0.54 - 79% of winners

Average

DI 1.08 / CD 0.05

Running Style

fr-2 / cp-4 / hu-8 - Hold up horses come out on top in this competitive handicap hurdle. Front runners have only managed 2 victories, struggling to lead from pillar to post in double figured fields.

Summary

Usually a competitive handicap and one that heavily favours the Dosage strong thoroughbred. 14/14 had 12 points or more in their profile and 9/14 had 16 points or more. Plenty of strongly fancied runners have failed to change this stat. Although a 2 mile hurdle race this is not an event that is dominated by speed heavy winners. In fact only 1 winner has had a DI above 2.00 (Verasi) and it is the other end of the scale that supplies most winners. 10/14 winners have had a DI of 1.13 or below with the same number having a CD of 0.18 and below. This is not to say this Listed hurdle is suited to a stamina heavy horse as only the talented Relkeel has managed to win the race with a DI below 0.57 and a CD below -0.43. 11 of the last 14 races have been run on good to soft or worse conditions so I suspect the testing ground and uphill finish have a major contributing factor in keeping the Dosage ratings on the low side.

Notable Defeats

'07 Breedsbreeze - **3-1-0-0-2 (6)** / 2.00 / 0.50 - sp 7/1
'05 Victram - **3-0-3-0-0 (6)** / 3.00 / 1.00 - sp 3/1
'03 Never - 9-5-11-1-0 (26) / **3.00** / **0.85** - sp 6/1
'02 Samon - **0-0-0-0-2 (2)** / 0.00 / -2.00 - sp 4/1

Tingle Creek Chase - Sandown

5th December - cl1 g1 - 2m - 4yo+

Dosage Strength

★★★★★

Year	Horse	DP	tot	DI	CD	Run sty	Field Size	Gng
2008	Master Minded	4-1-7-2-0	14	1.55	0.50	fr	7	gs
2007	Twist Magic	1-0-11-8-2	22	0.42	-0.45	hu	8	sft
2006	Kauto Star	2-2-6-10-2	22	0.47	-0.36	hu	7	sft
2005	Kauto Star	2-2-6-10-2	22	0.47	-0.36	cp	7	sft
2004	Moscow Flyer	3-1-6-4-0	14	1.00	0.21	cp	7	gs
2003	Moscow Flyer	3-1-6-4-0	14	1.00	0.21	cp	7	gd
2002	Cenkos	6-0-2-2-0	10	2.33	1.00	cp	6	sft
2001	Flagship Uberalles	6-1-7-4-0	18	1.40	0.50	hu	6	gs
2000	Flagship Uberalles	6-1-7-4-0	18	1.40	0.50	hu	7	sft
1999	Flagship Uberalles	6-1-7-4-0	18	1.40	0.50	hu	6	gd
1998	Direct Route	3-3-4-2-0	12	2.00	0.58	hu	10	gd
1997	Ask Tom	3-3-4-2-0	12	2.00	0.58	fr	7	gd
1996	Sound Man	4-0-2-4-4	14	0.56	-0.29	fr	4	gd
1995	Sound Man	4-0-2-4-4	14	0.56	-0.29	cp	5	gd
1994	Viking Flagship	6-1-7-2-2	18	1.40	0.39	cp	6	gd

DP

15/15 had 10 points or more in their Dosage Profile
14/15 had between 12 and 22 points in their Dosage profile

DI

14/15 had a DI of 2.00 and below
11/15 had a DI of 1.40 and below
0/15 had a DI below 0.42
Majority Range : 0.42 to 1.55 - 80% of winners

CD

15/15 had a CD of -0.45 and above
10/15 had a CD of 0.21 and above
1/15 had a CD above 0.58
Majority Range : -0.45 to 0.58 - 93% of winners

Average

DI 1.20 / CD 0.21

Running Style

fr-3 / cp-6 / hu-6 - Until Master Minded took the race from the front last year no front runner had won since Ask Tom in 1997. Close to pace runners and hold up horses share the honours in the Tingle Creek.

Summary

The top 2 mile chase outside of the festivals and one that has been dominated by Dosage strong animals. All 15 winners had 10 points or more in their Dosage Profile, interestingly 14 of them had between 10 and 22 points. This DP stat was the beating of Monet's Garden ('07) and Edredon Bleu ('98, '99, '01 and '02). The majority ranges are extremely strong with 14/15 having a CD between -0.45 and 0.58 and 12/15 having a DI of between 0.42 and 1.55. Although a Grade 1 race for the top 2 milers only 1 winner has had a DI above 2.00 and a CD above 0.58 (Cenkos - 2.33 / 1.00), this stat proving too much for Klairon Davis in the '97 renewal who simply had too much speed for the Tingle Creek. Looking at the Dosage Profiles we can see that every winner has had at least 1 point in the brilliant section of their profile, showing that at least the smallest amount of inherited speed is needed to take this race.

Notable Defeats

'07 Monet's Garden - **0-0-0-2-0 (2)** / 0.00 / -1.00 - sp 7/2
'07 Voy Por Ustedes - 1-0-6-1-4 (12) / 0.50 / **-0.58** - sp evens
'04 Azertyuiop - 2-0-2-8-2 (14) / **0.27** / **-0.57** - sp 5/6
'01 Edredon Bleu - **0-0-0-2-0 (2)** / 0.00 / -1.00 - sp 6/5
'97 Klairon Davis - 4-4-0-0-0 (8) / **inf** / **1.50** - sp 6/4

John Durkan Chase - Punchestown

6th December - g1 - 2m4f - 5yo+

Dosage Strength

★★★

Year	Horse	DP	tot	DI	CD	Run sty	Field Size	Gng
2008	Noland	7-6-19-0-0	32	2.37	0.63	cp	8	hvy
2007	The Listener	~~0-1-1-0-0~~	2	~~3.00~~	~~0.50~~	fr	10	hvy
2006	In Compliance	3-1-6-4-2	16	0.78	-0.06	cp	8	hvy
2005	Hi Cloy	5-0-5-0-0	10	3.00	1.00	hu	8	sft
2004	Kicking King	2-0-8-8-2	20	0.43	-0.40	cp	6	sft
2003	Beef Or Salmon	3-1-5-0-11	20	0.48	-0.75	cp	7	gs
2002	Native Upmanship	5-0-9-0-0	14	2.11	0.71	hu	5	sft
2001	Florida Pearl	0-0-4-8-6	18	0.13	-1.11	cp	4	sft
2000	Native Upmanship	5-0-9-0-0	14	2.11	0.71	cp	4	sft
1999	Buck Rogers	3-0-9-2-4	18	0.71	-0.22	cp	8	sft
1998	Imperial Call	3-3-4-0-2	12	2.00	0.42	fr	8	sft
1996	Royal Mountbrowne	~~2-2-0-0-2~~	6	~~2.00~~	~~0.33~~	cp	6	gs

DP

10/12 had 10 points or more in their Dosage Profile
9/12 had between 10 and 20 points in their Dosage Profile

DI

0/10 had a DI between 0.79 and 1.99
5/10 had a DI of 0.78 and below
5/10 had a DI of 2.00 and above
Majority Range : N/A

CD

0/10 had a CD between -0.05 and 0.41
5/10 had a CD of -0.06 and below
5/10 had a CD of 0.42 and above
Majority Range : N/A

Average

DI 1.41 / CD 0.09

Running Style

fr-2 / cp-8 / hu-2 - Running close to the pace is the place to be sitting in the John Durkan Chase, similar to 8 of the last 12 winners.

Summary

The strongest trends available in the John Durkan Chase comes from the 2 'gapping' stats unearthed above. 0/10 have had a DI between 0.79 and 1.99 and 0/10 have had a CD between -0.05 and 0.41. It is only correct to be wary of these 'gapping' trends when they appear, however there may be legitimate reasons for them. With solid evidence below in the notable defeats section there is no reason to ignore this trend at the moment. Apart from The Listener in '07 and Royal Mountbrowne in '96 every winner had 10 points or more in their Dosage Profile, pointing to another race for the Dosage strong animal.

Notable Defeats

'06 Nickname - 2-1-8-3-0 (14) / **1.00** / **0.14** - sp 7/2
'03 Tuitchev - 2-0-16-0-2 (20) / **1.00** / **0.00** - sp 11/2
'01 Rince Ri - 3-0-3-0-2 (8) / **1.29** / **0.25** - sp 9/4
'99 His Song - 5-1-8-4-0 (18) / **1.25** / **0.39** - sp 9/4

Peterborough Chase - Huntingdon

10th December - cl1 g2 - 2m5f - 4yo+

Dosage Strength

★

Year	Horse	DP	tot	DI	CD	Run sty	Field Size	Gng
2008	Monet's Garden	~~0-0-0-2-0~~	2	~~0.00~~	~~-1.00~~	cp	10	gs
2007	Racing Demon	2-0-6-4-0	12	0.71	0.00	fr	2	gd
2006	Racing Demon	2-0-6-4-0	12	0.71	0.00	cp	5	gd
2005	Impek	0-0-8-0-0	8	1.00	0.00	cp	11	gd
2004	Le Roi Miguel	3-1-4-2-0	10	1.50	0.50	hu	8	gs
2003	Jair Du Cochet	~~0-0-1-1-0~~	2	~~0.33~~	~~-0.50~~	fr	6	gs
2002	Best Mate	1-1-10-5-1	18	0.64	-0.22	fr	5	gs
2001	Edredon Bleu	~~0-0-0-2-0~~	2	~~0.00~~	~~-1.00~~	fr	4	gs
2000	Edredon Bleu	~~0-0-0-2-0~~	2	~~0.00~~	~~-1.00~~	fr	5	gs
1999	Edredon Bleu	~~0-0-0-2-0~~	2	~~0.00~~	~~-1.00~~	fr	4	gf
1998	Edredon Bleu	~~0-0-0-2-0~~	2	~~0.00~~	~~-1.00~~	fr	6	gd
1997	One Man	~~1-0-4-1-0~~	6	~~1.00~~	~~0.17~~	cp	6	gd
1996	Dublin Flyer	0-0-2-8-6	16	0.07	-1.25	cp	6	gs
1995	Travado	4-3-11-0-0	18	2.27	0.61	cp	7	gf
1994	Martha's Son	3-6-5-0-0	14	4.60	0.86	cp	4	gd

DP

8/15 had 8 points or more in their Dosage Profile
0/15 had more than 18 points in their Dosage Profile

DI

6/8 had a DI of 1.50 and below
5/8 had a DI of 1.00 and below
Majority Range : 0.64 to 1.50 - 63% of winners

CD

7/8 had a CD of -0.22 and above
6/8 had a CD of 0.00 and above
Majority Range : -0.22 to 0.00 - 50% of winners

Average

DI 1.44 / CD 0.06

Running Style

fr-7 / cp-7 / hu-1 - Huntingdon's tight turns are no place for hold up horses with only 1/14 taking the top honours. Front runners and close to pace runners share the honours.

Summary

Not a race with which we can rely too heavily on Dosage as only 8/15 were Dosage strong winners. This is due in the main to Edredon Bleu's 4 year dominance of the race between 1998 and 2001. An average field size of 6 may be the reason a high percentage of Dosage weak animals have won the Peterborough Chase. Of the Dosage figures we are able to analyse the strongest angle to concentrate on is that 7/8 had a CD of -0.22 or above - only Dublin Flyer fell below this. Although Huntingdon is a tight-fast track, a majority of the DI ratings are on the lower side with 6/8 at 1.50 or below. Narrowing it even further 5/8 had a DI of 1.00 and below.

Notable Defeats

'08 My Way De Solzen - 1-2-9-3-5 (20) / **0.60** / **-0.45** - sp 7/2
'04 Farmer Jack - 3-1-10-3-5 (22) / 0.69 / **-0.27** - sp 11/4

Dosage Fact

Had last years unlucky runner-up Snoopy Loopy won the race he would have been the fourth horse in a row to have had a CD rating of 0.00.

Bristol Novices' Hurdle - Cheltenham

12th December - cl1 g2 - 3m - 4yo+

Dosage Strength

Year	Horse	DP	tot	DI	CD	Run sty	Field Size	Gng
2007	Nenuphar Collonges	0-0-6-2-0	8	0.60	-0.25	cp	8	gd
2006	Flight Leader	4-2-2-4-4	16	0.78	-0.13	cp	8	sft
2005	Black Jack Ketchum	4-0-6-10-2	22	0.47	-0.27	hu	6	gs
2004	Brewster	~~0-0-3-1-0~~	4	~~0.60~~	~~-0.25~~	cp	10	gd
2003	Comply Or Die	2-0-6-4-0	12	0.71	0.00	cp	9	gs
2002	Iris's Gift	5-0-2-1-0	8	3.00	1.13	cp	7	gd
2000	Garruth	0-1-6-9-4	20	0.25	-0.80	cp	5	sft
1999	Bindaree	1-1-3-4-1	10	0.54	-0.30	fr	9	gs
1998	Bosuns Mate	1-1-8-4-2	16	0.60	-0.31	fr	6	gd
1997	Lord Jim	5-1-6-4-0	16	1.29	0.44	cp	9	gd
1996	Tarrs Bridge	1-1-7-1-2	12	0.85	-0.17	cp	9	gf

DP

10/11 had 8 points or more in their Dosage Profile
8/11 had 10 points or more in their Dosage Profile

DI

9/10 had a DI of 1.29 and below
8/10 had a DI of 0.85 and below
1/10 had a DI below 0.47
Majority Range : 0.25 to 0.85 - 80% of winners

CD

8/10 had a CD of 0.00 and below
7/10 had a CD of -0.13 and below
1/10 had a CD below -0.31
Majority Range : -0.31 to 0.00 - 70% of winners

Average

DI 0.91 / CD -0.07

Running Style

fr-2 / cp-8 / hu-1 - A race that has proven a graveyard for hold up horses with only the high class Black Jack Ketchum victorious from the position. Close to the pace is the ideal racing position with 8/11 holding that spot during the race.

Summary

This 3 mile slog around Prestbury Park in the middle of winter for novice hurdlers throws up no surprises with regards to Dosage ratings. 8 of the 10 winners had a CD of 0.00 and below with the same number having a DI of 0.85 and below, making this a race for stamina leaning Dosage profiles. The CD range can be narrowed further still with 7/10 having a rating of -0.13 and below. However, with only 1 winner having a CD below -0.31 this race does not play to the strengths of horses with deep reserves of stamina in their Dosage. This again is a race for the Dosage strong with 10/11 winners having 8 points or more in their Dosage Profile, only 2004 winner Brewster having less.

Notable Defeats

'07 Native Royal - 1-4-7-2-0 (14) / **1.55** / 0.29 - sp 7/2
'06 Labelthou - **2-0-2-0-0 (4)** / 3.00 / 1.00 - sp 13/8
'04 Idle Talk - 8-4-8-0-0 (20) / **4.00** / **1.00** - sp 7/2
'02 Ad Hoc - 3-3-4-0-0 (10) / **4.00** / **0.90** - sp 7/4
'98 Irish Banker - 6-0-4-0-0 (10) / **4.00** / **1.20** - sp 8/11

Boylesports Gold Cup - Cheltenham

12th December - cl1 g3 hcp - 2m 5f - 4yo+

Dosage Strength

★★★★

Year	Horse	DP	tot	DI	CD	Run sty	Field Size	Gng
2007	Tamarinbleu	1-3-10-6-0	20	0.82	-0.05	fr	16	gd
2006	Exotic Dancer	4-4-10-3-1	22	1.44	0.32	hu	12	sft
2005	Sir Oj	3-0-5-0-0	8	2.20	0.75	hu	16	gs
2004	Monkerhostin	3-3-6-3-1	16	1.29	0.25	hu	13	gd
2003	Iris Royal	4-3-12-7-0	26	1.00	0.15	cp	17	gs
2002	Fondmort	2-0-2-4-0	8	0.60	0.00	hu	9	gd
2000	Go Roger Go	1-1-6-0-0	8	1.67	0.38	hu	12	sft
1999	Legal Right	9-6-21-1-3	40	1.76	0.43	cp	9	gs
1998	Northern Starlight	5-1-8-0-0	14	2.50	0.79	fr	13	gd
1997	Senor El Betrutti	~~0-0-0-0-0~~	0	~~inf~~	~~inf~~	fr	9	gd
1996	Addington Boy	5-3-2-0-2	12	3.00	0.75	hu	10	gf
1994	Dublin Flyer	0-0-2-8-6	16	0.07	-1.25	fr	11	gs

DP

11/12 had 8 points or more in their Dosage Profile
8/12 had 12 points or more in their Dosage Profile

DI

10/11 had a DI of 0.60 and above
8/11 had a DI of 1.00 and above
Majority Range : 0.82 to 2.50 - 73% of winners

CD

10/11 had a CD of -0.05 and above
8/11 had a CD of 0.15 and above
Majority Range : -0.05 to 0.79 - 91% of winners

Average

DI 1.49 / CD 0.23

Running Style

fr-4 / cp-2 / hu-6 - Waiting out the back before unleashing your challenge is the key to the Boylesports Gold Cup with 6/12 hold up horses taking the honours. Front runners have a decent record but surprisingly close to pace runners fair worst with only 2/12 hitting the target.

Summary

This mid distance handicap is tailor made for horses with speed orientated Dosages. The strongest trend in the race comes from CD ratings with 10/11 winners having a CD of -0.05 and above. This range can be narrowed slightly further as 8/11 had a CD of 0.15 and above. DI ratings show that 10/11 had a rating of 0.60 and above, which is narrowed further with 8/11 having a rating of 1.00 and above. The one horse to fall well below the identified ranges was 1994 winner Dublin Flyer who used his vast stamina Dosage to grind out a win from the front. DP totals highlight the fact Dosage strong horses take the majority of renewals with 11/12 having 8 points or more. Senor El Betrutti was the only Dosage weak winner of the race.

Notable Defeats

'06 Taranis - 3-0-2-0-7 (12) / **0.50** / **-0.67** - sp 3/1
'05 Our Vic - 2-0-9-5-0 (16) / **0.68** / **-0.06** - sp 9/2
'03 Telemoss - 3-2-4-2-7 (18) / **0.64** / **-0.44** - sp 5/1
'97 Trying Again - 3-0-2-0-7 (12) / **0.50** / **-0.67** - sp 9/2

Dosage Fact

The Paddy Power Gold Cup, which is run over a distance a furlong shorter, actual has lower Dosage averages than the Boylesport Gold Cup. The Paddy Power averages are DI 0.80 & CD -0.17 compared to the Boylesport averages of DI 1.49 & CD 0.23.

International Hurdle - Cheltenham

12th December - cl1 g2 - 2m1f - 4yo+

Dosage Strength

Year	Horse	DP	tot	DI	CD	Run sty	Field Size	Gng
2007	Osana	0-0-8-0-0	8	1.00	0.00	fr	8	gd
2006	Detroit City	11-3-14-0-0	28	3.00	0.89	fr	4	sft
2005	Harchibald	5-4-13-2-0	24	1.82	0.50	hu	9	gs
2004	Back In Front	3-3-14-4-2	26	1.00	0.04	hu	7	gd
2003	Rigmarole	10-5-23-0-0	38	2.30	0.66	cp	7	gs
2002	Rooster Booster	6-6-6-4-2	24	1.67	0.42	cp	9	gd
2000	Geos	0-0-7-1-0	8	0.78	-0.13	cp	8	sft
1999	Relkeel	0-2-3-10-1	16	0.28	-0.63	hu	7	gs
1998	Relkeel	0-2-3-10-1	16	0.28	-0.63	hu	5	gd
1997	Relkeel	0-2-3-10-1	16	0.28	-0.63	hu	8	gd
1996	Large Action	2-0-14-0-4	20	0.82	-0.20	cp	7	gf
1994	Large Action	2-0-14-0-4	20	0.82	-0.20	cp	8	gs

DP

12/12 had 8 points or more in their Dosage Profile
10/12 had 16 points or more in their Dosage Profile

DI

10/12 had a DI of 1.82 and below
8/12 had a DI of 1.00 and below
Majority Range : 0.78 to 2.30 - 67% of winners

CD

10/12 had a CD of 0.50 and below
8/12 had a CD of 0.04 and below
Majority Range : -0.20 to 0.50 - 58% of winners

Average

DI 1.17 / CD 0.01

Running Style

fr-2 / cp-5 / hu-5 - Close to pace runners and hold up horses share the honours in the International Hurdle. After a barren 10 years front runners have taken the past 2 renewals.

Summary

A definite split is evident in the Dosage rating of the International Hurdle and this may be a case of where the race is heading rather than where it has come from. The last 6 results have seen winners with DI's of 1.00 and above and CD's of 0.00 and above, whereas in the previous 6 years every winner had a DI of 0.82 and below and a CD of -0.13 and below. From 1994 to 2000 the race was favouring stamina based runners but from 2002 onwards there is a definite leaning towards speed based horses. Although it would not be wise to completely ignore the results between 1994 and 2000 it looks like this Grade 2 hurdle race is now starting to favour horses with speedier Dosage ratings. The one trend that has stayed constant is the DP totals with all 12 winners having 8 or more points in their profile.

Notable Defeats *'02 Onwards*

'07 Katchit - 1-2-5-3-1 (12) / **0.85** / **-0.08** - sp 9/2
'04 Inglis Drever - 3-0-22-15-2 (42) / **0.50** / **-0.31** - sp 7/2
'04 Westender - 2-0-17-13-2 (34) / **0.45** / **-0.38** - sp 5/1
'02 Hors La Loi III - **2-0-0-4-0 (6)** / 0.50 / 0.00 - sp 13/2
'02 Landing Light - 3-3-19-13-10 (48) / **0.48** / **-0.50** - sp 6/1

Dosage Fact

11 of the last 12 runners-up also had 8 points or more in their Dosage Rating.

Relkeel Hurdle - Cheltenham

12th December - cl1 g2 - 2m5f 110yds - 4yo+

Dosage Strength

★★★★

Year	Horse	DP	tot	DI	CD	Run sty	Field Size	Gng
2007	Pouvoir	3-4-5-2-0	14	2.11	0.57	hu	8	gd
2006	Black Jack Ketchum	4-0-6-10-2	22	0.47	-0.27	cp	5	sft
2005	Mighty Man	7-2-6-0-1	16	3.00	0.88	hu	6	gs
2004	Lough Derg	~~0-0-3-2-1~~	6	~~0.33~~	~~-0.67~~	cp	6	gd
2003	Crystal D'ainay	~~0-0-1-3-0~~	4	~~0.14~~	~~-0.78~~	cp	7	gs
2002	Eternal Spring	5-2-6-7-0	20	1.00	0.25	fr	4	gd
2000	Mister Banjo	~~0-0-1-1-0~~	2	~~0.33~~	~~-0.50~~	cp	6	sft
1999	Heros Fatal	6-2-17-4-1	30	1.22	0.27	hu	3	gs
1998	Lady Rebecca	2-4-10-0-6	22	1.00	-0.18	cp	6	gd
1997	Daraydan	3-2-5-2-0	12	1.67	0.50	cp	4	gd
1996	Karshi	5-3-6-6-4	24	0.85	-0.04	fr	4	gf
1994	Fatack	7-8-11-4-4	34	1.52	0.29	cp	9	gs

DP

9/12 had 12 points or more in their Dosage Profile
6/12 had 20 points or more in their Dosage Profile

DI

8/9 had a DI of 0.85 and above
7/9 had a DI of 1.00 and above
1/9 had a DI above 2.11
Majority Range : 0.85 to 2.11 - 78% of winners

CD

9/9 had a CD of -0.27 and above
6/9 had a CD of 0.25 and above
1/9 had a CD above 0.57
Majority Range : -0.27 to 0.57 - 89% of winners

Average

DI 1.43 / CD 0.25

Running Style

fr-2 / cp-7 / hu-3 - Close to pace runners have been first past the post on 7 occasions, more than double the amount of any other running style.

Summary

With no winner having a CD rating below -0.27 this is not a race for a horse with masses of stamina in its Dosage. The Relkeel hurdle suits horses that have enough speed in their Dosage to sit behind the leaders and use their turn of pace to put the race to bed. 8/9 winners had a DI of 0.85 and above, which is narrowed further as 7/9 had a DI of 1.00 and above. As mentioned previously 9/9 winners had a CD of -0.27 and above - again this can be narrowed even more as 6/9 had a CD of 0.25 and above. With 3 of the last 7 winners having less than 8 points in their Dosage Profile this is not a race where we can confidently rule out Dosage weak animals. Of the 9 winners that were Dosage strong 6 of them had 20 or more points in their profile indicating this race has been won by some stoutly bred animals.

Notable Defeats

'07 My Turn Now - 3-3-21-13-2 (42) / **0.65** / **-0.19** - sp 4/1
'06 Blazing Bailey - 3-0-16-2-9 (30) / **0.58** / **-0.47** - sp 11/4
'03 Sh Boom - 0-1-4-0-7 (12) / **0.33** / **-1.08** - sp 9/4
'00 Doctor Goddard - 9-0-26-4-13 (52) / **0.73** / **-0.23** - sp 5/1

Barry and Sandra Kelly Memorial Novices' Hurdle - Navan

13th December - g1 - 2m4f - 4yo+

Dosage Strength

Year	Horse	DP	tot	DI	CD	Run sty	Field Size	Gng
2008	Mikael D'Haguenet	~~0-0-5-1-0~~	6	~~0.71~~	~~-0.17~~	cp	3	hvy
2007	Trafford Lad	2-1-16-2-1	22	1.00	0.05	cp	5	gs
2006	Aran Concerto	1-4-5-2-0	12	1.67	0.33	hu	6	hvy
2005	Travino	~~0-1-2-0-1~~	4	~~1.00~~	~~-0.25~~	fr	6	sft
2004	Peter The Knot	2-0-5-3-0	10	0.82	0.10	cp	9	sft
2003	Newmill	~~0-0-4-2-0~~	6	~~0.50~~	~~-0.33~~	hu	5	sft
2002	Solerina	3-1-8-2-0	14	1.33	0.36	fr	5	gs
2001	Over The Bar	2-0-0-6-0	8	0.33	-0.25	hu	7	gs
2000	Harbour Pilot	3-2-7-0-0	12	2.43	0.67	cp	8	hvy
1999	Aldino	2-0-5-4-3	14	0.47	-0.43	hu	7	hvy

DP

7/10 had 8 points or more in their Dosage Profile
6/10 had 10 points or more in their Dosage Profile

DI

6/7 had a DI of 1.67 and below
5/7 had a DI of 1.33 and below
Majority Range : 0.47 to 1.67 - 71% of winners

CD

7/7 had a CD of -0.43 and above
5/7 had a CD of 0.05 and above
1/7 had a CD above 0.36
Majority Range : -0.43 to 0.36 - 86% of winners

Average

DI 1.15 / CD 0.12

Running Style

fr-2 / cp-4 / hu-4 - An even split between close to pace runners and hold up horses with front runners fairing only slightly worse.

Summary

With only 7/10 of winners being classed as Dosage strong we cannot confidently rule out any runner with less than 8 points in their profile. The 7 that are left to analyse do however give strong Dosage pointers. 6/7 had a CD between -0.43 and 0.36, suggesting a well balanced individual is ideally suited to this novice hurdle. DI ratings offer a slightly larger scale but still give decent pointers to the type of horses needed for this Grade 1 hurdle. 6/7 had a DI of 1.67 and below which can be narrowed further as 5/7 had a DI of 1.33 and below. No winner had a DI below 0.33 so be wary of any runner falling below this range. Only the one winner (Harbour Pilot) had a rating above DI 1.67 & CD 0.36 with plenty of short priced runners since failing to overcome this statistic.

Notable Defeats

'08 Pandorama - 3-2-4-0-1 (10) / **2.33** / **0.60** - sp 2/7
'07 Gem Daly - 4-0-4-0-0 (8) / **3.00** / **1.00** - sp 6/4
'05 Powerstation - 3-3-0-2-0 (8) / **3.00** / **0.88** - sp 4/1
'04 Major Vernon - 5-2-8-0-1 (16) / **2.20** / **0.63** - sp 7/4
'02 Pizarro - 1-1-1-5-2 (10) / **0.33** / **-0.60** - sp 8/13

Dosage Fact

The 3 winners that had less than 8 points in their profile all went on to some form of success at the Cheltenham Festival. Mikael D' Haguenet and Newmill both recorded victories and Travino ran 3rd in a novice event.

Kennel Gate Novices Hurdle - Ascot

18th December - cl1 g2 - 2m - 4yo+

Dosage Strength

★★★★

Year	Horse	DP	tot	DI	CD	Run sty	Field Size	Gng
2008	Medermit	1-1-8-2-0	12	1.00	0.08	hu	8	gs
2007	Deep Purple	5-1-7-2-1	16	1.46	0.44	fr	6	gf
2006	Tagula Blue	~~0-0-2-4-0~~	6	~~0.20~~	~~-0.67~~	hu	10	gd
2003	Perle De Puce	0-0-6-0-12	18	0.20	-1.33	cp	10	gd
2002	Kopec	3-1-7-4-3	18	0.71	-0.17	hu	8	sft
2001	Never	9-5-11-1-0	26	3.00	0.85	hu	3	gd
2000	Ben Ewar	6-3-14-9-0	32	1.00	0.19	hu	8	hvy
1999	Monsignor	2-9-11-0-0	22	3.00	0.59	fr	6	sft
1998	Hidebound	3-0-9-2-4	18	0.71	-0.22	fr	7	sft
1997	Wahiba Sands	8-6-16-2-0	32	2.20	0.63	hu	9	gs
1996	Make A Stand	6-0-4-0-2	12	2.00	0.67	fr	9	gf
1995	Call Equiname	14-4-2-0-0	20	19.00	1.60	cp	10	gd
1994	Berude Not To	~~0-0-0-0-0~~	0	~~inf~~	~~inf~~	cp	8	gd

DP

11/13 had 12 points or more in their Dosage Profile
8/13 had 18 points or more in their Dosage Profile

DI

10/11 had a DI of 0.71 and above
8/11 had a DI of 1.00 and above
Majority Range : 0.71 to 2.20 - 64% of winners

CD

10/11 had a CD of -0.22 and above
8/11 had a CD of 0.08 and above
Majority Range : -0.22 to 0.67 - 73% of winners

Average

DI 3.12 / CD 0.30

Running Style

fr-4 / cp-3 / hu-6 - Held up out the back pays the biggest dividends in the Kennel Gate Novices' Hurdle. Front runners also get their fair share of glory and surprisingly it is close to pace runners that come out worse with only 3 winners.

Summary

This 2 mile novices' hurdle plays into the hands of the speed orientated. 10/11 winners had a DI of 0.71 and above and a CD of -0.22 and above. These ranges can be narrowed even further with 8/11 having a DI of 1.00 and above and 8/11 having a CD of 0.08 and above. Perhaps surprisingly, the ground does not get too testing at Ascot at this time of year and this stops the speedier types from getting bogged down in deep winter ground. However, on 2 of the occasions soft or worse ground appeared in the going description, 2 of the 3 winners with minus CD figures were victorious - Hidebound in '98 & Kopec in '02. DP totals highlight once more that it is the Dosage strong that take most renewals with 11/13 holding 12 points or more in their profile. Dosage Profiles also highlight the importance of speed with 10/11 winners having at least 1 point in the Brilliant section of their profile.

Notable Defeats

'08 Bergo - 0-0-5-2-3 (10) / **0.33** / **-0.80** - sp 7/2
'06 Pepporoni Pete - 0-0-9-3-0 (12) / **0.60** / **-0.25** - sp 10/11
'02 Puntal - 1-0-7-5-7 (20) / **0.29** / **-0.85** - sp 8/13
'02 Foreman - **1-0-3-1-1 (6)** / 0.71 / -0.17 - sp 7/2
'00 Artic Jack - 1-0-4-7-2 (14) / **0.27** / **-0.64** - sp 7/2

Dosage Fact

Two of the three winners with a minus CD rating (Perle De Puce & Kopeck) were also the biggest price of the last 13 winners, returning at an sp of 33-1.

Noel Novices Chase - Ascot

18th December - cl1 g2 - 2m3f - 4yo+

Dosage Strength

★★★

Year	Horse	DP	tot	DI	CD	Run sty	Field Size	Gng
2008	Deep Purple	5-1-7-2-1	16	1.46	0.44	fr	5	gs
2007	Hobbs Hill	2-1-8-6-7	24	0.41	-0.63	fr	4	gf
2006	Briareus	3-0-6-2-1	12	1.00	0.17	fr	5	gd
2003	Supreme Prince	4-2-2-4-4	16	0.78	-0.13	cp	4	sft
2002	Tarxien	3-1-9-6-1	20	0.74	-0.05	cp	6	sft
2001	Seebald	8-3-12-7-0	30	1.31	0.40	cp	4	gd
2000	Galant Moss	0-0-10-0-2	12	0.71	-0.33	hu	7	sft
1999	Toto Toscato	4-0-17-0-1	22	1.32	0.27	fr	5	gs
1998	Kurakka	2-0-2-8-6	18	0.20	-0.89	fr	7	gs
1997	Chief's Song	3-1-4-0-6	14	0.75	-0.36	cp	3	gs
1996	Simply Dashing	6-3-4-5-0	18	1.57	0.56	cp	8	gf
1995	Senor El Betrutti	~~0-0-0-0-0~~	0	~~inf~~	~~inf~~	fr	8	gd
1994	Book Of Music	4-0-2-0-2	8	1.67	0.50	hu	5	gd

DP

12/13 had 8 points or more in their Dosage Profile
11/13 had 12 points or more in their Dosage Profile

DI

12/12 had a DI of 1.67 and below
9/12 had a DI of 1.32 and below
2/12 had a DI below 0.71
Majority Range : 0.71 to 1.67 - 83% of winners

CD

11/12 had a CD of 0.50 and below
8/12 had a CD of 0.27 and below
0/12 had a CD below -0.89
Majority Range : -0.36 to 0.56 - 83% of winners

Average

DI 0.99 / CD 0.00

Running Style

fr-6 / cp-5 / hu-2 - Best to go from the front or sit close to the pace in the Noel Novices' Chase. Hold up horses have a tendency to get left behind with only 2/13 winning from out the back. Hold up horses have also drawn a blank in the past 6 years.

Summary

Not many races run at the 2m3f distance and not a race for horses with bags of speed in their Dosage. All 12 winners had a DI of 1.67 and below and 11/12 had a CD of 0.50 and below. Although the DI ratings do not rise too far they also don't often dip into stamina heavy territory with only 2/12 winners having a DI below 0.71. CD ratings show a similar trend with again only 2/12 have a rating below -0.36. Both horses that fell into the stamina heavy ranges used their Dosage to win the race from the front, making the race a stamina test that none of their opponents were able to live with. Only one winner, Senor El Betrutti, had less than 8 points in his DP with the majority of winners having 12 or more points.

Notable Defeats

'03 Lilium De Cotte - **0-0-0-0-4 (4)** / 0.00 / -2.00 - sp 4/6
'01 St Pirran - 5-0-11-0-0 (16) / **1.91** / **0.63** - sp 5/2
'00 Rugged River - 4-2-8-0-0 (14) / **2.50** / **0.71** - sp 3/1
'99 Good Vibes - 0-0-3-0-15 (18) / **0.09** / **-1.67** - sp11/4
'98 Billingsgate - 2-2-4-0-0 (8) / **3.00** / **0.75** - sp 3/1

Silver Cup Handicap Chase - Ascot

19th December - cl1 Lst - 3m - 4yo+

Dosage Strength

★★★

Year	Horse	DP	tot	DI	CD	Run sty	Field Size	Gng
2008	Niche Market	1-2-3-4-2	12	0.60	-0.33	cp	14	gs
2007	Vodka Bleu	2-0-8-2-2	14	0.75	-0.14	hu	13	gf
2006	Billyvoddan	5-1-6-8-0	20	0.82	0.15	hu	18	gs
2003	Horus	0-5-5-5-1	16	0.88	-0.13	hu	8	sft
2002	Behrajan	12-3-11-7-5	38	1.17	0.26	fr	7	sft
2001	Shooting Light	1-0-7-12-6	26	0.21	-0.85	hu	9	gd
2000	Legal Right	9-6-21-1-3	40	1.76	0.43	cp	7	sft
1999	Tresor De Mai	~~0-0-0-2-0~~	2	~~0.00~~	~~-1.00~~	hu	9	gs
1998	Torduff Express	2-2-13-8-1	26	0.68	-0.15	cp	7	gs
1997	Cool Dawn	2-2-8-0-0	12	2.00	0.50	fr	6	gs
1996	Go Ballistic	3-0-11-2-0	16	1.13	0.25	hu	9	gf
1995	Unguided Missile	9-0-7-0-2	18	2.27	0.78	hu	9	gd
1994	Raymylette	2-2-4-4-0	12	1.00	0.17	fr	8	gd

DP

12/13 had 12 points or more in their Dosage Profile
8/13 had 16 points or more in their Dosage Profile

DI

11/12 had a DI of 0.60 and above
9/12 had a DI of 0.75 and above
1/12 had a DI above 2.00
Majority Range : 0.60 to 1.17 - 67% of winners

CD

11/12 had a CD of -0.33 and above
10/12 had a CD of -0.15 and above
1/12 had a CD of above 0.50
Majority Range : -0.33 to 0.50 - 83% of winners

Average

DI 1.11 / CD 0.08

Running Style

fr-3 / cp-3 / hu-7 - Hold up horses have won the majority of Silver Cups with 7 victories. Front runners and close to pace runners shared 3 wins a piece.

Summary

This 3 mile handicap does not attract as many stamina based winners as may be expected. 11/12 winners had a CD of -0.33 and above which is narrowed further with 10/12 having a CD of -0.15 and above. DI ratings follow a similar pattern with 11/12 having a DI of 0.60 and above. However, looking at the 6 most recent renewals of this race indicates that no winner has had a DI above 1.17 - in fact only 3 of the past 13 have been above this range. Thoroughbreds with speed orientated Dosage ratings have struggled recently and this is something to bear in mind when looking at future renewals. 1999 winner Tresor De Mai is the only horse to be classed as Dosage weak showing that Dosage strong animals hold the upper hand with 12/13 holding 12 points or more in their profile.

Notable Defeats

'07 Alerburn - **0-0-1-0-5 (6)** / 0.09 / -1.67 - sp 4/1
'06 Copsale Lad - 2-0-1-4-5 (12) / **0.26** / **-0.83** - sp 6/1
'01 Ad Hoc - 3-3-4-0-0 (10) / **4.00** / **0.90** - sp 7/2
'99 Spendid - 5-5-0-2-0 (12) / **5.00** / **1.08** - sp 2/1
'95 Couldn't Be Better - **2-0-2-2-0 (6)** / 1.00 / 0.33 - sp 7/2

Long Walk Hurdle - Ascot

19th December - cl1 g1 - 3m1f - 4yo+

Dosage Strength

Year	Horse	DP	tot	DI	CD	Run sty	Field Size	Gng
2008	Punchestowns	2-1-9-0-0	12	1.67	0.42	hu	11	gs
2007	Lough Derg	~~0-0-3-2-1~~	6	~~0.33~~	~~-0.67~~	fr	9	gf
2006	Mighty Man	7-2-6-0-1	16	3.00	0.88	hu	9	gs
2003	Baracouda	2-3-8-1-2	16	1.29	0.13	hu	6	gd
2002	Deano's Beeno	5-1-6-10-6	28	0.47	-0.39	fr	5	sft
2001	Baracouda	2-3-8-1-2	16	1.29	0.13	hu	5	gd
2000	Baracouda	2-3-8-1-2	16	1.29	0.13	hu	9	hvy
1999	Anzum	0-1-6-0-13	20	0.25	-1.25	cp	6	sft
1998	Princeful	2-0-6-4-2	14	0.56	-0.29	cp	11	sft
1997	Paddys Return	3-0-5-8-2	18	0.44	-0.33	cp	7	gs
1996	Ocean Hawk	5-2-9-0-0	16	2.56	0.75	fr	6	gf
1995	Silver Wedge	3-3-16-0-0	22	1.75	0.41	fr	11	gd
1994	Hebridean	4-0-4-4-2	14	0.75	0.00	hu	8	gd

DP

12/13 had 12 points or more in their Dosage Profile
9/12 had 16 points or more in their Dosage Profile

DI

10/12 had a DI of 1.75 and below
8/12 had a DI of 1.29 and below
1/12 had a DI of 0.44 and below
Majority Range : 0.44 to 1.75 - 75% of winners

CD

10/12 had a CD of 0.42 and below
8/12 had a CD of 0.13 and below
1/12 had a CD below -0.39
Majority Range : -0.39 to 0.42 - 75% of winners

Average

DI 1.28 / CD 0.05

Running Style

fr-4 / cp-3 / hu-6 - Hold up horse have taken the most renewals with 6. Surprisingly front runners have managed to stave off the rest of the field in this 3m1f hurdle race on 4 occasions. Close to pace runners have drawn a blank in the last 7 renewals.

Summary

With only course specialist Lough Derg winning with less than 8 points in his profile this is a race for the Dosage strong - 12/13 have had 12 points or more in their Dosage Profile. Although a 3m1f race the CD ratings do not fall into the stamina territory very often with 11/12 having a CD of -0.39 and above, the range being narrowed further with 8/12 having a CD of 0.00 and above. A point to bear in mind is that only 2/12 have won with a CD rating above 0.42. DI ratings follow the same trend with only 2/12 having a DI above 1.75. The majority ranges mentioned above are very strong and make a good starting point when looking to analyse this race in future.

Notable Defeats

'08 Blazing Bailey - 3-0-16-2-9 (30) / **0.58** / **-0.47** - sp 4/1
'06 Neptune Collonges - **0-0-0-2-0 (2)** / 0.00 / -1.00 - sp 100/30
'97 Go-Informal - 4-1-3-0-0 (8) / **4.33** / **1.13** - sp 3/1
'96 Trainglot - 7-3-8-0-0 (18) / **3.50** / **0.94** - sp 9/4
'96 Pleasure Shared - 2-0-2-4-4 (12) / **0.33** / **-0.67** - sp 5/2

Feltham Novices' Chase - Kempton

26th December - cl1 g1 - 3m - 4yo+

Dosage Strength

★★

Year	Horse	DP	tot	DI	CD	Run sty	Field Size	Gng
2008	Breedsbreeze	~~3-1-0-0-2~~	6	~~2.00~~	~~0.50~~	cp	6	gd
2007	Joe Lively	3-3-5-0-1	12	2.43	0.58	fr	6	gs
2006	Ungaro	0-1-8-5-0	14	0.56	-0.29	hu	6	gs
2004	Ollie Magern	0-1-2-0-5	8	0.33	-1.13	fr	9	gs
2003	Strong Flow	2-1-11-0-0	14	1.55	0.36	cp	5	gd
2002	Jair Du Cochet	~~0-0-1-1-0~~	2	~~0.33~~	~~-0.50~~	cp	7	sft
2001	Maximize	8-6-0-2-0	16	7.00	1.25	fr	7	gd
2000	Bacchanal	4-7-16-1-0	28	2.11	0.50	cp	5	gs
1999	Gloria Victis	2-0-0-8-2	12	0.20	-0.67	cp	10	sft
1998	Lord Of The River	3-3-10-0-0	16	2.20	0.56	fr	7	gs
1997	Fiddling The Facts	2-1-3-0-2	8	1.29	0.13	hu	6	sft
1996	Djeddah	2-0-2-4-2	10	0.43	-0.40	cp	5	gf
1994	Brown Hall	1-0-3-0-4	8	0.45	-0.75	cp	6	sft

DP

11/13 had 8 pts or more in their Dosage Profile
8/13 had 10 pts or more in their Dosage Profile

DI

10/11 had a DI of 2.43 and below
7/11 had a DI of 1.55 and below
1/11 had a DI below 0.33
Majority Range : 0.33 to 1.55 - 56% of winners

CD

10/11 had a CD of 0.58 and below
7/11 had a CD of 0.36 and below
Majority Range : -0.67 to 0.58 - 73% of winners

Average

DI 1.69 / CD 0.01

Running Style

fr-4 / cp-7 / hu-2 - Hold up horses struggle round the sharp turns of Kempton Park with only 2 managing to take top honours. Close to pace runners are best situated to take this Grade 1 novice prize.

Summary

A difficult race for Dosage analysis with winning ranges covering a wide spectrum. Although high class pair Breedsbreeze and the ill fated Jair Du Cochet won with less than 8 points in their profile the DP totals provide the strongest trend. 11 of the past 13 were Dosage strong and plenty of short priced runners have tried and failed to win the Feltham with less than 8 points in their DP. Looking at the Dosage Profiles themselves tell that every winner had at least one point in the Brilliant or Intermediate sections of their profile, allowing them at least the smallest amount of inherited speed needed to take this top 3 mile novice chase.

Notable Defeats

'07 Silverburn - 0-1-1-6-2 (10) / **0.18** / **-0.90** - sp 11/8
'06 Bold Fire - **2-0-2-0-0 (4)** / 3.00 / 1.00 - sp 9/4
'02 Bold Investor - **3-1-0-2-0 (6)** / 2.00 / 0.83 - sp 7/2
'97 Ottowa - **1-0-5-0-0 (6)** / 1.40 / 0.33 - sp 4/1

Christmas Hurdle - Kempton

26th December - cl1 g1 - 2m - 4yo+

Dosage Strength

★★★★★

Year	Horse	DP	tot	DI	CD	Run sty	Field Size	Gng
2008	Harchibald	5-4-13-2-0	24	1.82	0.50	hu	7	gd
2007	Straw Bear	5-1-6-4-4	20	0.82	-0.05	cp	6	gs
2006	Jazz Messenger	4-0-2-1-1	8	1.67	0.63	cp	7	gs
2004	Harchibald	5-4-13-2-0	24	1.82	0.50	hu	7	gs
2003	Intersky Falcon	5-1-16-0-0	22	1.75	0.50	hu	6	gd
2002	Intersky Falcon	5-1-16-0-0	22	1.75	0.50	cp	6	sft
2001	Landing Light	3-3-19-13-10	48	0.48	-0.50	cp	5	gd
2000	Geos	0-0-7-1-0	8	0.78	-0.13	cp	7	gs
1999	Dato Star	5-1-7-4-1	18	1.12	0.28	cp	4	sft
1998	French Holly	4-16-13-11-6	50	1.13	0.02	cp	5	sft
1997	Kerawi	6-1-15-0-0	22	1.93	0.59	fr	5	sft
1994	Absalom's Lady	7-4-5-0-4	20	2.08	0.50	hu	6	sft

DP

12/12 had 8 points or more in their Dosage Profile
10/12 had 18 points or more in their Dosage Profile

DI

11/12 had a DI of 0.78 and above
9/12 had a DI of 1.12 and above
1/12 had a DI above 1.93
Majority Range : 0.78 to 1.93 - 83% of winners

CD

11/12 had a CD of -0.13 and above
9/12 had a CD of 0.02 and above
0/12 had a CD above 0.63
Majority Range : -0.13 to 0.63 - 92% of winners

Average

DI 1.43 / CD 0.28

Running Style

fr-1 / cp-7 / hu-4 - With all the renewals having been contested by seven or less runners it is perhaps surprising there has only been the one front running winner. Close to pace runners are the majority call with 7 successes.

Summary

It pays to be leaning on the speed side and be Dosage strong in this Grade 1 - two mile hurdle race around the flat Kempton track. All 12 winners had 8 points or more in their Dosage Profile with 10/12 actually having 18 points or more. Champion Hurdle winner Hors La Loi III fell foul of this stat in the '02 & '01 renewals. DI ratings show that 11/12 had a DI of 0.78 and above and a CD of -0.13 and above, with only Landing Light managing to defy this stat in the 2001 race. Both ratings can be narrowed further with 9/12 having a DI of 1.12 and above and a CD of 0.02 and above. Both ranges do however have upper limits as no winner had a rating above DI 2.08 or CD 0.63. The flat/sharp configuration of Kempton seems to play into the hands of the speedier 2 mile hurdlers leaving the stamina based Dosage horses floundering slightly.

Notable Defeats

'02 Hors La Loi III - **2-0-0-4-0 (6) /** 0.50 / 0.00 - sp 11/4
'01 Azertyuiop - 2-0-2-8-2 (14) / **0.27** / **-0.57 -** sp 7/2
'00 Mister Morose - **2-0-0-4-0 (6) /** 0.50 / 0.00 - sp 5/1

Dosage Fact

Every runner up had 8 points or more in their Dosage Profile making the Christmas Hurdle a particularly potent race for the Dosage strong.

King George VI Chase - Kempton

26th December - cl1 g1 - 3m - 4yo+

Dosage Strength

★★★★★

Year	Horse	DP	tot	DI	CD	Run sty	Field Size	Gng
2008	Kauto Star	2-2-6-10-2	22	0.47	-0.36	cp	10	gd
2007	Kauto Star	2-2-6-10-2	22	0.47	-0.36	hu	7	gs
2006	Kauto Star	2-2-6-10-2	22	0.47	-0.36	cp	9	gs
2004	Kicking King	2-0-8-8-2	20	0.43	-0.40	cp	13	gs
2003	Edredon Bleu	~~0-0-0-2-0~~	2	~~0.00~~	~~-1.00~~	fr	12	gd
2002	Best Mate	1-1-10-5-1	18	0.64	-0.22	cp	10	sft
2001	Florida Pearl	0-0-4-8-6	18	0.13	-1.11	cp	8	gd
2000	First Gold	2-0-0-4-2	8	0.33	-0.50	cp	9	gs
1999	See More Business	0-0-3-6-1	10	0.18	-0.80	cp	9	sft
1998	Teeton Mill	0-0-4-4-2	10	0.25	-0.80	cp	9	sft
1997	See More Business	0-0-3-6-1	10	0.18	-0.80	cp	8	sft
1996	One Man	~~1-0-4-1-0~~	6	~~1.00~~	~~0.17~~	cp	5	gf
1994	Algan	~~1-0-1-0-2~~	4	~~0.60~~	~~-0.50~~	hu	9	sft

DP

10/13 had 8 points or more in their Dosage Profile

9/13 had between 10 & 22 points in their Dosage Profile

DI

10/10 had a DI of 0.64 and below

9/10 had a DI of 0.47 and below

Majority Range : 0.13 to 0.64 - 100% of winners

CD

10/10 had a CD of -0.22 and below

9/10 had a CD of -0.36 and below

Majority Range : -1.11 to -0.22 - 100% of winners

Average

DI 0.38 / CD -0.57

Running Style

fr-1 / cp-10 / hu-2 - Quite simply you don't want to set the race up for others from the front and you don't want to have to make up ground coming from the back. Close to pace runners hold sway here with a commanding 10 victories.

Summary

Dosage weak animals can win the King George, as demonstrated by Edredon Bleu, One Man & Algan, but a majority of winners (10/13) have had 8 points or more. The strongest stat in this Grade 1 race comes from the fact that no winner in the past 15 years has had a DI above 0.64 or a CD above -0.22. This suggests that 3 miles around Kempton is not as "easy" a 3 miles as people are led to believe and any horse lining up in this race without the required stamina based Dosage is in trouble even before the tapes go up. Surprisingly, none of these stamina horses utilised their staying power and took the race from the front, only the Dosage weak Edredon Bleu managed that task. One of the strongest Dosage races on the calendar and I would be shocked if the trends identified did not continue.

Notable Defeats

'07 Exotic Dancer - 4-4-10-3-1 (22) / **1.44** / **0.32** - sp 9/2

'02 Bacchanal - 4-7-16-1-0 (28) / **2.11** / **0.50** - sp 100/30

'02 Flagship Uberalles - 6-1-7-4-0 (18) / **1.40** / **0.50** - sp 10/1

'99 Looks like Trouble - 1-4-5-2-0 (12) / **1.67** / **0.33** - sp 7/2

'98 Imperial Call - 3-3-4-0-2 (12) / **2.00** / **0.42** - sp 7/2

Dosage Fact

A look at Desert Orchid's Dosage Rating shows how much of a wonder horse he really was. A dosage of 4-2-6-0-0 (12) / 3.00 / 0.83 does not fit anywhere near the race profile yet he still managed to capture four King George's!

Rowland Meyrick Chase - Wetherby

26th December - cl1 g3 hcp - 3m1f - 4yo+

Dosage Strength

★★★★

Year	Horse	DP	tot	DI	CD	Run sty	Field Size	Gng
2008	Nozic	1-1-8-2-4	16	0.60	-0.44	cp	8	sft
2007	Lothian Falcon	~~3-1-2-0-0~~	6	~~5.00~~	~~1.17~~	hu	6	gs
2006	Leading Man	3-0-11-6-0	20	0.74	0.00	hu	10	sft
2005	The Real Bandit	3-3-6-0-2	14	1.80	0.36	hu	10	sft
2004	Truckers Travern	2-0-6-0-0	8	1.67	0.50	hu	7	gs
2003	Gunner Welburn	5-0-1-1-1	8	2.20	0.88	fr	8	gs
2001	Behrajan	12-3-11-7-5	38	1.17	0.26	cp	12	gs
1998	Random Harvest	3-3-4-2-0	12	2.00	0.58	fr	4	sft
1997	Strath Royal	2-0-10-0-0	12	1.40	0.33	cp	4	sft
1994	Cogent	5-2-6-5-2	20	1.00	0.15	fr	3	gd

DP

9/10 had 8 points or more in their Dosage Profile
7/10 had 12 points or more in their Dosage Profile

DI

9/9 had a DI of 0.60 and above
7/9 had a DI of 1.00 and above
0/9 had a DI above 2.20
Majority Range : 1.00 to 2.20 - 78% of winners

CD

9/9 had a CD of -0.44 and above
8/9 had a CD of 0.00 and above
0/9 had a CD above 0.88
Majority Range : 0.00 to 0.58 - 78% of winners

Average

DI 1.40 / CD 0.29

Running Style

fr-3 / cp-3 / hu-4 - A very even spread amongst running styles in the Rowland Meyrick Chase, hold up runners just coming out on top with 4 victories.

Summary

A race that until the last 2 renewals had very strong Dosage trends. Last years winner Nozic was the first horse to have a CD below 0.00 and the first to have a DI below 0.74. 2007 winner Lothian Falcon was the first winner to have less than 8 points in his Dosage Profile. Two results do not, however, make this a poor Dosage race, indeed, even when Nozic's Dosage ratings are incorporated strong trends are still at play. 9/9 winners had a DI of 0.60 and above with 7/9 having a DI of 1.00 and above. No winner has had a rating above 2.20 so out and out speedsters are likely to struggle in Wetherby's winter conditions. CD rating show even stronger trends with 8/9 having a rating of 0.00 and above. It is a slight surprise that there has only been one winner with a stamina based Dosage rating, as one would expect 3m1f round Wetherby's galloping track in the heart of winter to develop into quiet a slog. The stats however cannot be ignored.

Notable Defeats

'08 State of Play - 2-0-11-2-5 (20) / **0.60** / **-0.40** - sp 4/1
'07 Flying Enterprise - 3-1-12-6-4 (26) / **0.63** / **-0.27** - sp 4/1
'06 King Killone - 1-0-5-4-0 (10) / **0.54** / **-0.20** - sp2/1
'05 My Will - **0-0-1-1-0 (2)** / 0.33 / -0.50 - sp 11/4
'03 Artic Jack - 1-0-4-7-2 (14) / **0.27** / **-0.64** - sp 5/2

Durkan Juvenile Hurdle - Leopardstown

26th December - g1 - 2m - 3yo

Dosage Strength

★★★★

Year	Horse	DP	tot	DI	CD	Run sty	Field Size	Gng
2008	Lethal Weapon	8-0-11-1-0	20	2.08	0.75	cp	11	sft
2007	Won In The Dark	7-1-13-5-0	26	1.26	0.38	cp	13	gd
2006	Lounaos	3-1-11-3-2	20	0.90	0.00	cp	13	sft
2005	Clear Riposte	7-1-10-10-2	30	0.76	0.03	cp	12	gs
2004	Arch Rebel	4-3-20-1-0	28	1.55	0.36	hu	9	sft
2003	Top Strategy	8-0-17-2-5	32	1.06	0.13	hu	14	sft
2002	Party Airs	7-2-12-0-1	22	2.14	0.64	hu	9	hvy
2001	Newhall	2-0-2-8-6	18	0.20	-0.89	hu	11	gs
2000	Pittsburgh Phil	7-2-19-8-0	36	1.06	0.22	cp	13	sft
1999	Calladine	1-1-4-8-6	20	0.25	-0.85	hu	11	sft
1998	Knife Edge	1-4-15-2-0	22	1.32	0.18	cp	6	sft
1997	Rainbow Frontier	6-4-8-0-4	22	1.75	0.36	fr	9	hvy
1996	Grimes	4-0-4-0-2	10	1.50	0.40	cp	16	gs

DP

13/13 had 10 points or more in their Dosage Profile
11/13 had 20 points or more in their Dosage Profile

DI

11/13 had a DI of 0.76 and above
9/13 had a DI of 1.06 and above
0/13 had a DI above 2.14
Majority Range : 0.76 to 1.75 - 69% of winners

CD

11/13 had a CD of 0.00 and above
9/13 had a CD of 0.13 and above
0/13 had a CD above 0.75
Majority Range : 0.00 to 0.40 - 69% of winners

Average

DI 1.22 / CD 0.13

Running Style

fr-1 / cp-7 / hu-5 - Front runners have a terrible record in this juvenile hurdle with only the 1 success from the last 13. Close to pace runners just shade it with 7 wins compared to 5 for hold up runners.

Summary

A race for the Dosage strong with all winners holding 10 points or more in their profile. The majority (11/13) of Durkan Juvenile Hurdle winners actually had 20 or more points in their DP's - any Dosage weak animal lining up in this race should probably ply their trade elsewhere. DI and CD ratings highlight the need for winners to have a Dosage heading towards speed with 9/13 winners having a DI of 1.06 and above and 11/13 having a CD of 0.00 and above. Leopardstown's galloping track does not play into the hands of exceptionally fast juveniles as no winner has had a DI above 2.14 or a CD above 0.75. Plenty of ex flat horses with speed heavy Dosage ratings have attempted to win this race but all have been left floundering by Leopardstown's soft winter ground.

Notable Defeats

'02 Golden Cross - 8-2-12-0-0 (22) / **2.67** / **0.82** - sp 5/4
'00 Golden Storm - 5-0-3-0-0 (8) / **4.33** / **1.23** - sp 100/30
'99 Fable - 10-3-6-2-1 (22) / **2.67** / **0.86** - sp 100/30
'98 Golden Rule - 3-5-6-0-0 (14) / **3.67** / **0.79** - sp 7/4
'98 Simulacrum - 2-0-12-2-8 (24) / **0.50** / **-0.58** - sp 3/1

Durkan Novices' Chase - Leopardstown

26th December - g1 - 2m1f - 4yo+

Dosage Strength

★★★★★

Year	Horse	DP	tot	DI	CD	Run sty	Field Size	Gng
2008	Follow The Plan	6-1-7-4-2	20	1.11	0.25	hu	7	sft
2007	Sky's The Limit	1-1-6-2-0	10	1.00	0.10	cp	4	gd
2006	Schindler's Hunt	2-0-6-2-0	10	1.00	0.20	cp	9	sft
2005	Missed That	1-0-4-6-1	12	0.33	-0.50	cp	8	gs
2004	Mariah Rollins	2-0-10-2-0	14	1.00	0.14	hu	10	sft
2003	Central House	2-1-8-4-5	20	0.54	-0.45	cp	8	sft
2002	Le Coudray	1-0-8-4-5	18	0.38	-0.67	fr	5	hvy
2001	Moscow Flyer	3-1-6-4-0	14	1.00	0.21	cp	8	gs
2000	Knife Edge	1-4-15-2-0	22	1.32	0.18	cp	4	sft
1999	Native Upmanship	5-0-9-0-0	14	2.11	0.71	hu	8	sft
1998	His Song	5-1-8-4-0	18	1.25	0.39	cp	9	sft
1997	Dardjini	5-1-20-8-0	34	0.89	0.09	cp	9	hvy
1996	Danoli	2-2-12-0-4	20	1.00	-0.10	cp	9	gs

DP

13/13 had 10 points or more in their Dosage Profile
10/13 had 14 points or more in their Dosage Profile

DI

12/13 had a DI of 1.32 and below
9/13 had a DI of 1.00 and below
0/13 had a DI above 2.11
Majority Range : 0.54 to 1.32 - 77% of winners

CD

12/13 had a CD of 0.39 and below
11/13 had a CD of 0.25 and below
0/13 had a CD below -0.67
Majority Range : -0.10 to 0.39 - 69% of winners

Average

DI 0.99 / CD 0.04

Running Style

fr-1 / cp-9 / hu-3 - The lack of speedy winners is highlighted by the poor showing of front runners with only 1 hitting the mark. Close to pace runners come out well on top with 9 winners.

Summary

A strong Dosage race giving plenty of solid trends to work with. Although run over 2m1f this race has only produced one winner with a DI above 1.32 and a CD above 0.39; Native Upmanship in 1999. 12/13 had a DI of 1.32 and below and a CD of 0.39 and below, highlighting the poor record of speed orientated Dosage ratings. The John Durkan Novices' Chase is also not an ideal hunting ground for novice chasers with a large stock of stamina in their Dosage as no winner has had a DI below 0.33 or a CD below -0.67. The Dosage averages point to a well balanced individual being the ideal sort for this race and amazingly 5 winners have won this race with a DI of exactly 1.00. DP totals throw up another positive trend with 13/13 winners having 10 points or more in their Dosage Profile, stressing the dominance of Dosage strong runners in this race.

Notable Defeats

'08 Tatenen - 3-1-7-1-0 (12) / **1.67** / **0.50** - sp 4/6
'07 Perce Rock - 2-2-6-0-0 (10) / **2.33** / **0.60** - sp 7/4
'06 Glenfinn Captain - 0-0-3-0-7 (10) / **0.18** / **-1.40** - sp 11/4
'99 Quinze - 6-2-3-5-0 (16) / **1.46** / **0.56** - sp 3/1
'96 Jeffell - **2-3-1-0-0 (6)** / 11.00 / 1.17 - sp 5/2

Wayward Lad Novices' Chase - Kempton

27th December - cl1 g2 - 2m - 4yo+

Dosage Strength

★★★★★

Year	Horse	DP	tot	DI	CD	Run sty	Field Size	Gng
2008	Original	1-1-7-3-0	12	0.85	0.00	hu	6	gd
2007	Mahogany Blaze	5-2-13-3-1	24	1.29	0.29	cp	4	gs
2006	Jack The Giant	2-1-8-1-2	14	1.00	0.00	cp	6	gs
2003	Caracciola	1-2-5-0-2	10	1.22	0.00	fr	3	gd
2002	Epervier D'or	0-1-7-0-0	8	1.29	0.13	cp	5	sft
2001	Fondmort	2-0-2-4-0	8	0.60	0.00	cp	4	gd
2000	Dusk Duel	7-4-13-8-4	36	0.95	0.06	hu	4	gs
1998	Hoh Express	2-0-6-0-0	8	1.67	0.50	cp	2	sft
1997	Angelo's Double	4-3-7-0-0	14	3.00	0.79	fr	4	sft
1996	Greenback	4-0-0-0-4	8	1.00	0.00	cp	4	gf
1994	High Baron	~~3-0-1-2-0~~	6	~~1.40~~	~~0.67~~	fr	6	sft

DP

10/11 had 8 points or more in their Dosage Profile
8/11 had between 8 and 14 points in their Dosage Profile

DI

9/10 had a DI of 1.67 and below
8/10 had a DI of 1.29 and below
0/10 had a DI below 0.60
Majority Range : 0.60 to 1.29 - 80% of winners

CD

10/10 had a CD of 0.00 and above
1/10 had a CD above 0.50
Majority Range : 0.00 to 0.29 - 80% of winners

Average

DI 1.29 / CD 0.18

Running Style

fr-3 / cp-6 / hu-2 - Last years winner Original was only the second horse to come from out the back, most winners taking up the close to pace position in the Wayward Lad Novices' Chase.

Summary

Not a minus CD figure in sight in this novice chase. Every winner had a CD of 0.00 and above, indicating that horses with a stamina based Dosage will struggle around Kempton Park's sharp turns over this 2 mile trip. Oddly, 5 of the 10 winners had a CD of exactly 0.00. A balanced Dosage rating rather than a speed based rating is preferable as only '97 winner Angelo's Double had a DI above 1.67 and a CD above 0.50 although he put his speed to good use by front running his way to victory. The majority ranges highlighted above show just how strong a Dosage race this is and they are an excellent starting point for future handicapping. DP totals give a strong pointer, with only '94 winner High Baron having less than 8 points in his profile. Every other winner was classed as Dosage strong.

Notable Defeats

'09 Oumeyade - **0-2-4-0-0 (6)** / 2.00 / 0.33 - sp 8/11
'06 Twist Magic - 1-0-11-8-2 (22) / **0.42** / **-0.45** - sp 11/8
'94 Brief Gale - 5-3-4-0-0 (12) / **5.00** / **1.08** - sp 100/30

Dosage Fact

Ironically, Wayward Lad (who this race is named after) had a minus CD rating of -0.20.

Future Champions Novices' Hurdle - Leopardstown

27th December - Leopardstown - g2 - 2m - 4yo+

Dosage Strength

Year	Horse	DP	tot	DI	CD	Run sty	Field Size	Gng
2008	Hurricane Fly	2-1-9-4-0	16	0.88	0.06	cp	7	gs
2007	Whatuthink	0-1-1-4-2	8	0.23	-0.88	fr	9	gd
2006	De Valira	5-2-12-4-1	24	1.18	0.25	hu	8	hvy
2005	Mr Nosie	6-4-5-1-0	16	3.57	0.94	cp	6	sft
2004	Royal Paradise	1-2-8-3-0	14	1.00	0.07	fr	6	sft
2003	Mariah Rollins	2-0-10-2-0	14	1.00	0.14	hu	6	sft
2002	Solerina	3-1-8-2-0	14	1.33	0.36	fr	2	hvy
2001	Sacundai	8-0-17-2-7	34	0.94	0.00	hu	6	gs
2000	Ned Kelly	5-0-7-0-0	12	2.43	0.83	cp	9	sft
1999	Youlneverwalkalone	3-2-4-2-7	18	0.64	-0.44	cp	7	sft
1998	Joe Mac	~~0-0-1-5-0~~	6	~~0.09~~	~~-0.83~~	hu	6	hvy
1997	His Song	5-1-8-4-0	18	1.25	0.39	cp	8	hvy
1996	Istabraq	11-9-26-10-0	56	1.43	0.38	cp	5	gs

DP

12/13 had 8 points or more in their Dosage Profile
10/13 had 14 points or more in their Dosage Profile

DI

10/12 had a DI of 1.43 and below
8/12 had a DI of 1.25 and below
1/12 had a DI below 0.64
Majority Range : 0.64 to 1.43 - 75% of winners

CD

10/12 had a CD of 0.00 and above
2/12 had a CD above 0.39
Majority Range : 0.00 to 0.39 - 67% of winners

Average

DI 1.32 / CD 0.18

Running Style

fr-3 / cp-6 / hu-4 - Close to pace runners hold the advantage in this novice hurdle with 6 wins. Not much to choose between held up runners and pace setters with 4 and 3 wins respectively.

Summary

Not much in the way of stamina based Dosage ratings in this Grade 2 novice hurdle. 10/12 winners had a CD of 0.00 and above with only '99 winner Youlneverwalkalone and '07 winner Whatuthink falling below this. At the the top end of the scale only 2 winners had a CD above 0.39 giving a decent 67% majority range of 0.00 to 0.39 to work with in future renewals. DI ratings also provide a strong Dosage range to work with as 75% of winners fall within 0.64 and 1.43. DP totals point towards the Dosage strong runners with only '98 winner Joe Mac having less than 8 points in his profile.

Notable Defeats

'04 Rocket Ship - 0-2-8-4-2 (16) / **0.60** / **-0.38** - sp 11/8
'03 Mark The Man - 4-1-4-5-4 (18) / **0.64** / **-0.22** - sp 2/1
'03 Newmill - **0-0-4-2-0 (6)** / 0.50 / -0.33 - sp 9/4
'02 Central House - 2-1-8-4-5 (20) / **0.54** / **-0.45** - sp 7/4
'00 Bust Out - 3-0-3-8-6 (20) / **0.29** / **-0.70** - sp 7/2

Paddy Power Dial-A-Bet Chase - Leopardstown

27th December - g1 - 2m1f - 5yo+

Dosage Strength

★★★

Year	Horse	DP	tot	DI	CD	Run sty	Field Size	Gng
2008	Big Zeb	4-0-8-8-2	22	0.57	-0.18	hu	7	gs
2007	Mansony	~~1-1-4-0-0~~	6	~~2.00~~	~~0.50~~	cp	6	gd
2006	Nickname	2-1-8-3-0	14	1.00	0.14	hu	6	hvy
2005	Hi Cloy	5-0-5-0-0	10	3.00	1.00	hu	5	sft
2004	Central House	2-1-8-4-5	20	0.54	-0.45	fr	4	sft
2003	Moscow Flyer	3-1-6-4-0	14	1.00	0.21	cp	6	sft
2002	Moscow Flyer	3-1-6-4-0	14	1.00	0.21	cp	6	hvy
2001	Knife Edge	1-4-15-2-0	22	1.32	0.18	cp	8	gs
2000	Papillon	0-1-4-1-6	12	0.33	-1.00	fr	4	sft
1999	Merry Gale	5-3-4-0-2	14	2.50	0.64	fr	10	sft

DP

9/10 had 10 points or more in their Dosage Profile
7/10 had between 14 and 22 points in their Dosage Profile

DI

7/9 had a DI of 1.32 and below
6/9 had a DI of 1.00 and below
0/9 had a DI below 0.33
Majority Range : 0.33 to 1.32 - 78% of winners

CD

8/9 had a CD of -0.45 and above
7/9 had a CD of -0.18 and above
1/9 had a CD above 0.64
Majority Range : -0.45 to 0.21 - 67% of winners

Average

DI 1.25 / CD 0.08

Running Style

fr-3 / cp-4 / hu-3 - No real advantage to any running style in this Grade 1 chase. A point to note is that only 1 front runner has won in the past 8 renewals.

Summary

With a majority of runners having a DI of 1.32 and below and a CD of 0.21 and below this is not a 2m1f race that suits speed heavy horses. Winter ground must have a bearing on this as only Hi Cloy and Merry Gale have had Dosage ratings with vast amounts of inherited speed in them. The majority of winners are well balanced individuals as highlighted by the Dosage averages for the race. Only 2007 winner Mansony was classed as Dosage weak, with every other running going to a horse with 8 points or more in their profile.

Notable Defeats

'04 Rathgar Beau - **1-0-3-2-0 (6)** / 0.71 / 0.00 - sp 8/11
'01 Killultagh Storm - 8-6-0-2-0 (16) / **7.00** / **1.25** - sp 9/2
'00 Miles Byrne - 4-0-10-0-0 (14) / **1.80** / **0.57** - sp 3/1

Future Champions Finale Juvenile Hurdle - Chepstow

28th December - cl1 g1 - 2m - 3yo

Dosage Strength

Year	Horse	DP	tot	DI	CD	Run sty	Field Size	Gng
2008	Walkon	1-1-3-3-0	8	0.78	0.00	hu	10	sft
2007	Franchoek	6-1-11-0-0	18	2.27	0.72	cp	12	sft
2006	Good Bye Simon	1-3-6-2-0	12	1.40	0.25	cp	12	sft
2005	Blue Shark	1-0-8-3-2	14	0.56	-0.36	cp	15	gs
2004	Phar Bleu	1-0-6-1-2	10	0.67	-0.30	hu	16	hvy
2003	Sun Ray	3-1-11-5-0	20	0.90	0.10	hu	8	sft
2002	Nas Na Riogh	6-0-15-4-1	26	1.08	0.23	cp	8	hvy
2001	Tempo D'Or	4-0-14-0-0	18	1.57	0.44	cp	10	gs
2000	Jair Du Cochet	~~0-0-1-1-0~~	2	~~0.33~~	~~-0.50~~	cp	8	sft
1999	Mister Banjo	~~0-0-4-1-0~~	2	~~0.33~~	~~-0.50~~	cp	8	hvy
1998	Hunt Hill	5-2-9-2-6	24	0.92	-0.08	cp	5	hvy
1997	Rain Watch	10-0-21-11-6	48	0.75	-0.06	fr	6	hvy

DP

10/12 had 8 points or more in their Dosage Profile
7/12 had 14 points or more in their Dosage Profile

DI

9/10 had a DI of 1.57 and below
7/10 had a DI of 1.08 and below
0/10 had a DI below 0.56
Majority Range : 0.56 to 1.57 - 90% of winners

CD

10/10 had a CD of -0.36 and above
8/10 had a CD of -0.08 and above
1/10 had a CD of above 0.44
Majority Range : -0.36 to 0.44 - 90% winners

Average

DI 1.09 / CD 0.09

Running Style

fr-1 / cp-8 / hu-3 - Front runners are up against it around Chepstow's testing track with only 1 horse (Rain Watch) winning from the front. Close to pace runners have taken the majority of renewals.

Summary

Juveniles with a vast amount of speed in their Dosage are liable to struggle in this Grade 1 juvenile hurdle. With all 12 runnings having taken place on good to soft or much worse ground, mixed with Chepstow's galloping-undulating nature, speedy youngsters would be better served staying at home. 9/10 winners had a DI of 1.57 or below, the range being reduced further with 7/10 having a DI of 1.08 and below. Bear in mind this is still a 2 mile hurdle race so DI ratings do not dip too low, 0.56 being the cut off point. Strong pointers also come from CD ratings with 9/10 falling between -0.36 and 0.44. There have been 2 winners with less than 8 points in their Dosage Profile but the figures still show a preference for a Dosage strong winner.

Notable Defeats

'04 Salut Saint Cloud - 2-2-4-0-0 (8) / **3.00** / **0.75** - sp 5/2
'02 Lougaroo - 3-0-9-2-8 (22) / **0.52** / **-0.55** - sp 9/2
'01 Live The Dream - 4-4-8-0-0 (16) / **3.00** / **0.75** - sp 7/4

Welsh National - Chepstow

28th December - cl1 g3 hcp - 3m5f - 4yo+

Dosage Strength

★★★

Year	Horse	DP	tot	DI	CD	Run sty	Field Size	Gng
2008	Notre Pere	~~0-0-3-1-0~~	4	~~0.60~~	~~-0.25~~	hu	20	sft
2007	Miko De Beauchene	~~0-0-0-0-0~~	0	~~inf~~	~~inf~~	cp	18	sft
2006	Halcon Genelardais	2-0-7-5-0	14	0.65	-0.07	hu	18	sft
2005	L'Aventure	2-0-0-4-2	8	0.33	-0.50	cp	18	gs
2004	Silver Birch	2-0-4-8-6	20	0.25	-0.80	hu	17	hvy
2003	Bindaree	1-1-3-4-1	10	0.54	-0.30	cp	14	sft
2002	Mini Sensation	3-1-10-0-0	14	1.80	0.50	hu	16	hvy
2001	Supreme Glory	6-1-1-8-6	22	0.52	-0.32	cp	13	gs
2000	Jocks Cross	2-1-7-0-6	16	0.68	-0.44	cp	19	sft
1999	Edmond	0-0-6-0-2	8	0.60	-0.50	fr	16	hvy
1998	Kendal Cavalier	~~2-0-0-0-0~~	2	~~inf~~	~~2.00~~	cp	14	hvy
1997	Earth Summit	3-0-11-2-0	16	1.13	0.25	fr	14	hvy

DP

9/12 had 8 points or more in their Dosage Profile
6/12 had between 14 and 22 points in their Dosage Profile

DI

8/9 had a DI of 1.13 and below
7/9 had a DI of 0.68 and below
0/9 had a DI above 1.80
Majority Range : 0.25 to 0.68 - 78% of winners

CD

8/9 had a CD of 0.25 and below
7/9 had a CD of -0.07 and below
0/9 had a CD above 0.50
Majority Range : -0.80 to -0.07 - 78% of winners

Average

DI 0.72 / CD -0.24

Running Style

fr-2 / cp-6 / hu-4 - Sitting close to the pace is the percentage call in the Welsh National. Front runners have not won since the turn of the century, Edmond being the last in 1999.

Summary

A testing track, soft winter ground and a marathon distance all conspire to produce winners with low DI and CD ratings. With a stiff uphill finish also to contend with at the end of 3 and a half miles plus, winners of the Welsh National generally need to be stamina orientated. 7/9 winners had a DI of 0.68 and below and a CD of -0.07 and below. Only Mini Sensation has won with a Dosage rating above DI 1.13 and CD 0.25. The last two winners of this race both had less than 8 points in their Dosage Profile making 3 of the last 12 winners Dosage weak. When handicapping future races it would be prudent to give Dosage weak animals at least a second look.

Notable Defeats

'08 Officier De Reserve - 1-3-2-0-2 (8) / **1.67** / 0.13 - sp 13/2
'07 Gungadu - 4-0-5-3-0 (12) / **1.18** / **0.42** - sp 4/1
'03 Sir Rembrandt - 10-6-0-2-0 (18) / **8.00** / **1.33** - sp 2/1
'02 Gunner Welburn - 5-0-1-1-1 (8) / **2.20** / **0.88** - sp 5/2
'00 Moral Support - 1-4-5-2-0 (12) / **1.67** / **0.33** - sp 2/1

Dosage Fact

In the last 20 runnings of the Welsh National no winner has had a DI above 1.80 and only 1992 winner Run For Free has had a CD higher than 0.50 with his CD of 0.56.

G1 Novice Chase - Leopardstown

28th December - g1 - 3m -4yo+

Dosage Strength

Year	Horse	DP	tot	DI	CD	Run sty	Field Size	Gng
2008	Casey Jones	2-0-10-8-2	22	0.47	-0.36	hu	8	gs
2007	Notre Pere	~~0-0-3-1-0~~	4	~~0.60~~	~~-0.25~~	cp	12	gd
2006	Cailin Alainn	1-9-6-2-0	18	2.60	0.50	cp	11	hvy
2005	Southern Vic	2-1-7-4-0	14	0.87	0.07	cp	10	sft
2004	Forget The Past	6-1-3-0-0	10	5.67	1.30	fr	7	sft
2003	Pizarro	1-1-1-5-2	10	0.33	-0.60	cp	8	sft
2002	Be My Belle	3-0-7-0-0	10	1.86	0.60	fr	7	hvy
2001	Give Over	3-3-10-0-0	16	2.20	0.56	cp	9	gs
2000	Over The Furze	2-0-8-0-0	10	1.50	0.40	hu	4	hvy
1999	Saxophone	4-1-1-6-4	16	0.52	-0.31	hu	7	sft
1998	Nick Dundee	6-1-3-4-4	18	0.89	0.06	cp	9	sft
1997	Boss Doyle	2-0-6-0-2	10	1.00	0.00	cp	8	hvy
1996	Dorans Pride	~~2-0-2-0-2~~	6	~~1.00~~	~~0.00~~	fr	4	gd

DP

11/13 had 10 points or more in their Dosage profile
10/13 had between 10 and 18 points in their Dosage Profile

DI

9/11 had a DI of 0.52 and above
8/11 had a DI of 0.87 and above
Majority Range : 0.87 to 2.20 - 55% of winners

CD

10/11 had a CD of -0.36 and above
8/11 had a CD of 0.00 and above
1/11 had a CD above 0.60
Majority Range : -0.36 to 0.60 - 82% of winners

Average

DI 1.63 / CD 0.20

Running Style

fr-3 / cp-7 / hu-3 - Close to pace runners have got their heads in front on most occasions in this 3 mile novice chase. Front runners and hold up horses share the spoils with 3 a piece.

Summary

Although run on testing ground for 11 of the 13 renewals this 3 mile novice chase does not supply many stamina heavy Dosage winners. Only 3 horses have won with a negative CD rating, the other 8 have all had a CD of 0.00 and above. DI ratings follow a similar path with 9/11 winners having a rating of 0.52 and above and 8/11 having a DI of 0.87 and above. The explanation for the lack of stamina based winners may be due to the general slow pace this race has been run at, allowing the slightly faster animals to track in behind the leaders before unleashing their winning run. DP totals point to the Dosage Strong with 11/13 winners having 10 points or more in their Dosage Profiles. Only the high class pair of Notre Pere and Dorans Pride being able to overcome this stat.

Notable Defeats

'04 Mark The Man - 4-1-4-5-4 (18) / **0.64** / **-0.22** - sp4/7
'03 Satco Express - **2-0-0-0-0 (2)** / inf / 2.00 - sp 4/1
'01 Colonel Braxton - 1-0-11-2-4 (18) / **0.57** / **-0.44** - sp 11/8
'99 Sallies Girl - 1-0-6-3-6 (16) / **0.33** / **-0.81** - sp 7/2

Lexus Chase - Leopardstown

28th December - g1 - 3m -5yo+

Dosage Strength

★★★

Year	Horse	DP	tot	DI	CD	Run sty	Field Size	Gng
2008	Exotic Dancer	4-4-10-3-1	22	1.44	0.32	hu	9	gs
2007	Denman	0-1-1-6-2	10	0.18	-0.90	fr	6	gd
2006	The Listener	~~0-1-1-0-0~~	2	~~3.00~~	~~0.50~~	fr	6	hvy
2005	Beef Or Salmon	3-1-5-0-11	20	0.48	-0.75	hu	5	sft
2004	Beef Or Salmon	3-1-5-0-11	20	0.48	-0.75	hu	6	sft
2003	Best Mate	1-1-10-5-1	18	0.64	-0.22	cp	8	sft
2002	Beef Or Salmon	3-1-5-0-11	20	0.48	-0.75	hu	7	hvy
2001	Foxchapel King	~~0-2-0-2-0~~	4	~~1.00~~	~~0.00~~	cp	8	gs
2000	Rince Ri	3-0-3-0-2	8	1.29	0.25	cp	7	hvy
1999	Rince Ri	3-0-3-0-2	8	1.29	0.25	cp	6	sft
1998	Dorans Pride	~~2-0-2-0-2~~	6	~~1.00~~	~~0.00~~	cp	6	sft
1997	Imperial Call	3-3-4-0-2	12	2.00	0.42	cp	4	hvy
1996	Johnny Setaside	~~2-2-2-0-0~~	6	~~5.00~~	~~1.00~~	cp	7	gd

DP

9/13 had 8 points or more in their Dosage Profile
7/13 had between 10 and 22 points in their Dosage Profile

DI

8/9 had a DI of 1.44 and below
7/9 had a DI of 1.29 and below
Majority Range : 0.48 to 1.44 - 78% of winners

CD

9/9 had a CD of 0.42 and below
7/9 had a CD of 0.25 and below
5/9 had a CD of -0.22 and below
Majority Range : -0.75 to 0.32 - 78% of winners

Average

DI 0.92 / CD -0.24

Running Style

fr-2 / cp-7 / hu-4 - Although close to pace runners have the best record they have actually only won once in the last 7 races. Until Denman and The Listener won from the front in '07 & '06 front runners had drawn a blank in the previous 10 runnings.

Summary

Typically speed does not feature in the profile of a Lexus Chase winner. This is backed up by the fact that a plethora of speed based stayers have failed to taste success in recent years. 7/9 winners had a DI of 1.29 and below while 7/9 had a CD of 0.25 and below. Looking at the Dosage Profiles, every winner had at least 1 point in the Professional section of their DP and interestingly only Denman failed to have at least one point in the Brilliant section of his profile. While throwing up some decent DP, DI and CD pointers this is not a straightforward race for the Dosage strong, with 4 winners in the past 13 having less than 8 points in their profile. If Notre Pere were to line up in this years renewal he would be an interesting Dosage weak contender.

Notable Defeats

'05 Forget The Past - 6-1-3-0-0 (10) / **5.67** / **1.30** - sp 11/2
'01 Paris Pike - 6-0-2-0-0 (8) / **7.00** / **1.50** - sp 11/2
'00 Native Upmanship - 5-0-9-0-0 (14) / **2.11** / **0.71** - sp 11/8
'97 Merry Gale - 5-3-4-0-2 (14) / **2.50** / **0.64** - sp 3/1
'96 Idiots Venture - 0-6-6-0-0 (12) / **3.00** / **0.50** - sp 5/2

Dosage Fact

Had British raider Neptune Collonges not departed at the 2nd last fence when still 2 lengths in the lead in last years renewal, he could have become the fifth Dosage weak winner in the past 13 renewals.

Christmas Hurdle - Leopardstown

28th December - g2 - 3m -4yo+

Dosage Strength

★★★★

Year	Horse	DP	tot	DI	CD	Run sty	Field Size	Gng
2008	Catch Me	3-3-3-0-1	10	3.00	0.70	cp	6	gs
2007	Sweet Kiln	0-0-5-3-0	8	0.45	-0.38	hu	10	gd
2006	Celestial Wave	2-0-9-1-0	12	1.18	0.25	fr	8	sft
2005	Rosaker	3-9-13-6-3	34	1.19	0.09	cp	5	gs
2004	Emotional Moment	2-5-6-0-1	14	2.50	0.50	cp	5	sft
2003	Sacundai	8-0-17-2-7	34	0.94	0.00	cp	7	gs
2002	Limestone Lad	3-3-2-2-2	12	1.40	0.25	fr	6	hvy
2001	Bannow Bay	0-1-6-11-4	22	0.22	-0.82	cp	4	gs
2000	Bannow Bay	0-1-6-11-4	22	0.22	-0.82	hu	9	hvy
1999	Limestone Lad	3-3-2-2-2	12	1.40	0.25	fr	5	sft
1998	Commanche Court	4-0-5-2-13	24	0.37	-0.83	cp	5	sft
1997	Nocksky	2-0-17-4-11	34	0.45	-0.65	cp	4	hvy
1996	What A Question	3-0-14-1-4	22	0.83	-0.14	fr	5	gs
1994	Dorans Pride	~~2-0-2-0-2~~	6	~~1.00~~	~~0.00~~	hu	5	hvy

DP

13/14 had 8 pts or more in their Dosage Profile
11/14 had 12 pts or more in their Dosage Profile

DI

11/13 had a DI of 1.40 and below
9/13 had a DI of 1.19 and below
7/13 had a DI of 0.94 and below
Majority Range : 0.22 to 1.40 - 85% of winners

CD

11/13 had a CD of 0.25 and below
8/13 had a CD of 0.09 and below
0/13 had a CD below -0.83
Majority Range : -0.83 to 0.25 - 85% of winners

Average

DI 1.09 / CD -0.12

Running Style

fr-4 / cp-7 / hu-3 - Hold up runners can struggle to make an impact in this 3m Hurdle race with only 3 victories to their name. Close to pace runners have taken 50% of the last 14 runnings. 3 of the 4 front running winners had a DI of 1.18 and above.

Summary

A lack of winners with speed based Dosage ratings is no surprise in this 3m-Grade 2 hurdle race, especially as 13 of the last 14 runnings have been contested on good to soft or worse ground. 9/13 had a DI of 1.19 and below with 8/13 having a CD of 0.09 and below. The majority ranges emphasized above also give negatives to speed heavy runners. Catch Me struck a blow for the Dosage fast in last years renewal, however he only just clung on to victory by the small margin of a head from the Dosage correct Whatuthink, who's Dosage figures fitted into the majority ranges perfectly. Persistent Dosage breaker Dorans Pride notched up a success for the Dosage weak, however he has been the only victor with less than 8 points in his profile.

Notable Defeats

'07 Sonnyanjoe - **0-0-3-1-0 (4)** / 0.60 / -0.25 - sp 7/2
'05 Solerina - 3-1-8-2-0 (14) / 1.33 / **0.36** - 4/5
'00 Catch Ball - **2-0-0-4-0 (6)** / 0.50 / 0.00 - sp 3/1
'97 Cockney Lad - 6-0-0-0-2 (8) / **3.00** / **1.00** - sp evens

Challow Novices' Hurdle - Newbury

29th December - cl1 g1 - 2m5f -4yo+

Dosage Strength

★

Year	Horse	DP	tot	DI	CD	Run sty	Field Size	Gng
2008	Diamond Harry	7-3-7-0-1	18	3.00	0.83	cp	6	gs
2007	Souffleur	6-0-20-14-2	42	0.62	-0.14	hu	9	sft
2006	Wichita Lineman	4-0-11-5-2	22	0.76	-0.05	cp	8	gs
2004	Brewster	~~0-0-3-1-0~~	4	~~0.60~~	~~-0.25~~	cp	8	gs
2003	Cornish Rebel	1-1-10-5-1	18	0.64	-0.22	hu	6	gs
2002	Coolnagorna	3-11-4-0-0	18	8.00	0.94	fr	7	hvy
2001	Classified	~~2-2-0-0-0~~	4	~~inf~~	~~1.50~~	cp	6	gd
1999	King's Road	~~2-0-0-4-0~~	6	~~0.50~~	~~0.00~~	fr	5	hvy
1994	Be Rude Not To	~~0-0-0-0-0~~	0	~~inf~~	~~inf~~	cp	8	hvy

DP

5/9 had 18 points or more in their Dosage Profile

DI

2/5 had a DI of 3.00 and above
3/5 had a DI between 0.64 and 0.76
Majority Range : 0.62 to 0.76 - 60% of winners

CD

2/5 had a CD of 0.83 and above
3/5 had a CD between -0.22 and -0.05
Majority Range : -0.22 to -0.05 - 60% of winners

Average

DI 2.60 / CD 0.27

Running Style

fr-2 / cp-5 / hu-2 - Close to pace runners have taken the top spot on most occasions. Front running Coolnagorna had the fastest Dosage rating by a wide margin.

Summary

The weakest race on the calendar for Dosage analysis. With 4 Dosage weak winners in the past 9 renewals, this does not leave a very large group of ratings to analyse. One positive point to note is that 5 of the last 6 winners were Dosage strong. This suggests that the Challow Hurdle may be starting to become a race for more stoutly bred individuals. Of the ratings available to analyse 3/5 fall into a very small band, as highlighted in the Majority ranges. This may be the area to concentrate on in future renewals as this is the range I would expect to come to prominence over this distance round Newbury's galloping track on winter softened ground. However, at the moment this can only be deemed as a very cautious estimate.

Notable Defeats

N/A

Dosage Fact

2002 winner Coolnagorna had an extremely fast Dosage rating and his opponents never saw which way he went, leading from pillar to post to win by a massive 29 lengths.

December Festival Hurdle - Leopardstown

29th December - g1 - 2m -4yo+

Dosage Strength

★★★★★

Year	Horse	DP	tot	DI	CD	Run sty	Field Size	Gng
2008	Sublimity	9-1-12-4-0	26	1.60	0.58	hu	9	gs
2007	Al Eile	5-4-14-0-5	28	1.33	0.14	cp	6	gd
2006	Brave Inca	0-1-7-9-9	26	0.21	-1.00	fr	4	hvy
2005	Brave Inca	0-1-7-9-9	26	0.21	-1.00	cp	5	sft
2004	Macs Joy	4-4-3-3-2	16	1.46	0.31	cp	6	sft
2003	Golden Cross	8-2-12-0-0	22	2.67	0.82	hu	7	gs
2002	Liss A Paoraigh	5-2-6-0-1	14	2.50	0.71	fr	5	hvy
2001	Istabraq	11-9-26-10-0	56	1.43	0.38	cp	6	gs
2000	Moscow Flyer	3-1-6-4-0	14	1.00	0.21	cp	7	hvy
1999	Istabraq	11-9-26-10-0	56	1.43	0.38	cp	6	sft
1998	Istabraq	11-9-26-10-0	56	1.43	0.38	cp	3	hvy
1997	Istabraq	11-9-26-10-0	56	1.43	0.38	hu	5	hvy
1996	Theatreworld	7-2-23-8-0	40	1.05	0.20	fr	6	gs

DP

13/13 had 14 points or more in their Dosage Profile
10/13 had 22 points or more in their Dosage Profile

DI

11/13 had a DI of 1.00 and above
8/13 had a DI of 1.33 and above
2/13 had a DI above 1.60
Majority Range : 1.00 to 1.60 - 69% of winners

CD

11/13 had a CD of 0.14 and above
10/13 had a CD of 0.20 and above
2/13 had a CD above 0.58
Majority Range : 0.14 to 0.58 - 69% of winners

Average

DI 1.37 / CD 0.19

Running Style

fr-3 / cp-7 / hu-3 - Sitting close to the pace has been the key to this Grade 1 hurdle with 7 taking up the position during the race. Front runners and hold up horses share 3 wins each.

Summary

A race that leans reasonably strongly on the side of speed with regards to Dosage ratings. 11/13 winners had a DI of 1.00 and above and 11/13 had a CD of 0.14 and above, dual winner and continual Dosage buster Brave Inca being the only horse that had a rating fall below this strong trend. Ratings can be reduced further as 8/13 had a DI of 1.33 and above and 10/13 had a CD of 0.20 and above. With the ground regularly on the soft side the Dosage ratings have only twice risen above DI 1.60 and CD 0.38 - this is a factor to be wary of when narrowing the field in future. With 13/13 having 14 points or more in their Dosage Profile this is a race that is heavily in favour of the Dosage strong, more so when we consider that 10/13 had 22 points or more in their profile. The Dosage Profiles themselves offer up a final clue as, excluding Brave Inca, every winner had at least 3 points in the brilliant section of their profile.

Notable Defeats

'08 Sizing Europe - 2-2-6-0-0 (10) / **2.33** / **0.60** - sp 15/8
'06 Iktitaf - 12-4-10-0-0 (26) / **4.20** / **1.08** - sp 4/6
'03 Rhinestone Cowboy - 3-0-10-1-2 (16) / 1.00 / **0.06** - sp 11/10
'03 Back In Front - 3-3-14-4-2 (26) / 1.00 / **0.04** - sp 5/2
'96 Cockney lad - 6-0-0-0-2 (8) / **3.00** / **1.00** - sp 6/4

Dosage Fact

Golden Cross, who had the fastest Dosage rating of the past 15 winners, was not only a negative with regards to Dosage but he also was a negative in the betting ring when winning at an sp of 66/1.

Tolworth Hurdle - Sandown

2nd January - cl1 g1 - 2m - 4yo+

Dosage Strength

★★★★

Year	Horse	DP	tot	DI	CD	Run sty	Field Size	Gng
2008	Breedsbreeze	~~3-1-0-0-2~~	6	~~2.00~~	~~0.50~~	hu	10	sft
2007	Silverburn	0-1-1-6-2	10	0.18	-0.90	hu	7	hvy
2006	Noland	7-6-19-0-0	32	2.37	0.63	cp	5	sft
2005	Marcel	~~2-0-0-0-0~~	2	~~inf~~	~~2.00~~	cp	9	gs
2004	Lingo	3-4-11-6-0	24	1.09	0.17	hu	5	gs
2000	Monsignor	2-9-11-0-0	22	3.00	0.59	cp	6	sft
1999	Behrajan	12-3-11-7-5	38	1.17	0.26	cp	6	sft
1998	French Holly	4-16-13-11-6	50	1.13	0.02	cp	8	sft
1996	Right Win	4-3-6-0-1	14	2.50	0.64	hu	9	gs
1995	Silver Wedge	3-3-16-0-0	22	1.75	0.41	cp	5	sft

DP

8/10 had 10 points or more in their Dosage Profile
6/10 had 22 points or more in their Dosage Profile

DI

7/8 had a DI of 1.09 and above
5/8 had a DI of 1.17 and above
Majority Range : 1.09 to 2.50 - 75% of winners

CD

7/8 had a CD of 0.02 and above
5/8 had a CD of 0.26 and above
0/8 had a CD above 0.64
Majority Range : 0.02 to 0.64 - 88% of winners

Average

DI 1.65 / CD 0.23

Running Style

fr-0 / cp-6 / hu-4 - Front runners have nothing to show for their efforts in this Grade 1 novice hurdle with 0/10 hitting the mark. Close to pace runners shade it over hold up runners by 6 to 4.

Summary

A strong Dosage race to start the new year with and one that places a big negative against horses with stamina based Dosage ratings. Novices carrying more stamina than speed should pray for heavy ground at the Esher track as on the only occasion when this occured did a horse with a negative CD rating and a DI below 1.09 win the Tolworth. Silverburn being the horse in question. Silverburn apart, every winner had a DI of 1.09 and above and a CD of 0.02 and above. The highest CD rating was held by '96 winner Right Win at 0.64 - no winner has won with a CD rating above this. DP totals show that 8/10 winners have been Dosage strong with 6/10 having 22 points or more in their profile.

Notable Defeats

'06 Lennon - 1-0-6-5-2 (14) / **0.40** / **-0.50** - sp 15/8
'05 Wild Passion - 2-0-0-1-5 (8) / **0.33** / **-0.88** - sp 5/2
'04 Bourbon Manhattan - 2-1-8-2-5 (18) / **0.64** / **-0.39** - sp 9/4
'00 Best Mate - 1-1-10-5-1 (18) / **0.64** / **-0.22** - sp 4/1
'99 Hidebound - 3-0-9-2-4 (18) / **0.71** / **-0.22** - sp 2/5

Pierse Handicap Chase - Leopardstown

10th January - Grade A hcp - 3m - 5yo+

Dosage Strength

★★★

Year	Horse	DP	tot	DI	CD	Run sty	Field Size	Gng
2009	Schindlers Hunt	2-0-6-2-0	10	1.00	0.20	cp	10	gs
2008	Mister Top Notch	1-9-6-0-2	18	2.60	0.39	hu	15	hvy
2007	Point Barrow	3-3-2-2-2	12	1.40	0.25	hu	19	sft
2006	What A Native	3-1-6-0-0	10	2.33	0.70	cp	12	hvy
2005	Marcus Du Berlais	~~0-0-0-0-0~~	0	~~inf~~	~~inf~~	hu	14	hvy
2004	Cloudy Bays	8-3-7-0-6	24	1.53	0.29	fr	9	sft
2003	Youlneverwalkalone	3-2-4-2-7	18	0.64	-0.44	hu	11	sft
2002	Lyreen Wonder	6-0-8-0-0	14	2.50	0.86	fr	8	gs
2001	Micko's Dream	2-1-7-2-4	16	0.68	-0.31	cp	8	sft
2000	Buck Rogers	3-0-9-2-4	18	0.71	-0.22	hu	12	sft
1999	Hollybank Buck	2-3-7-2-4	18	0.89	-0.17	hu	14	hvy
1998	Una's Choice	2-0-2-0-16	20	0.18	-1.40	cp	8	hvy
1997	Time For A Run	7-0-11-0-2	20	1.67	0.50	hu	8	gs
1996	Royal Mountbrowne	~~2-2-0-0-2~~	6	~~2.00~~	~~0.33~~	fr	12	hvy
1994	High Peak	2-0-2-2-2	8	0.60	-0.25	cp	9	sft

DP

13/15 had 8 points or more in their Dosage Profile
11/15 had between 10 and 20 points in their Dosage Profile

DI

12/13 had a DI of 0.60 and above
8/13 had a DI of 0.89 and above
0/13 had a DI above 2.60
Majority Range : 0.60 to 1.67 - 69% of winners

CD

12/13 had a CD of -0.44 and above
10/13 had a CD of -0.25 and above
2/13 had a CD above 0.50
Majority Range : -0.44 to 0.50 - 77% of winners

Average

DI 1.29 / CD 0.03

Running Style

fr-3 / cp-5 / hu-7 - Hold up horses have the best record in this competitive handicap, winning 7 of the last 15. Front runners have the worst record, only 3 having managed to lead from pillar to post.

Summary

One of the major staying handicaps run in Ireland and a race that has historically seen horses with a heavy leaning towards stamina in their Dosage struggle to win. 12/13 had a CD of -0.44 and above, only Una's Choice in 1998 fell below this. DI trends follow the same pattern with 12/13 having a DI of 0.60 and upwards, again Una's Choice being the odd one out. DP totals point us towards the Dosage strong as only Marcus Du Berlais in '05 and Royal Mountbrowne in '96 have had less than 8 points. Looking closely at the Dosage Profiles indicates that every winner had at least 1 point in the Brilliant section of their profile, a fact that helps keep the Dosage ratings from slipping towards stamina based horses.

Notable Defeats

'09 Kilcrea Castle - 4-1-2-5-0 (10) / 1.50 / **0.60** - sp 11/2
'08 Notable D'Estruval - **0-1-3-0-0 (4)** / 1.67 / 0.25 - sp 7/2
'04 Timbera - 0-3-8-0-13 (24) / **0.41** / **-0.83** - sp 3/1
'03 Foxchapel King - **0-2-0-2-0 (4)** / 1.00 / 0.00 - sp 13/2

Pierse Handicap Hurdle - Leopardstown

10th January - Grade B hcp - 2m - 4yo+

Dosage Strength

★★★★★

Year	Horse	DP	tot	DI	CD	Run sty	Field Size	Gng
2009	Penny's Bill	2-2-5-0-1	10	1.86	0.40	cp	30	gs
2008	Barker	~~0-0-1-1-0~~	2	~~0.33~~	~~-0.50~~	hu	28	hvy
2007	Spring The Que	2-2-8-4-2	18	0.80	-0.11	cp	30	sft
2006	Studmaster	2-5-12-0-11	30	0.76	-0.43	cp	27	hvy
2005	Essex	7-1-25-13-0	46	0.80	0.04	cp	21	sft
2004	Dromlease Express	4-0-4-2-0	10	1.50	0.60	hu	19	sft
2003	Xenophon	1-1-6-2-0	10	1.00	0.10	hu	28	sft
2002	Adamant Approach	8-6-2-4-2	22	2.14	0.64	cp	26	gs
2001	Grinkov	6-4-16-0-0	26	2.25	0.62	cp	24	sft
2000	Mantles Prince	4-5-7-0-0	16	3.57	0.81	cp	14	sft
1999	Archive Footage	11-3-24-8-0	46	1.30	0.37	hu	25	hvy
1998	Graphic Equaliser	5-1-14-4-0	24	1.18	0.29	hu	25	gs
1997	Master Tribe	4-3-9-2-0	18	1.77	0.50	cp	23	gs
1996	Dance Beat	4-0-12-2-0	18	1.25	0.33	cp	22	hvy
1995	Anusha	5-4-14-1-0	24	2.00	0.54	hu	17	gs

DP

14/15 had 10 points or more in their Dosage Profile
11/15 had 16 points or more in their Dosage Profile

DI

14/14 had a DI of 0.76 and above
11/14 had a DI of 1.00 and above
9/15 had a DI of 1.25 and above
Majority Range : 0.76 to 2.00 - 79% of winners

CD

13/14 had a CD of -0.11 and above
12/14 had a CD of 0.04 and above
10/14 had a CD of 0.29 and above
Majority Range : 0.04 to 0.64 - 79% of winners

Average

DI 1.58 / CD 0.34

Running Style

fr-0 / cp-9 / hu-6 - A terrible race for front runners who have not managed a single victory in the past 15 runnings. Close to pace runners have taken top honours on 9 occasions with hold up runners winning the remaining 6.

Summary

Despite the large fields that usually contest this handicap, Dosage ratings give strong pointers on all fronts. CD ratings indicate very strong preferences at play with 13/14 having a rating of -0.11 and above, being narrowed further with 12/14 having a CD of 0.04 and above. The lowest CD rating came from '06 winner Studmaster at -0.43. DI ratings are similarly strong with all 14 winners having a rating of 0.76 and above, which can again be narrowed to 11/14 with a DI of 1.00 and above. These figures show that any horse entering this race with masses of stamina in their Dosage is likely to be heavily outpaced by the more speed favoured animals. DP totals once more point to a race for the Dosage strong as only 2007 winner Barker had less than 8 points. The final important piece of Dosage info available to us concerns the fact that all winners had at least 1 point in the Brilliant section of their Dosage Profile, with 13/14 actually having at least 2 inherited Brilliant points.

Notable Defeats

'08 Do The Trick - 5-1-4-0-0 (10) / **4.00** / **1.10** - sp 5/1
'07 View Mount Prince - 0-0-3-5-0 (8) / **0.23** / **-0.63** - sp 8/1
'06 No Where To Hyde - 2-0-3-5-0 (10) / **0.54** / **-0.10** - sp 6/1
'06 Victram - **3-0-3-0-0 (6)** / 3.00 / 1.00 - sp 4/1
'04 Beechcourt - **1-2-2-0-1 (6)** / 2-00 / 0.33 - sp 6/1

Champion Hurdle Trial - Haydock

23rd January - c1 g2 - 2m - 4yo+

Dosage Strength

Year	Horse	DP	tot	DI	CD	Run sty	Field Size	Gng
2009	Songe	3-3-17-2-5	30	0.94	-0.10	hu	8	gd
2007	Afsoun	3-0-10-3-2	18	0.80	-0.06	cp	8	hvy
2006	Al Eile	5-4-14-0-5	28	1.33	0.14	hu	7	hvy
2005	Inglis Drever	3-0-22-15-2	42	0.50	-0.31	hu	7	hvy
2004	Rooster Booster	6-6-6-4-2	24	1.67	0.42	cp	6	gd
2003	Flame Creek	2-0-4-1-1	8	1.00	0.13	hu	7	gs
2002	Rodock	3-5-9-0-1	18	2.27	0.50	hu	5	sft
2000	Dato Star	5-1-7-4-1	18	1.12	0.28	cp	5	sft
1999	Master Beveled	4-2-8-0-0	14	2.50	0.71	hu	6	sft
1998	Dato Star	5-1-7-4-1	18	1.12	0.28	fr	5	sft
1997	Mistinguett	4-3-8-5-0	20	1.22	0.30	fr	10	gf
1996	Mysilv	6-2-2-8-6	24	0.60	-0.25	fr	6	sft
1995	Relkeel	0-2-3-10-1	16	0.28	-0.63	cp	4	hvy
1994	Flakey Dove	~~2-0-2-0-0~~	4	~~3.00~~	~~1.00~~	cp	5	sft

DP

13/14 had 8 pts or more in their Dosage Profile
12/14 had 14 pts or more in their Dosage Profile

DI

12/13 had a DI of 0.50 and above
10/13 had a DI of 0.94 and above
2/13 had a DI above 1.67
Majority Range : 0.50 to 1.67 - 77% of winners

CD

12/13 had a CD of -0.31 and above
10/13 had a CD of -0.10 and above
1/13 had a CD above 0.50
Majority Range : -0.31 to 0.42 - 77% of winners

Average

DI 1.18 / CD 0.11

Running Style

fr-3 / cp-5 / hu-6 - Not much between close to pace runners and hold up horses in this Champion Hurdle trial. Although 3 renewals have gone to front runners they have not won for the past 9 years.

Summary

With this being a trial for the big one at Cheltenham in March it is to be expected that stoutly bred individuals run well here. The DP totals back up this sentiment with 13/14 winners being classed as Dosage strong - only 1994 winner Flakey Dove fails on this score. Not a race for horses with large quantities of stamina in their Dosage with 12/13 having a DI of 0.50 and above and a CD of -0.31 and above. These ranges can be narrowed even further with 10/13 having a DI of 0.94 and above and a CD of -0.10 and above. Speed horses can also struggle with only 2 winners, '02 winner Rodock & '99 winner Master Beveled, having a DI above 1.67 and a CD above 0.42. A stat to keep an eye on is that 3 of the last 4 winners had a DI below 1.00 and a negative CD rating. Whether this is a blip in the trends or an indication of where the race is heading remains to be seen.

Notable Defeats

'06 Faasel - 10-7-13-4-0 (34) / 2.24 / **0.68** - sp 2/1
'04 Hasty Prince - 3-1-6-2-10 (22) / **0.47** / **-0.68** - sp 9/2
'03 Ilnamar - **0-0-0-4-0 (4)** / 0.00 / -1.00 - sp 11/10
'02 The French Furze - 13-7-13-5-0 (38) / **2.30** / **0.74** - sp 6/5
'99 Wahiba Sands - 8-6-16-2-0 (32) / 2.20 / **0.63** - sp 11/4

Dosage Fact

In theory this should be a good trial for the Champion Hurdle as the Dosage averages for both races are not too dissimilar. However the only horse to go on to Cheltenham glory in the same season was the Dosage weak Flakey Dove.

Peter Marsh Chase - Haydock

23rd January - c1 g2 Lmtd Hcp - 3m - 5yo+

Dosage Strength

★★★★

Year	Horse	DP	tot	DI	CD	Run sty	Field Size	Gng
2009	Cloudy Lane	2-1-13-4-0	20	0.90	0.05	hu	10	sft
2007	The Outlier	~~0-0-0-0-0~~	0	~~inf~~	~~inf~~	cp	9	hvy
2006	Ebony Light	2-0-9-3-4	18	0.57	-0.39	cp	5	hvy
2005	Lord Transcend	3-3-6-0-2	14	1.80	0.36	fr	7	hvy
2004	Artic Jack	1-0-4-7-2	14	0.27	-0.64	fr	5	gd
2003	Truckers Tavern	2-0-6-0-0	8	1.67	0.50	hu	9	gs
2002	Red Striker	~~5-0-1-0-0~~	6	~~11.00~~	~~1.67~~	hu	15	sft
2000	The Last Fling	2-2-0-10-2	16	0.33	-0.50	cp	7	sft
1999	General Wolfe	3-4-13-0-6	26	1.08	-0.08	cp	10	sft
1998	General Wolfe	3-4-13-0-6	26	1.08	-0.08	cp	9	sft
1997	Jodami	2-0-6-8-6	22	0.29	-0.73	hu	6	gf
1996	Scotton Banks	1-2-5-4-0	12	0.85	0.00	fr	6	sft
1995	Earth Summit	3-0-11-2-0	16	1.13	0.25	cp	4	hvy
1994	Zetas Lad	3-0-9-0-0	12	1.67	0.50	hu	6	sft

DP

12/14 had 8 points or more in their Dosage Profile
11/14 had 12 points or more in their Dosage Profile

DI

12/12 had a DI of 1.80 and below
9/12 had a DI of 1.13 and below
Majority Range : 0.27 to 1.13 - 75% of winners

CD

10/12 had a CD of 0.36 and below
8/12 had a CD of 0.05 and below
0/12 had a CD below -0.73
Majority Range : -0.50 to 0.50 - 83% of winners

Average

DI 0.97 / CD -0.06

Running Style

fr-3 / cp-6 / hu-5 - Not much advantage to any running style in the Peter Marsh Chase, although close to pace runners just come out on top with 6 wins. Front runners won all their races in fields of 7 or less.

Summary

Horses with speed heavy Dosage ratings have a tough time of it in the Peter Marsh Handicap Chase. All 12 winners had a DI of 1.80 and below and 10/12 had a CD of 0.36 and below. The DI range can be reduced significantly as 9/12 had a rating of 1.13 and below, as can the CD range with 8/12 having a CD of 0.05 and below. The good to soft or worse ground found at Haydock Park at this time of year has a big effect on any speed horses attempting this race and I suspect this is a big factor in keeping the Dosage ranges low. With only 2 winners having less than 8 points in their profile we should once more be looking at the Dosage strong in future renewals.

Notable Defeats

'09 Dear Villez - 5-1-6-0-2 (14) / **1.80** / **0.50** - sp 3/1
'07 Snakebite - **1-0-2-1-0 (4)** / 1.00 / 0.25 - sp 11/4
'05 Chives - 0-1-6-11-4 (22) / **0.22** / **-0.82** - sp 11/4
'02 Banker Count - 3-5-2-0-0 (10) / **9.00** / **1.10** - sp 4/1
'00 Spendid - 5-5-0-2-0 (12) / **5.00** / **1.08** - sp 100/30

Irish Arkle Challenge Cup - Leopardstown

24th January - g1 - 2m1f - 5yo+

Dosage Strength

★★★★

Year	Horse	DP	tot	DI	CD	Run sty	Field Size	Gng
2009	Golden Silver	1-2-10-3-0	16	1.00	0.06	cp	4	hvy
2008	Thyne Again	2-1-6-9-6	24	0.33	-0.67	cp	6	sft
2007	Schindlers Hunt	2-0-6-2-0	10	1.00	0.20	cp	7	sft
2006	Missed That	1-0-4-6-1	12	0.33	-0.50	hu	7	gs
2005	Ulaan Baatar	9-0-11-0-0	20	2.64	0.90	hu	8	hvy
2004	Kicking King	2-0-8-8-2	20	0.43	-0.40	cp	7	gs
2003	Bust Out	3-0-3-8-6	20	0.29	-0.70	cp	8	sft
2002	Assesssed	5-2-4-0-7	18	1.00	-0.11	cp	7	hvy
2001	Well Ridden	1-0-9-0-2	12	0.85	-0.17	cp	7	sft
2000	Frozen Groom	3-0-12-4-3	22	0.69	-0.18	cp	5	gs
1999	His Song	5-1-8-4-0	18	1.25	0.39	cp	6	hvy
1998	Private Peace	~~0-0-0-2-0~~	2	~~0.00~~	~~-1.00~~	cp	5	gs
1997	Mulligan	5-7-4-0-2	18	3.50	0.72	fr	6	gs
1996	Manhattan Castle	5-3-4-6-2	20	1.00	0.15	cp	6	sft
1994	Atone	4-0-0-4-4	12	0.50	-0.33	hu	7	sft

DP

14/15 had 10 pts or more in their Dosage Profile
10/15 had 16 pts or more in their Dosage Profile

DI

12/14 had a DI of 1.25 and below
11/14 had a DI of 1.00 and below
Majority Range : 0.29 to 1.25 - 86% of winners

CD

12/14 had a CD of 0.39 and below
11/14 had a CD of 0.20 and below
9/14 had a CD of 0.06 and below
Majority Range : -0.50 to 0.39 - 71% of winners

Average

DI 1.06 / CD -0.05

Running Style

fr-1 / cp-11 / hu-3 - The lack of speed based winners is shown in the running styles with only the speedy Mulligan taking the race from the front. Close to pace runners hold a huge advantage here with 11 winners.

Summary

A surprising clutch of trends for the Irish version of the Arkle Chase with this very much being a race in which speed based runners struggle. The strongest pointer comes from DI stats with 12/14 having a rating of 1.25 and below, being narrowed a touch with 11/14 having a DI of 1.00 and below. The DI majority ranges show that a massive 86% of runners fell between 0.29 and 1.25 - this is a very strong stat to consider when looking at future renewals. CD ratings also point towards stamina with 11/14 having a rating of 0.20 and below, being narrowed again with 9/14 having a CD of 0.06 and below. This Grade 1 novice race points strongly towards the Dosage strong with 14/15 winners falling into this category.

Notable Defeats

'09 Jayo - 10-1-11-6-0 (28) / **1.43** / **0.54** - sp 15/8
'06 Justified - 3-6-6-0-1 (10) / **3.00** / **0.63** - sp 5/2
'05 Foreman - **1-0-3-1-1 (6)** / 0.71 / -0.17 - sp 13/8
'00 Grimes - 4-0-4-0-2 (10) / **1.50** / **0.40** - sp 6/4
'98 Magical Lady - 3-8-9-2-0 (22) / **2.38** / **0.55** - sp 6/4

Dosage Fact

A surprising omission from the winners roster is superstar gelding Moscow Flyer. His Dosage figures of DI 1.00 & CD 0.21 would have fitted ideally into the ranges for this race. Unfortunately he was a faller when 4/6 favourite in the 2002 renewal.

AIG Europe Champion Hurdle - Leopardstown

24th January - g1 - 2m - 4yo+

Dosage Strength

★★★★

Year	Horse	DP	tot	DI	CD	Run sty	Field Size	Gng
2009	Brave Inca	0-1-7-9-9	26	\	-1.00	cp	9	hvy
2008	Sizing Europe	2-2-6-0-0	10	2.33	0.60	cp	6	gs
2007	Hardy Eustace	4-2-6-0-2	14	1.80	0.43	fr	8	sft
2006	Brave Inca	0-1-7-9-9	26	0.21	-1.00	fr	7	gs
2005	Macs Joy	4-4-3-3-2	16	1.46	0.31	cp	6	hvy
2004	Foreman	~~1-0-3-1-1~~	6	~~0.71~~	~~-0.17~~	cp	8	gs
2003	Like-A-Butterfly	3-2-4-0-7	16	0.78	-0.38	cp	5	gs
2002	Ned Kelly	5-0-7-0-0	12	2.43	0.83	cp	8	hvy
2001	Istabraq	11-9-26-10-0	56	1.43	0.38	cp	7	sft
2000	Istabraq	11-9-26-10-0	56	1.43	0.38	cp	6	gs
1999	Istabraq	11-9-26-10-0	56	1.43	0.38	cp	6	hvy
1998	Istabraq	11-9-26-10-0	56	1.43	0.38	cp	7	gs
1997	Cockney Lad	6-0-0-0-2	8	3.00	1.00	hu	7	gs
1996	Collier Bay	4-8-20-0-0	32	2.20	0.50	hu	11	sft
1994	Fortune And Fame	4-0-0-2-4	10	0.67	-0.20	hu	7	sft

DP

14/15 had 8 points or more in their Dosage profile
11/15 had 12 points or more in their Dosage Profile

DI

12/14 had a DI of 0.67 and above
10/14 had a DI of 1.43 and above
0/14 had a DI above 3.00
Majority Range : 1.43 to 2.43 - 64% of winners

CD

12/14 had a CD of -0.38 and above
10/14 had a CD of 0.31 and above
Majority Range : -0.38 to 0.60 - 71% of winners

Average **DI 1.49 / CD 0.19**

Running Style **fr-2 / cp-10 / hu-3 -** Close to pace runners have taken most renewals with 10 wins. A hold up runner has not won since Cockney Lad in 1997.

Summary The Dosage strong win out in the AIG Europe Champion Hurdle with 14/15 winners having 8 points or more in their profile. Only 2004 winner Foreman was classed as Dosage weak. Not surprisingly this race favours the more speed orientated hurdler with 10/14 having a DI of 1.43 and above and a CD of 0.31 and above. Not for the first time Brave Inca doesn't stick by the rules and his Dosage ratings fall quite a bit out with the majority ranges and Dosage averages. At the top end of the scale only Cockney Lad had a DI above 2.43 with his rating of 3.00. Any runners with a rating higher than this in future runnings may struggle in the likely testing conditions.

Notable Defeats

'08 Aitmatov - 1-0-9-3-5 (18) / **0.44** / **-0.61** - sp 5/1
'03 Scottish Memories - 3-0-3-4-2 (12) / **0.60** / -0.17 - sp 3/1
'01 Stage Affair - 3-2-18-7-4 (34) / **0.70** / **-0.21** - sp 11/2
'96 Elas Image - 5-8-3-0-16 (32) / 0.83 / **-0.44** sp 9/2

Trophy Handicap Chase - Cheltenham

30th January - c1 g3 Hcp - 2m5f - 5yo+

Dosage Strength

Year	Horse	DP	tot	DI	CD	Run sty	Field Size	Gng
2009	The Sawyer	4-0-8-1-1	14	1.33	0.36	cp	13	hvy
2008	Maljimar	0-3-8-3-0	14	1.00	0.00	hu	11	gs
2007	Whispered Secret	7-1-14-4-0	26	1.36	0.42	hu	10	hvy
2005	Buckby Lane	~~1-0-1-4-0~~	6	~~0.33~~	~~-0.33~~	fr	16	gs
2004	Hunters Tweed	7-0-9-2-4	22	1.10	0.18	cp	13	gs
2003	Lady Cricket	4-4-1-1-2	12	2.43	0.58	cp	15	gs
2002	Foly Pleasant	2-0-8-0-2	12	1.00	0.00	cp	10	hvy
2001	Young Spartacus	0-2-8-4-0	14	0.75	-0.14	cp	11	sft
2000	Makounji	2-0-8-4-4	18	0.50	-0.44	fr	7	gs
1999	Dr Leunt	12-5-10-5-4	36	1.57	0.44	fr	6	sft
1998	Papillon	0-1-4-1-6	12	0.33	-1.00	hu	6	gs
1997	Dublin Flyer	0-0-2-8-6	16	0.07	-1.25	fr	7	gf
1995	Couldn't Be Better	~~2-0-2-2-0~~	6	~~1.00~~	~~0.33~~	cp	10	hvy
1994	Waterloo Boy	9-0-7-2-0	18	2.27	0.78	cp	8	sft

DP

12/14 had 12 points or more in their Dosage Profile
10/14 had between 12 and 22 points in their Dosage Profile

DI

10/12 had a DI of 0.50 and above
8/12 had a DI of 1.00 and above
2/12 had a DI above 1.57
Majority Range : 0.33 to 1.57 - 75% of winners

CD

10/12 had a CD of -0.44 and above
8/12 had a CD of 0.00 and above
2/12 had a CD above 0.44
Majority Range : -0.44 to 0.44 - 67% of winners

Average

DI 1.14 / CD -0.01

Running Style

fr-4 / cp-7 / hu-3 - Hold up horses fair worst in this handicap chase although 2 of the last 3 have gone to horses from out the back. Close to pace is the percentage call with 7 winners.

Summary

This middle distance handicap chase hasn't been a happy hunting ground for stamina based runners, especially in recent years. The last 6 Dosage strong winners all had a DI of 1.00 and above and a CD of 0.00 above, hinting that this race is becoming more about speed than stamina. Cheltenham's gruelling track does not ,however, play to speed heavy runners as no winner had a DI above 2.43 and only 1 winner had a CD above 0.58. Dosage strong winners have the upper hand here with 12/14 having 12 points or more in their Dosage Profile.

Notable Defeats

'07 New Alco - **0-0-0-4-0 (4)** / 0.00 / -1.00 - sp 4/1
'04 Whereareyounow - 3-9-6-0-0 (18) / **5.00** / **0.83** - sp 100/30
'99 Monnaie Forte - 5-3-6-0-0 (14) / **3.67** / **0.93** - sp 7/2
'97 Addington Boy - 5-3-2-0-2 (12) / **3.00** / **0.75** - sp 2/1
'95 Beachy Head - 13-3-6-2-0 (24) / **3.80** / **1.13** - sp 4/1

Cotswold Chase - Cheltenham

30th January - c1 g2 - 3m1f - 5yo+

Dosage Strength

★★★★

Year	Horse	DP	tot	DI	CD	Run sty	Field Size	Gng
2009	Joe Lively	3-3-5-0-1	12	2.43	0.58	cp	8	hvy
2008	Knowhere	3-3-7-0-1	14	2.11	0.50	hu	8	gs
2007	Exotic Dancer	4-4-10-3-1	22	1.44	0.32	hu	9	hvy
2005	Grey Abbey	2-1-4-4-1	12	0.71	-0.08	fr	7	gs
2004	Jair Du Cochet	~~0-0-1-1-0~~	2	~~0.33~~	~~-0.50~~	cp	6	gs
2003	Behrajan	12-3-11-7-5	38	1.17	0.26	fr	6	gs
2002	Rince Ri	3-0-3-0-2	8	1.29	0.25	fr	6	hvy
2001	See More Business	0-0-3-6-1	10	0.18	-0.80	fr	4	sft
2000	Looks Like Trouble	1-4-5-2-0	12	1.67	0.33	fr	6	gs
1999	Cyfor Malta	2-0-10-6-2	20	0.54	-0.30	hu	5	sft
1998	See More Business	0-0-3-6-1	10	0.18	-0.80	hu	7	gs
1997	One Man	~~1-0-4-1-0~~	6	~~1.00~~	~~0.17~~	hu	4	gf
1995	Master Oats	9-0-3-2-0	14	3.00	1.14	hu	7	hvy
1994	Dubacilla	2-2-14-10-0	28	0.65	-0.14	hu	5	sft

DP

12/14 had 8 points or more in their Dosage Profile
9/14 had 12 points or more in their Dosage Profile

DI

10/12 had a DI of 0.54 and above
8/12 had a DI of 0.71 and above
7/12 had a DI of 1.17 and above
Majority Range : 0.54 to 1.67 - 58% of winners

CD

10/12 had a CD of -0.30 and above
8/12 had a CD of -0.08 and above
1/12 had a CD above 0.58
Majority Range : -0.30 to 0.58 - 75% of winners

Average

DI 1.28 / CD 0.11

Running Style

fr-5 / cp-2 / hu-7 - Sitting close to the pace is not a tactic that has paid much dividends in the Cotswold Chase with only 2 winners successful from that position. It is best to either set the pace or preferably have the pace made for you, as was the case for 7 of the 14 winners who came from out the back.

Summary

Although the Cotswold chase is seen as a trial for the Cheltenham Gold Cup the Dosage averages for both races are in fact quiet different. Where as the Gold Cup attracts horses with a stamina based Dosage rating, the Cotswold chase plays more to the strengths of slightly speedier individuals. The reason for this could of course be due to this race being a furlong shorter than the Gold Cup, however it is more likely to be because of the much more sedate pace this trial is run at. With regards to the ratings, 10/12 had a DI above 0.54 and a CD of -0.30 and above. Both of these can be narrowed further with 8/12 having a DI of 0.71 and above and a CD of -0.08 and above. High class pair Jair Du Cochet and One Man were the only 2 winners with less than 8 points in their Dosage Profile, every other winner was Dosage strong.

Notable Defeats

'09 Nozic - 1-1-8-2-4 (16) / **0.60** / **-0.44** - sp 9/2
'08 Neptune Collonges - **0-0-0-2-0 (2)** / 0.00 / -1.00 - sp 3/1
'08 State Of Play - 2-0-11-2-5 (20) / **0.60** / **-0.40** - sp 5/1
'05 Ollie Magern - 0-1-2-0-5 (8) / **0.33** / **-1.13** - sp 4/1
'04 Sir Rembrandt - 10-6-0-2-0 (18) / **8.00** / **1.33** - sp 7/2

Wragge & Co Juvenile Novices' Hurdle - Cheltenham

30th January - c1 g2 - 2m1f - 4yo

Dosage Strength

Year	Horse	DP	tot	DI	CD	Run sty	Field Size	Gng
2009	Walkon	1-1-3-3-0	8	0.78	0.00	cp	7	hvy
2008	Franchoek	6-1-11-0-0	18	2.27	0.72	fr	11	gs
2007	Katchit	1-2-5-3-1	12	0.85	-0.08	cp	8	hvy
2005	Akilak	3-0-10-3-0	16	1.00	0.19	hu	16	gs
2004	Mondul	~~0-0-0-0-0~~	0	~~inf~~	~~inf~~	cp	10	gs
2003	Moneytrain	~~0-0-0-1-1~~	2	~~0.00~~	~~-1.50~~	cp	11	gs
2002	Vol Solitaire	2-2-18-0-2	24	1.18	0.08	cp	7	hvy
2001	Jair Du Cochet	~~0-0-1-1-0~~	2	~~0.33~~	~~-0.50~~	fr	7	sft
2000	Mister Banjo	~~0-0-1-1-0~~	2	~~0.33~~	~~-0.50~~	fr	6	gs
1999	Hors La Loi III	~~2-0-0-4-0~~	6	~~0.50~~	~~0.00~~	cp	9	sft
1998	Zafarabad	10-3-7-8-8	36	0.85	-0.03	hu	6	gs
1997	Shooting Light	1-0-7-12-6	26	0.21	-0.85	cp	8	gf
1995	Brave Tornado	~~6-0-0-0-0~~	6	~~inf~~	~~2.00~~	hu	10	hvy
1994	Pridwell	6-1-21-10-0	38	0.85	0.08	hu	7	sft

DP

8/14 had 8 points or more in their Dosage Profile
7/14 had 12 points or more in their Dosage Profile

DI

7/8 had a DI of 1.18 and below
6/8 had a DI of 1.00 and below
1/8 had a DI below 0.78
Majority Range : 0.78 to 1.18 - 75% of winners

CD

7/8 had a CD of 0.19 and below
6/8 had a CD of 0.08 and below
1/8 had a CD below -0.08
Majority Range : -0.08 to 0.19 - 75% of winners

Average

DI 1.00 / CD 0.01

Running Style

fr-3 / cp-7 / hu-4 - This juvenile hurdle has gone the way of close to pace runners on a majority of occasions with 7 taking the top spot.

Summary

Depending on which angle this race is analysed from it could be viewed in one of two ways; either a strong Dosage race or a poor Dosage race. With 6 winners being classed as Dosage weak this race could very easily be viewed as difficult to handicap using Dosage. However, the 8 Dosage strong winners supply very strong trends and it is best to concentrate on this angle for future handicapping. The majority ranges and Dosage averages point towards a well balanced horse as the ideal candidate for this race. 6/8 winners had a DI between 0.78 and 1.18 and 6/8 winners had a CD between -0.08 and 0.19. 2008 winner Franchoek used his speedier Dosage to front run his way to victory, however most horses with a Dosage leaning towards speed have struggled in this race.

Notable Defeats

'08 Tatenen - 3-1-7-1-0 (12) / **1.67** / **0.50** - sp 2/1
'07 Predateur - 4-1-5-2-0 (12) / **1.67** / **0.58** - sp 7/2
'04 Howle Hill - 3-0-5-2-0 (10) / **1.22** / **0.40** - sp 7/2
'03 Don Fernando - 8-6-18-0-6 (38) / **1.53** / **0.26** - sp 7/4
'02 Tempo D'or - 4-0-14-0-0 (18) / **1.57** / **0.44** - sp 6/5

Sandown Handicap Hurdle - Sandown

6th February - cl1 g3 - 2m6f - 4yo+

Dosage Strength

★★★

Year	Horse	DP	tot	DI	CD	Run sty	Field Size	Gng
2009	Chief Yeoman	13-4-19-4-4	44	1.51	0.41	hu	14	sft
2008	The Tother One	5-1-6-4-0	16	1.29	0.44	cp	15	sft
2007	Taranis	~~0-0-6-0-0~~	6	~~1.00~~	~~0.00~~	hu	16	sft
2006	Ungaro	0-1-8-5-0	14	0.56	-0.29	hu	18	gd
2005	Supreme Serenade	4-2-2-4-4	16	0.78	-0.13	hu	14	gs
2004	Baracouda	2-3-8-1-2	16	1.29	0.13	hu	9	sft
2003	Chopneyev	5-3-18-0-0	26	1.89	0.50	cp	13	hvy
2002	Iris Royal	4-3-12-7-0	26	1.00	0.15	fr	14	sft
2001	The Extra Man	4-0-14-2-0	20	1.22	0.30	fr	18	hvy
2000	Rubhahunish	3-1-8-2-4	18	0.80	-0.17	hu	12	gs
1999	Teaatral	5-2-11-4-0	22	1.32	0.36	cp	13	gs
1998	Buckhouse Boy	4-2-2-10-0	18	0.64	0.00	hu	14	gd
1997	Tullymurry Toff	2-0-0-8-2	12	0.20	-0.67	cp	13	gf
1996	Trainglot	7-3-8-0-0	18	3.50	0.94	cp	14	gf
1995	Miracle Man	2-0-0-4-4	10	0.25	-0.80	hu	12	hvy

DP

14/15 had 10 points or more in their Dosage Profile
11/15 had 16 points or more in their Dosage Profile

DI

12/14 had a DI of 0.56 and above
8/14 had a DI of 1.00 and above
1/14 had a DI above 1.89
Majority Range : 0.56 to 1.89 - 79% of winners

CD

12/14 had a CD of -0.29 and above
9/14 had a CD of 0.00 and above
1/14 had a CD above 0.50
Majority Range : -0.29 to 0.50 - 79% of winners

Average

DI 1.16 / CD 0.08

Running Style

fr-2 / cp-5 / hu-8 - Making the pace in this handicap hurdle can be difficult with only 2/15 managing to achieve this feat. Hold up horses have taken the majority of renewals with 5 of the last 6 also going the way of horses coming from out the back.

Summary

DP totals give the strongest trends pointer with 14/15 winners having 10 points or more in their Dosage Profile. The Paul Nicholls trained Taranis was the exception to the rule. Only 1996 winner Trainglot had Dosage figures above DI 1.89 and CD 0.50 although he did have the benefit of good to firm ground to help his speed orientated Dosage rating. 12/14 winners had a DI of 0.56 and above which is narrowed further with 8/14 having a DI of 1.00 and above. CD figures follow a comparable path with 12/14 having a CD of -0.29 and above, with this being narrowed further to 9/14 with a CD of 0.00 and above. When looking to narrow the field in future renewals the majority ranges highlighted are an excellent starting point as 79% of previous winners are incorporated within these figures.

Notable Defeats

'06 Be Be King - 3-4-13-0-0 (20) / **2.08** / **0.50** - sp 9/4
'02 Vrin - 6-2-2-1-1 (12) / **3.00** / **0.92** - 7/2
'00 Brandon Court - 8-4-9-4-1 (26) / **1.74** / **0.54** - sp 11/2
'99 Moondigua - 8-0-4-2-0 (14) / **2.50** / **1.00** - sp 2/1

Challengers (Scilly Isles) Novices' Chase - Sandown

6th February - cl1 g1 - 2m4f - 5yo+

Dosage Strength

Year	Horse	DP	tot	DI	CD	Run sty	Field Size	Gng
2009	Herecomesthetruth	0-1-1-4-2	8	0.23	-0.88	fr	5	gs
2008	Silverburn	0-1-1-6-2	10	0.18	-0.90	fr	5	sft
2007	New Little Bric	2-3-9-2-2	18	1.12	0.06	fr	4	gs
2006	Napolitain	4-4-8-4-0	20	1.50	0.40	fr	4	gf
2005	El Vaquero	0-0-7-3-2	12	0.41	-0.58	cp	5	gd
2004	Patricksnineteenth	1-9-6-2-0	18	2.60	0.50	cp	7	sft
2003	Tarxien	3-1-9-6-1	20	0.74	-0.05	cp	4	hvy
2002	Golden Goal	2-4-5-1-0	12	2.43	0.58	hu	6	gs
2001	Best Mate	1-1-10-5-1	18	0.64	-0.22	cp	8	hvy
2000	Upgrade	9-1-10-2-0	22	2.14	0.77	fr	6	gd
1999	Hoh Express	2-0-6-0-0	18	1.67	0.50	fr	9	gd
1998	Jack Doyle	5-0-5-4-2	16	0.88	0.13	hu	6	gd
1997	Stately Home	6-3-13-4-2	28	1.24	0.25	fr	6	gf
1996	Senor El Betrutti	~~0-0-0-0-0~~	0	~~inf~~	~~inf~~	fr	6	gf
1995	Banjo	1-0-7-4-4	16	0.39	-0.63	fr	8	sft

DP

14/15 had 8 points or more in their Dosage Profile
10/15 had 16 points or more in their Dosage Profile

DI

11/14 had a DI of 1.67 and below
9/14 had a DI of 1.24 and below
Majority Range : 0.39 to 1.67 - 64% of winners

CD

12/14 had a CD of 0.50 and below
9/14 had a CD of 0.25 and below
Majority Range : -0.22 to 0.50 - 57% of winners

Average

DI 1.16 / CD -0.01

Running Style

fr-9 / cp-4 / hu-2 - An excellent race for front runners with 9 (including the last 4) leading from pillar to post. Hold up horses are at a major disadvantage in this Novice chase with only 2 coming home in front.

Summary

Not a solid race for Dosage analysis due to the wide range of ratings the winning animals covered. DP totals once again give the strongest indicator with 14 of the 15 winners having 8 points or more in their profile - only Senor El Betrutti could be classed as Dosage weak. Numerous Dosage weak animals have tried and failed to take this race since Senor El Betrutti's victory and any short priced runner with this kind of profile should be viewed with caution in future renewals. DI ratings show that 11/14 had a DI of 1.67 and below hinting that preference is for animals with lesser amounts of speed in their Dosage. CD ratings also suggest the same as 12/14 had a CD of 0.50 and below which can be narrowed further to 9/14 having a CD of 0.25 and below.

Notable Defeats

'09 Araldur - **0-3-3-0-0 (6)** / 3.00 / 0.50 - sp 15/8
'07 Aztec Warrior - **2-1-2-1-0 (6)** / 2.00 / 0.67 - sp 7/2
'04 Ladalko - **0-0-1-1-0 (2)** / 0.30 / -0.50 - sp 2/1
'02 Bounce Back - 7-1-8-0-0 (16) / **3.00** / **0.94** - sp 7/2

Tote Handicap Chase - Sandown

6th February - cl2 hcp - 3m - 5yo+

Dosage Strength

Year	Horse	DP	tot	DI	CD	Run sty	Field Size	Gng
2009	Can't Buy Time	8-1-3-4-4	20	1.11	0.25	hu	9	gs
2008	Gungadu	4-0-5-3-0	12	1.18	0.42	cp	11	sft
2007	Rambling Minster	1-0-11-3-11	26	0.33	-0.88	hu	18	gs
2006	Dunbrody Millar	3-3-6-4-2	18	1.00	0.06	fr	11	gf
2005	Innox	0-0-6-4-0	10	0.43	-0.40	cp	12	gd
2004	Kings Mistral	3-3-6-0-0	12	3.00	0.75	fr	16	sft
2003	Iris Bleu	0-0-4-6-2	12	0.20	-0.83	hu	14	hvy
2002	Billingsgate	2-2-4-0-0	8	3.00	0.75	cp	9	gs
2001	Storm Damage	2-0-6-0-0	8	1.67	0.50	cp	9	hvy
2000	Trouble Ahead	~~2-0-0-0-2~~	4	~~1.00~~	~~0.00~~	cp	9	gd
1999	Clever Remark	8-4-7-1-0	20	3.44	0.95	hu	6	gd
1998	Court Melody	~~4-0-2-0-0~~	6	~~5.00~~	~~1.33~~	cp	4	gd

DP

10/12 had 8 points or more in their Dosage profile
7/12 had 12 points or more in their Dosage Profile

DI

7/10 had a DI of 1.00 and above
Majority Range : N/A

CD

7/10 had a CD of 0.06 and above
6/10 had a CD of 0.25 and above
Majority Range : 0.06 to 0.75 - 60% of winners

Average

DI 1.54 / CD 0.16

Running Style

fr-2 / cp-6 / hu-4 - Close to pace runners have the best record in this 3 mile chase. Front runners struggle slightly with only 2 from 12 scoring.

Summary

A competitive mid season handicap chase, however one, that does not throw up many strong Dosage pointers. The strongest trend this race produces comes from the DP totals with 10/12 being classed as Dosage strong, only 2000 winner Trouble Ahead and 1998 winner Court Melody fall down on this score. The prominence of this trend is highlighted by the fact that the last 9 winners have all been Dosage strong. DI ratings are a bit of a mixed bag, ranging from 0.20 right up to 3.44. CD ratings do ,however, provide a small trend to help the cause with 7/10 having a rating of 0.06 and above.

Notable Defeats

'06 Ladalko - **0-0-1-1-0 (2)** / 0.30 / -0.50 - sp 7/4
'04 Hersov - **0-1-1-0-0 (2)** / 3.00 / 0.50 - sp 5/1
'00 Montroe - **0-0-0-4-0 (4)** / 0.00 / -1.00 - sp 9/4

Towton Novices' Chase - Wetherby

6th February - cl1 g2 - 3m1f - 5yo+

Dosage Strength

Year	Horse	DP	tot	DI	CD	Run sty	Field Size	Gng
2009	Kornati Kid	2-0-10-6-0	18	0.64	-0.11	cp	5	sft
2007	Heltornic	3-4-7-2-0	16	1.91	0.50	fr	7	gs
2006	Halcon Genelardais	2-0-7-5-0	14	0.65	-0.07	cp	5	sft
2005	Ollie Magern	0-1-2-0-5	8	0.33	-1.13	fr	6	gs
2004	Royal Emperor	~~0-0-2-0-0~~	2	~~1.00~~	~~0.00~~	cp	7	sft
2003	Keen Leader	4-2-2-6-4	18	0.64	-0.22	hu	6	gs
2000	Arctic Camper	3-3-2-0-0	8	7.00	1.13	hu	4	sft
1999	Kadou Nonantais	1-0-4-3-6	14	0.27	-0.93	fr	5	hvy
1998	Escartefigue	2-2-16-0-0	20	1.50	0.30	cp	7	sft
1996	Mr Mulligan	2-3-7-4-2	18	0.89	-0.06	fr	8	gs

DP

9/10 had 8 points or more in their Dosage Profile
7/10 had between 14 and 20 points in their Dosage Profile

DI

7/9 had a DI of 1.50 and below
6/9 had a DI of 0.89 and below
Majority Range : 0.27 to 0.89 - 67% of winners

CD

7/9 had a CD of 0.30 and below
6/9 had a CD of -0.06 and below
Majority Range : -0.22 to 0.30 - 56% of winners

Average

DI 1.54 / CD -0.07

Running Style

fr-4 / cp-4 / hu-2 - A definite advantage to be setting the pace or sitting close to the pace as these positions have shared 4 wins a piece. Hold up horses have found it difficult to make up the ground in this novice chase.

Summary

Three miles one furlong around Wetherby's galloping easy bends is tailor made for stamina types and a bit tricky for horses with speed based Dosage ratings. 6/9 winners had a DI rating of 0.89 and below and a CD rating of -0.06 and below. The DI average for the race is slightly misleading as Arctic Camper's high DI of 7.00 pulls the total deceptively high. The small field that took part in 2000 is probably the reason for this abnormal result. The DP totals lead us in the direction of the Dosage strong with 9/10 having 8 points or more in their profile - Royal Emperor in 2004 being the only Dosage weak winner.

Notable Defeats

'06 Rebel Rhythm - 4-3-17-0-0 (24) / **1.82** / **0.46** - sp 7/2
'96 Senor El Betrutti - **0-0-0-0-0 (0)** / inf / inf - sp 6/1

Deloitte Novices' Hurdle Hurdle - Leopardstown

7th February - g1 - 2m2f - 5yo+

Dosage Strength

★★★

Year	Horse	DP	tot	DI	CD	Run sty	Field Size	Gng
2009	Pandorama	3-2-4-0-1	10	2.33	0.60	fr	4	sft
2008	Forpadydeplasterer	5-1-8-4-0	18	1.25	0.39	cp	7	gs
2007	Aran Concerto	1-4-5-2-0	12	1.67	0.33	cp	4	hvy
2006	Mr Nosie	6-4-5-1-0	16	3.57	0.94	cp	7	gs
2005	Royal Paradise	1-2-8-3-0	14	1.00	0.07	cp	8	sft
2004	Brave Inca	0-1-7-9-9	26	0.21	-1.00	hu	7	sft
2003	Solerina	3-1-8-2-0	14	1.33	0.36	fr	6	sft
2002	Like-A-Butterfly	3-2-4-0-7	16	0.78	-0.38	cp	10	hvy
2001	Colonel Braxton	1-0-11-2-4	18	0.57	-0.44	cp	8	hvy
2000	Youlneverwalkalone	3-2-4-2-7	18	0.64	-0.44	cp	11	gs
1999	Alexander Banquet	0-1-6-7-0	14	0.40	-0.43	fr	5	sft
1998	Native Estates	5-0-5-0-0	10	3.00	1.00	hu	11	gs
1997	Istabraq	11-9-26-10-0	56	1.43	0.38	hu	7	gs
1996	Bolino Star	~~0-0-0-0-0~~	0	~~inf~~	~~inf~~	hu	11	sft
1995	Hotel Minella	4-3-9-0-2	18	1.77	0.39	hu	9	sft

DP

14/15 had 10 points or more in their Dosage profile
12/15 had between 10 and 18 points in their Dosage profile

DI

11/14 had a DI of 1.77 and below
9/14 had a DI of 1.43 and below
1/14 had a DI below 0.40
Majority Range : 0.40 to 1.77 - 71% of winners

CD

11/14 had a CD of 0.39 and below
2/14 had a CD above 0.60
1/14 had a CD below -0.44
Majority Range : -0.44 to 0.39 - 71% of winners

Average

DI 1.43 / CD 0.13

Running Style

fr-3 / cp-7 / hu-5 - Sitting close to the pace has had the most success in this novice hurdle with 7 victories. Hold up horses have only managed 1 win in the past 11 races with the tough Brave Inca in 2004.

Summary

Another race that favours Dosage strong runners with 14 of the 15 winners having 10 points or more in their DP, '96 winner Bolino Star the only winner to be classed as Dosage weak. The DI and CD trends sit very much in the middle ground with the majority ranges suggesting negatives for stamina and speed orientated runners. 11/14 had a DI of 1.77 and below ,however, only our old friend Brave Inca fell below 0.40. 11/14 had a CD of 0.39 and below with again Brave Inca being the odd horse out as he was the only winner to have his CD fall below -0.44.

Notable Defeats

'08 Whatuthink - 0-1-1-4-2 (8) / **0.23** / **-0.88** - sp 100/30
'04 Watson Lake - 4-1-5-0-0 (10) / **3.00** / **0.90** - sp 9/10
'01 Liss A Paoraigh - 5-2-6-0-1 (14) / **2.50** / **0.71** - sp 2/1
'99 Native Upmanship - 5-0-9-0-0 (14) / 2.11 / **0.71** - sp 4/1

Moriarty Novices' Chase - Leopardstown

7th February - g1 - 2m5f - 5yo+

Dosage Strength

★★

Year	Horse	DP	tot	DI	CD	Run sty	Field Size	Gng
2009	Cooldine	0-0-5-3-0	8	0.45	-0.38	fr	7	sft
2008	J'Y Vole	~~0-0-6-0-0~~	6	~~1.00~~	~~0.00~~	fr	7	gs
2007	Mister Top Notch	1-9-6-0-2	18	2.60	0.39	cp	10	hvy
2006	The Railway Man	0-1-3-8-6	18	0.16	-1.06	hu	10	gs
2005	Carrigeen Victor	2-0-6-6-0	14	0.56	-0.14	cp	7	sft
2004	Pizarro	1-1-1-5-2	10	0.33	-0.60	cp	9	gs
2003	Barrow Drive	9-0-3-0-0	12	7.00	1.50	fr	7	gs
2002	Harbour Pilot	3-2-7-0-0	12	2.43	0.67	cp	10	hvy
2001	Sackville	2-1-5-2-2	12	0.85	-0.08	cp	3	hvy
2000	Native Upmanship	5-0-9-0-0	14	2.11	0.71	hu	7	gs
1999	Nick Dundee	6-1-3-4-4	18	0.89	0.06	fr	6	sft
1998	Florida Pearl	0-0-4-8-6	18	0.13	-1.11	cp	5	gs
1997	Dorans Pride	~~2-0-2-0-2~~	6	~~1.00~~	~~0.00~~	fr	4	gs
1996	Major Rumpus	1-3-2-2-2	10	1.00	-0.10	cp	7	sft
1995	Harcon	4-0-2-8-4	18	0.38	-0.44	cp	5	sft

DP

13/15 had 8 points or more in their Dosage profile
12/15 had between 10 and 18 points in their Dosage profile

DI

9/13 had a DI of 1.00 and below
0/13 had a DI between 1.01 and 2.10
Majority Range : 0.13 to 1.00 - 69% of winners

CD

10/13 had a CD of 0.39 and below
9/13 had a CD of 0.06 and below
2/13 had a CD below -0.60
Majority Range : -0.60 to 0.39 - 62% of winners

Average

DI 1.45 / CD -0.04

Running Style

fr-5 / cp-8 / hu-2 - Hold up horses have a poor record in this mid distance novice chase with only 2 successes. Close to pace runners have struck gold on most occasions with 8 winners.

Summary

Although this novice chase is run over an intermediate distance it is the runners with a Dosage rating in the middle ground that suffer the most, 0/13 winners having a CD rating between 1.01 and 2.10. The majority of winners have had stamina based Dosage ratings with 9/13 having a DI of 1.00 and below and the same number having a CD of 0.06 and below. This race has produced 4 speed heavy winners, with DI ratings of 2.11 and above and CD ratings of 0.39 and above, although it is the stamina heavy horses that win out in the long run. Ground conditions at Leopardstown have had an impact on the Dosage ratings with the ground officially riding good to soft or worse on every occasion. DP totals as usual favour the Dosage strong with only '08 winner J'Y Vole and the consistent Dosage breaker Dorans Pride in '97 having less than 8 points in their Dosage Profile.

Notable Defeats

'06 Sher Beau - **1-0-3-2-0 (6)** / 0.71 / 0.00 - sp 100/30
'05 Newmill - **0-0-4-2-0 (6)** / 0.50 / -0.33 - sp 9/4
'02 Truckers Tavern - 2-0-6-0-0 (8) / **1.67** / **0.50** - sp 9/4
'99 Native Estates - 5-0-5-0-0 (10) / **3.00** / **1.00** - sp 9/2

Hennessy Gold Cup Chase - Leopardstown

7th February - g1 - 3m - 5yo+

Dosage Strength

★★★★★

Year	Horse	DP	tot	DI	CD	Run sty	Field Size	Gng
2009	Neptune Collonges	~~0-0-0-2-0~~	2	~~0.00~~	~~-1.00~~	cp	6	sft
2008	The Listener	~~0-1-1-0-0~~	2	~~3.00~~	~~0.50~~	fr	8	gs
2007	Beef Or Salmon	3-1-5-0-11	20	0.48	-0.75	cp	5	hvy
2006	Beef Or Salmon	3-1-5-0-11	20	0.48	-0.75	hu	7	gs
2005	Rule Supreme	4-1-3-4-4	16	0.68	-0.19	cp	7	sft
2004	Florida Pearl	0-0-4-8-6	18	0.13	-1.11	hu	7	gs
2003	Beef Or Salmon	3-1-5-0-11	20	0.48	-0.75	hu	5	gs
2002	Alexander Banquet	0-1-6-7-0	14	0.40	-0.43	cp	5	hvy
2001	Florida Pearl	0-0-4-8-6	18	0.13	-1.11	cp	7	hvy
2000	Florida Pearl	0-0-4-8-6	18	0.13	-1.11	cp	7	gs
1999	Florida Pearl	0-0-4-8-6	18	0.13	-1.11	cp	7	sft
1998	Dorans Pride	~~2-0-2-0-2~~	6	~~1.00~~	~~0.00~~	cp	8	gs
1997	Danoli	2-2-12-0-4	20	1.00	-0.10	fr	8	gs
1996	Imperial Call	3-3-4-0-2	12	2.00	0.42	fr	8	sft
1995	Jodami	2-0-6-8-6	22	0.29	-0.73	hu	6	sft

DP

12/15 had 12 points or more in their Dosage Profile

11/15 had between 14 and 22 points in their Dosage Profile

DI

11/12 had a DI of 1.00 and below

10/12 had a DI of 0.68 and below

Majority Range : 0.13 to 0.68 - 83% of winners

CD

11/12 had a CD of -0.10 and below

9/12 had a CD of -0.43 and below

Majority Range : -1.11 to -0.10 - 92% of winners

Average

DI 0.53 / CD -0.64

Running Style

fr-3 / cp-8 / hu-4 - Running close to the pace is the ideal position to win the Irish Hennessy from with 8 of the last 15 adopting that position. 2 of the 3 front running winners, Imperial Call and Danoli, also had the 2 speediest Dosage ratings.

Summary

A race for the stayers with 11/12 having a CD of -0.10 and below and a DI of 1.00 and below. Furthermore, 9/12 had a CD of -0.43 and below and a DI of 0.48 and below. A possible contributing factor to this may be that ground conditions have ridden good to soft or worse on all 15 occasions. Add to this the galloping nature of the Leopardstown track and it becomes clear that a horse with a large stock of stamina in its Dosage is going to be ideally suited by the rigours of this Grade 1 chase. The last 2 runnings have gone to British raiders, both of whom had less than 8 points in their Dosage Profile. However, the majority call is still to go with Dosage strong horses as with 12/15 of the previous winners. Looking forward it would be interesting if Denman were to line-up in this seasons renewal as his Dosage figures look ready made for this race.

Notable Defeats

'08 Snowy Morning - 3-2-9-4-0 (18) / **1.12** / **0.22** - sp 11/4

'07 Forget The Past - 6-1-3-0-0 (10) / **5.67** / **1.30** - sp 9/2

'06 Hedgehunter - 8-3-8-2-7 (28) / **1.15** / **0.11** - sp 100/30

'99 Escartefigue - 2-2-16-0-0 (20) / **1.50** / **0.30** - sp 100/30

Dosage Fact

Imperial Call is the only horse in the races history to have won with a positive CD rating.

Game Spirit Chase - Newbury

13th February - cl1 g2 - 2m1f - 5yo+

Dosage Strength

★★★★★

Year	Horse	DP	tot	DI	CD	Run sty	Field Size	Gng
2008	Master Minded	4-1-7-2-0	14	1.55	0.50	fr	6	gs
2007	Well Chief	6-1-9-2-0	18	1.77	0.61	hu	8	sft
2005	Azertyuiop	2-0-2-8-2	14	0.27	-0.57	cp	6	gs
2004	Azertyuiop	2-0-2-8-2	14	0.27	-0.57	cp	6	gd
2003	Kadarann	3-0-8-1-0	12	1.40	0.42	cp	5	gs
2002	Lady Cricket	4-4-1-1-2	12	2.43	0.58	hu	7	sft
2001	Function Dream	3-3-4-2-0	12	2.00	0.58	cp	6	sft
2000	Flagship Uberalles	6-1-7-4-0	18	1.40	0.50	cp	3	gs
1999	Celibate	8-1-11-2-4	26	1.26	0.27	cp	6	gs
1998	Ask Tom	3-3-4-2-0	12	2.00	0.58	cp	4	gd
1997	Double Symphony	2-0-4-0-2	8	1.00	0.00	hu	3	gd
1996	Viking Flagship	6-1-7-2-2	18	1.40	0.39	cp	6	gs
1995	Nakir	3-0-3-2-0	8	1.29	0.50	fr	3	hvy
1994	Viking Flagship	6-1-7-2-2	18	1.40	0.39	cp	5	sft

DP

14/14 had 8 points or more in their Dosage Profile
13/14 had between 8 and 18 points in their Dosage Profile

DI

12/14 had a DI of 1.00 and above
11/14 had a DI of 1.26 and above
1/14 had a DI above 2.00
Majority Range : 1.00 to 2.00 - 79% of winners

CD

12/14 had a CD of 0.00 and above
11/14 had a CD of 0.27 and above
0/14 had a CD above 0.61
Majority Range : 0.00 to 0.61 - 86% of winners

Average

DI 1.39 / CD 0.30

Running Style

fr-2 / cp-9 / hu-3 - Close to pace runners hold a big advantage in the Game Spirit Chase with 9/14 winning. Until Master Minded front ran his way to victory in 2008 no other front runner had won since Nakir in 1995.

Summary

The Game Spirit Chase provides very strong Dosage trends on all fronts. DP totals indicate that all 14 winners were Dosage strong. DP totals also offer up its own little mini stat with 13/14 winners having between 8 and 18 points in their profile. 12/14 winners had a DI of 1.00 and above with the same number having a CD of 0.00 and above. This can be narrowed further with 11/14 having a DI of 1.26 and above and 11/14 having a CD of 0.27 and above. The DI ratings have an upper limit of 2.43 and the CD ratings cap at 0.61, leaving some robust majority ranges to use in future renewals. The only horse to fall out with these parameters was dual winner and serial Dosage buster Azertyuiop, who's Dosage rating was more akin to a Gold Cup winner rather than the 2 mile champion chaser he was.

Notable Defeats

'08 Voy Por Ustedes - 1-0-6-1-4 (12) / **0.50** / **-0.58** - sp evens
'07 Foreman - **1-0-3-1-1 (6)** / 0.71 / -0.17 - sp 9/2
'03 Cenkos - 6-0-2-2-0 (10) / **2.33** / **1.00** - 5/6
'02 Fadalko - 2-0-5-5-0 (12) / **0.60** / **-0.08** - sp 7/4
'99 Mulligan - 5-7-4-0-2 (18) / **3.50** / **0.72** - sp 7/2

Dosage Fact

Every winner of this race (since 1988) has been Dosage strong with 8 points or more in their profile.

Aon Chase - Newbury

13th February - cl1 g2 - 3m - 5yo+

Dosage Strength

Year	Horse	DP	tot	DI	CD	Run sty	Field Size	Gng
2008	Denman	0-1-1-6-2	10	0.18	-0.90	fr	4	gs
2007	Kauto Star	2-2-6-10-2	22	0.47	-0.36	hu	6	sft
2005	Farmer Jack	3-1-10-3-5	22	0.69	-0.27	cp	8	gs
2004	Shooting Light	1-0-7-12-6	26	0.21	-0.85	cp	8	gd
2003	Valley Henry	1-4-10-3-2	20	1.00	-0.05	cp	6	gd
2002	Bacchanal	4-7-16-1-0	28	2.11	0.50	fr	7	sft
2001	Shotgun Willy	3-1-10-0-0	14	1.80	0.50	cp	5	sft
2000	See More Business	0-0-3-6-1	10	0.18	-0.80	cp	6	gs

DP

8/8 had 10 points or more in their Dosage Profile
5/8 had 20 points or more in their Dosage Profile

DI

6/8 had a DI of 1.00 and below
5/8 had a DI of 0.69 and below
1/8 had a DI above 1.80
Majority Range : 0.18 to 1.00 - 75% of winners

CD

6/8 had a CD of -0.05 and below
5/8 had a CD of -0.27 and below
0/8 had a CD above 0.50
Majority Range : -0.90 to -0.05 - 75% of winners

Average

DI 0.83 / CD -0.28

Running Style

fr-2 / cp-5 / hu-1 - Hold up horses have struggled to be competitive in the Aon Chase with only the great Kauto Star winning from a help up position. Close to the pace is the ideal position to strike from as with 5 of the previous 8 winners.

Summary

The Aon Chase is touted as a trial for the Gold Cup in March and judging by the Dosage ratings of the winners it is the perfect race for Cheltenham hopefuls to put their credentials on the line. Three miles around Newbury's wide galloping track is just the place for stayers with stamina based Dosage ratings. 6/8 winners had a DI of 1.00 and below with the same number having a CD of -0.05 and below. Both ranges can be narrowed even more as 5/8 had a DI of 0.69 and below and 5/8 had a CD of -0.27 and below. DP totals point to Dosage strong individuals with all 8 winners having 8 points or more in their profile.

Notable Defeats

'05 Strong Flow - 2-1-11-0-0 (14) / **1.55** / **0.36** - sp 2/1
'05 Celestial Gold - **1-1-0-2-0 (4)** / 1.00 / 0.25 - sp 2/1
'04 Sir Rembrandt - 10-6-0-2-0 (18) / **8.00** / **1.33** - sp 4/1
'03 Marlborough - 3-3-4-0-0 (10) / **4.00** / **0.90** - sp 6/4

Totesport Trophy Hurdle - 13th February

Newbury - cl1 g3 hcp - 2m - 4yo+

Dosage Strength

★★★★

Year	Horse	DP	tot	DI	CD	Run sty	Field Size	Gng
2008	Wingman	3-2-22-13-2	42	0.62	-0.21	cp	24	gs
2007	Heathcote	13-3-15-2-1	34	2.24	0.74	hu	20	sft
2005	Essex	7-1-25-13-0	46	0.80	0.04	cp	25	gs
2004	Geos	0-0-7-1-0	8	0.78	-0.13	hu	25	gd
2003	Spirit Leader	6-3-3-4-4	20	1.11	0.15	hu	27	gd
2002	Copeland	3-0-9-4-0	16	0.88	0.13	cp	16	sft
2001	Landing Light	3-3-19-13-10	48	0.48	-0.50	hu	20	sft
2000	Geos	0-0-7-1-0	8	0.78	-0.13	cp	17	gs
1999	Decoupage	2-1-6-9-14	32	0.23	-1.00	hu	18	gd
1998	Sharpical	5-1-10-0-0	16	2.20	0.69	hu	14	gd
1997	Make A Stand	6-0-4-0-2	12	2.00	0.67	fr	18	gd
1996	Squire Silk	2-4-6-4-0	16	1.29	0.25	hu	18	gs
1995	Mysilv	6-2-2-8-6	24	0.60	-0.25	fr	8	hvy
1994	Large Action	2-0-14-0-4	20	0.82	-0.20	cp	11	sft

DP

14/14 had 8 points or more in their Dosage Profile
11/14 had 16 points or more in their Dosage Profile

DI

11/14 had a DI of 1.29 and below
9/14 had a DI of 0.88 and below
1/14 had a DI below 0.48
0/14 had a DI above 2.24
Majority Range : 0.48 to 1.29 - 71% of winners

CD

11/14 had a CD of 0.25 and below
10/14 had a CD of 0.15 and below
1/14 had a CD below -0.50
Majority Range : -0.25 to 0.25 - 64% of winners

Average

DI 1.06 / CD 0.02

Running Style

fr-2 / cp-5 / hu-7 - Leading from the front, and staying there, against the large fields usually found in the Totesport Trophy has proved too difficult for all bar 2. The front running Mysilv had an easier task than most with only 7 opponents. Hold up horses have taken the most renewals with 7.

Summary

Although a 2 mile handicap the Totesport Trophy has not been won by that many speed based horses. 11/14 winners had a DI of 1.29 and below and 11/14 had a CD of 0.25 and below. These figures are reduced slightly with 9/14 having a DI of 0.88 and below and 10/14 having a CD of 0.15 and below. Stamina based horses have also struggled in the Totesport Trophy with only 1999 winner Decoupage having a DI below 0.48 and a CD below -0.50. The strongest trend to come out of this race involves the DP totals, with all 14 winners being classed as Dosage strong.

Notable Defeats

'08 Five Dream - **1-1-4-0-0 (6)** / 2.00 / 0.50 - sp 7/2
'05 Roman Ark - 0-2-0-6-2 (10) / **0.25** / **-0.80** - sp 7/1
'03 Non So - 1-9-2-2-0 (14) / **3.67** / **0.64** - sp 9/2
'01 Grinkov - 6-4-16-0-0 (26) / **2.45** / **0.62** - sp 6/1

Grade 2 National Hunt Flat Race - Newbury

13th February - cl1 g2 - 2m 110yds - 4-6yo

Dosage Strength

★★★

Year	Horse	DP	tot	DI	CD	Run sty	Field Size	Gng
2008	Mad Max	2-0-13-5-0	20	0.47	-0.05	hu	9	gs
2007	Crocodiles Rock	1-2-9-2-4	18	0.71	-0.33	fr	10	sft
2005	Karanja	0-0-3-4-7	14	0.12	-1.29	cp	17	gs
2004	Secret Ploy	4-2-14-2-4	26	1.00	0.00	cp	24	gd
2003	Cornish Rebel	1-1-10-5-1	18	0.64	-0.22	hu	23	gd
2002	Iris's Gift	5-0-2-1-0	8	3.00	1.13	cp	14	sft
2001	Redde	3-1-6-4-6	20	0.54	-0.45	cp	18	sft
2000	Patriarch	6-4-11-1-0	22	2.38	0.68	hu	16	gs

DP

8/8 had 8 points or more in their Dosage Profile
7/8 had 14 points or more in their Dosage Profile

DI

6/8 had a DI of 1.00 and below
5/8 had a DI of 0.71 and below
Majority Range : 0.47 to 1.00 - 63% of winners

CD

6/8 had a CD of 0.00 and below
5/8 had a CD of -0.05 and below
Majority Range : -0.45 to 0.00 - 63% of winners

Average

DI 1.11 / CD -0.07

Running Style

fr-1 / cp-4 / hu-3 - Front runners struggle in this graded bumper race with only the 1 victory. Much better for these inexperienced horses to have cover and sit either close to the pace or held up out the back.

Summary

Dosage figures span quite a spectrum in this Grade 2 national hunt flat race. Although there is only 8 runnings to analyse, there is enough information to narrow the figures down slightly. The most obvious trend comes from the DP totals with every winner having 8 points or more in their profile, in fact 7 of the 8 winners had 14 points or more in their profile. DI ranges point in the direction of stamina based runners with 6/8 having a rating of 1.00 and below - being narrowed again with 5/8 having a DI of 0.71 and below. CD figures reveal the same with 6/8 having a rating of 0.00 and below. This makes perfect sense as this is essentially a flat race over 2 miles and half a furlong on a wide galloping track so winners are going to need at least a touch of stamina to last home. This is highlighted by every winner having at least 1 point in either the Solid or Professional section of their Dosage Profile.

Notable Defeats

'07 Seven Is My Number - 4-1-9-0-0 (14) / **2.11** / **0.64** - 15/8
'05 Mr Pointment - 2-0-7-4-5 (18) / **0.44** / **-0.56** - sp 9/2
'03 Control Man - 0-0-5-7-0 (12) / **0.26** / **-0.58** - sp 4/1
'03 Cloudy Grey - **0-0-0-2-0 (2)** / 0.00 / -1.00 - sp 9/2

Reynoldstown Novices' Chase - Ascot

20th February - cl1 g2 - 3m - 5yo+

Dosage Strength

★★★★

Year	Horse	DP	tot	DI	CD	Run sty	Field Size	Gng
2009	Carruthers	2-1-11-6-0	20	0.74	-0.05	fr	4	hvy
2008	Albertas Run	5-1-6-6-0	18	1.00	0.28	hu	7	gd
2007	Gungadu	4-0-5-3-0	12	1.18	0.42	fr	7	gs
2004	Our Vic	2-0-9-5-0	16	0.68	-0.06	cp	6	gd
2003	Keen leader	4-2-2-6-4	18	0.64	-0.22	hu	4	gs
2002	Jimmy Tennis	0-0-8-0-0	8	1.00	0.00	cp	5	gs
2001	Bacchanal	4-7-16-1-0	28	2.11	0.50	cp	3	sft
2000	Beau	1-4-7-2-0	14	1.55	0.29	fr	4	gs
1999	Lord Of The River	3-3-10-0-0	16	2.20	0.56	fr	6	gd
1998	The Toiseach	2-0-6-0-0	8	1.67	0.50	fr	5	gd
1997	Djeddah	2-0-2-4-2	10	0.43	-0.40	hu	5	gf
1996	Mr Mulligan	2-3-7-4-2	18	0.89	-0.06	fr	10	gs
1995	Sweet Duke	1-0-19-0-6	26	0.68	-0.38	fr	10	sft
1994	One Man	~~1-0-4-1-0~~	6	~~1.00~~	~~0.17~~	cp	9	sft

DP

13/14 had 8 points or more in their Dosage Profile
10/14 had 12 points or more in their Dosage profile

DI

13/13 had a DI of 2.20 and below
11/13 had a DI of 1.67 and below
0/13 had a DI below 0.43
Majority Range : **0.43 to 1.18 - 69% of winners**

CD

13/13 had a CD of -0.40 and above
10/13 had a CD of -0.06 and above
0/13 had a CD above 0.56
Majority Range : **-0.40 to 0.56 - 100% of winners**

Average

DI 1.14 / CD 0.11

Running Style

fr-7 / cp-4 / hu-3 - The Reynoldstown seems to dispel the theory that Ascot is a graveyard for front runners with 7/14 renewals going to those racing from the front.

Summary

Apart from the perennial Dosage buster One Man every winner of this top novice event had 8 points or more in their Dosage Profile. Plenty of Dosage weak animals have tried and failed since One Man's victory in 1994, as highlighted by beaten favourites Breedsbreeze and Air Force One in the past 2 runnings. CD ratings throw up a strong, if slightly large, range to work with as all winners had CD between -0.40 and 0.56. No winner had a DI below 0.43 so although this is a 3 mile chase stamina heavy horses are likely to struggle to get their heads in front. Apart from '02 winner Jimmy Tennis every other Dosage strong winner had at least 1 point in the brilliant section of their Dosage Profile. This is in contrast to only 4 winners having any points in the professional section of their profile.

Notable Defeats

'09 Breedsbreeze - **3-1-0-0-2 (6)** / 2.00 / 0.50 - sp 5/4
'08 Air Force One - **1-2-3-0-0 (6)** / 3.00 / 0.67 - sp 15/8
'03 Jair Du Cochet - **0-0-1-1-0 (2)** / 0.33 / -0.50 - sp Evens
'02 Artic Jack - 1-0-4-7-2 (14) / **0.27** / **-0.64** - sp 6/5

Ascot Chase - Ascot

20th February - cl1 g1 - 2m5f - 5yo+

Dosage Strength

★★★

Year	Horse	DP	tot	DI	CD	Run sty	Field Size	Gng
2009	Voy Por Ustedes	1-0-6-1-4	12	0.50	-0.58	cp	4	hvy
2008	Kauto Star	2-2-6-10-2	22	0.47	-0.36	cp	9	gd
2007	Monet's Garden	~~0-0-0-2-0~~	2	~~0.00~~	~~-1.00~~	hu	7	gs
2004	Hand Inn Hand	4-1-10-2-5	22	0.83	-0.14	hu	7	sft
2003	Tiutchev	2-0-16-0-2	20	1.00	0.00	cp	7	gs
2002	Tresor De Mai	~~0-0-0-2-0~~	2	~~0.00~~	~~-1.00~~	hu	5	gs
2001	Tiutchev	2-0-16-0-2	20	1.00	0.00	cp	4	sft
2000	Rockforce	3-3-4-4-0	14	1.33	0.36	hu	5	gs
1999	Teeton Mill	0-0-4-4-2	10	0.25	-0.80	fr	7	gd
1998	One Man	~~1-0-4-1-0~~	6	~~1.00~~	~~0.17~~	cp	3	gd
1997	Strong Promise	4-5-5-2-0	16	2.56	0.69	cp	4	gf
1996	Sound Man	4-0-2-4-4	14	0.56	-0.29	hu	5	gs
1995	Martha's Son	3-6-5-0-0	14	4.60	0.86	hu	6	sft

DP

10/13 had 10 points or more in their Dosage Profile
8/13 had between 14 and 22 points in their Dosage Profile

DI

8/10 had a DI of 1.33 and below
7/10 had a DI of 1.00 and below
Majority Range : 0.25 to 1.33 - 80% of winners

CD

8/10 had a CD of 0.36 and below
7/10 had a CD of 0.00 and below
0/10 had a CD below -0.80
Majority Range : -0.58 to 0.36 - 70% of winners

Average

DI 1.31 / CD -0.03

Running Style

fr-1 / cp-6 / hu-6 - Front runners have a tough time of it in this Grade 1 Chase with only Teeton Mill scoring from the head of affairs. Close to pace and hold up horses share the honours with 6 wins each.

Summary

This Grade 1 chase has shown a preference for stamina based Dosage ratings in recent times. Every Dosage strong winner in the past 9 runnings of this race has had a DI of 1.33 and below and a CD of 0.36 and below. This can be narrowed slightly as 8 winners have had a DI of 1.00 and below and a CD of 0.00 and below. Dosage strong horses haven't had it their own way in this race as 3 Dosage weak winners have taken the Ascot Chase in the past 13 renewals. The Dosage Profiles themselves show that every winner bar Martha's Son had at least 2 points in either the solid or professional sections of their Dosage Profile.

Notable Defeats

'07 Thisthatandtother - 1-2-13-**0-0** (16) / **1.46** / 0.25 - sp 4/1
'04 Le Roi Miguel - 3-1-4-2-0 (10) / **1.50** / **0.50** - sp 4/1
'02 Banker Count - 3-5-2-**0-0** (10) / **9.00** / **1.10** - sp 5/4
'02 Exit To Wave - 5-5-7-1-0 (18) / **3.00** / **0.78** - sp 11/4
'00 Nordance Prince - 4-6-11-1-2 (24) / **1.82** / **0.38** - sp 11/4

Gold Cup Handicap Chase - Haydock

20th February - cl1 g3 hcp - 3m4f - 5yo+

Dosage Strength

Year	Horse	DP	tot	DI	CD	Run sty	Field Size	Gng
2009	Rambling Minster	1-0-11-3-11	26	0.33	-0.80	hu	16	hvy
2008	Miko De Beauchene	~~0-0-0-0-0~~	0	~~inf~~	~~inf~~	cp	16	gs
2007	Heltornic	3-4-7-2-0	16	1.91	0.50	cp	16	hvy
2006	Ossmoses	~~0-0-0-0-2~~	2	~~0.00~~	~~-2.00~~	cp	14	hvy
2005	Forest Gunner	9-0-1-0-0	10	19.00	1.80	fr	11	sft
2004	Jurancon II	0-0-5-0-5	10	0.33	-1.00	cp	10	gd
2003	Shotgun Willy	3-1-10-0-0	14	1.80	0.50	cp	17	gd
2001	Frantic Tan	1-4-8-3-0	16	1.29	0.19	fr	18	sft
2000	The Last Fling	2-2-0-10-2	16	0.33	-0.50	fr	7	sft
1999	Young Kenny	1-0-8-0-11	20	0.33	-1.00	cp	13	sft
1998	Dom Samourai	0-1-9-0-0	10	1.22	0.10	cp	15	gd
1997	Suny Bay	~~2-0-2-0-0~~	4	~~3.00~~	~~1.00~~	fr	5	gd
1996	Lo Stregone	7-0-13-0-4	24	1.29	0.25	cp	11	sft
1995	Nuaffe	8-0-0-0-2	10	4.00	1.20	hu	10	hvy

DP

11/14 had 10 points or more in their Dosage Profile
9/14 had between 10 and 20 points in their Dosage Profile

DI

7/11 had a DI of 1.22 and above
2/11 had a DI of 1.91 and above
0/11 had a DI between 0.34 and 1.21
Majority Range : N/A

CD

7/11 had a CD of 0.10 and above
2/11 had a CD above 0.50
0/11 had a CD between -0.49 and 0.09
Majority Range : N/A

Average

DI 2.89 / CD 0.11

Running Style

fr-4 / cp-8 / hu-2 - Trawling along at the back around this 3m4f race is not a recipe for success with only Rambling Minster and Nuaffe taking the honours from a hold up position. Close to pace runners are the champions with 8 victories to their name.

Summary

It is possibly best to concentrate on the negative trends in the Haydock Gold Cup Handicap Chase. This is a race that brings a set of gapping stats to the table with 0/11 having a DI between 0.34 and 1.21 or a CD between -0.49 and 0.09. If taking this trend literally then a number of runners will have a negative mark against themselves in future renewals. Whether this stat is strong enough to hold up remains to be seen but it is definitely one to be aware of. Looking at more conventional stats shows that only 2/11 winners had a DI above 1.91 or a CD above 0.50, the front running gelding Forest Gunner being one of them with his massive DI rating of 19.00 and similarly high CD of 1.80. 3 Dosage weak animals have taken this handicap although it may still be best to side with Dosage strong animals as 11/14 fell into this category.

Notable Defeats

'08 Geeveem - 4-1-3-6-4 (18) / **0.57** / **-0.28** - sp 11/2
'07 Cloudy Lane - 2-1-3-4-0 (20) / **0.90** / **0.05** - sp 11/2
'06 What A Native - 3-1-6-0-0 (10) / **2.33** / **0.70** - sp 4/1
'06 Joaaci - 1-2-1-4-2 (10) / **0.54** / **-0.40** - sp 11/2
'04 Joe Blake - 4-2-7-0-1 (14) / **2.11** / **0.57** - sp 4/1

Kingwell Hurdle - Wincanton

20th February - cl1 g2 - 2m - 4yo+

Dosage Strength

Year	Horse	DP	tot	DI	CD	Run sty	Field Size	Gng
2009	Ashkazar	7-1-23-9-2	42	0.87	0.05	cp	9	sft
2008	Katchit	1-2-5-3-1	12	0.85	-0.08	cp	6	gs
2007	Straw Bear	5-1-6-4-4	20	0.82	-0.05	fr	5	sft
2006	Briareus	3-0-6-2-1	12	1.00	0.17	fr	9	gs
2005	Inglis Drever	3-0-22-15-2	42	0.50	-0.31	fr	7	gs
2004	Rigmarole	10-5-23-0-0	38	2.30	0.66	hu	8	gd
2003	Rhinestone Cowboy	3-0-10-1-2	16	1.00	0.06	hu	6	gs
2002	Hors La Loi III	~~2-0-0-4-0~~	6	~~0.50~~	~~0.00~~	hu	6	gs
2001	Azertyuiop	2-0-2-8-2	14	0.27	-0.57	cp	9	gd
2000	Hors La Loi III	~~2-0-0-4-0~~	6	~~0.50~~	~~0.00~~	cp	4	gd
1999	Grey Shot	4-4-4-0-0	12	5.00	1.00	cp	6	gs
1998	I'm Supposin	4-7-26-2-1	40	1.50	0.28	cp	7	gf
1997	Dreams End	9-0-15-10-4	38	0.77	0.00	hu	8	gs
1995	Alderbrook	2-0-5-0-11	18	0.33	-1.00	hu	7	sft
1994	Valfinet	~~2-2-0-0-0~~	4	~~inf~~	~~1.50~~	fr	5	gs

DP

12/15 had 12 points or more in their Dosage Profile
8/15 had 18 points or more in their Dosage Profile

DI

10/12 had a DI of 1.50 and below
9/12 had a DI of 1.00 and below
0/12 had a DI below 0.27
Majority Range : 0.27 to 1.00 - 75% of winners

CD

10/12 had a CD of 0.28 and below
8/12 had a CD of 0.06 and below
1/12 had a CD below -0.57
Majority Range : -0.31 to 0.28 - 67% of winners

Average

DI 1.27 / CD 0.02

Running Style

fr-4 / cp-6 / hu-5 - Not much in it with regards to running styles but close to pace runners just shade it with 6 wins.

Summary

This trial for the Champion Hurdle in March has a produced a distinct lack of speed heavy winners. 10/12 winners had a DI of 1.50 and below and a CD of 0.28 and below. These ranges are narrowed slightly with 9/12 having a DI of 1.00 and below and 8/12 having a CD of 0.06 and below. At the bottom end of the range only 1995 winner Alderbrook has had a CD below -0.57 with his stamina heavy rating of -1.00, although his victory was aided by soft ground conditions. DP totals show that the race has been won on 3 occasions by a Dosage weak animal however 2 of those occasions was by 2002 Champion Hurdler Hors La Loi III, so it still pays to side with the Dosage strong in the Kingwell. The majority ranges highlighted give a strong indicator of the type of horses needed to win the Kingwell Hurdle.

Notable Defeats

'08 Blythe Knight - 11-1-12-2-2 (28) / **1.80** / **0.61** - sp 100/30
'06 Chief Yeoman - 13-4-19-4-4 (44) / **1.51** / **0.41** - sp 7/2
'04 Intersky Falcon - 5-1-16-0-0 (22) / **1.75** / **0.50** - sp 8/13
'99 Midnight Legend - 6-4-8-2-0 (20) / **2.33** / **0.70** - sp 5/1

Bobbyjo Chase - Fairyhouse

20th February - g2 - 3m1f - 5yo+

Dosage Strength

Year	Horse	DP	tot	DI	CD	Run sty	Field Size	Gng
2009	Black Apalachi	2-0-8-4-0	14	0.75	0.00	fr	5	sft
2008	Afistfullofdollars	3-0-8-1-0	12	1.40	0.42	cp	8	gs
2007	Homer Wells	4-0-4-4-0	12	1.00	0.33	cp	7	hvy
2006	Forget The Past	6-1-3-0-0	10	5.67	1.30	cp	9	sft
2005	Hedgehunter	8-3-8-2-7	28	1.15	0.11	fr	6	sft
2004	Takagi	3-3-5-0-1	12	2.43	0.58	fr	6	sft
2003	Rince Ri	3-0-3-0-2	8	1.29	0.25	fr	5	gs

DP

7/7 had 8 points or more in their Dosage Profile
6/7 had between 8 and 14 points in their Dosage Profile

DI

7/7 had a DI of 0.75 and above
6/7 had a DI of 1.00 and above
1/7 had a DI above 2.43
Majority Range : 0.75 to 1.40 - 71% of winners

CD

7/7 had a CD of 0.00 and above
6/7 had a CD of 0.11 and above
1/7 had a DI above 0.58
Majority Range : 0.00 to 0.58 - 86% of winners

Average

DI 1.96 / CD 0.43

Running Style

fr-4 / cp-3 / hu-0 - The last place you want to be during the race is out the back as no hold up horse has yet tasted victory. Front runners hold a slender advantage over close to pace runners.

Summary

A relatively young race but one that is starting to show a strong, if slightly unexpected, Dosage bias. The first thing that is evident is that no winner has had a negative CD rating, every winner has had a CD of 0.00 and above. For a 3m1f race this is slightly odd but the stats are their for all to see. DI ratings also point in the direction of more speed orientated runners with 6/7 winners having a DI of 1.00 and above. What is also surprising about this set of trends is the fact all runnings of this race have taken place on ground that was either good to soft or worse, conditions that would usually favour stamina based horses over the longer distances. DP totals also provide a healthy trend with all winners having 8 points or more in their profile.

Notable Defeats

'08 One Cool Cookie - 3-1-6-4-2 (16) / **0.78** / **-0.06** - sp 7/2
'07 Numbersixvalverde - 2-0-0-6-2 (10) / **0.25** / **-0.60** - sp 7/2
'05 Pizarro - 1-1-1-5-2 (10) / **0.33** / **-0.60** - sp 11/10
'04 Alexander Banquet - 0-1-6-7-0 (14) / **0.40** / **-0.43** - sp 2/1
'04 Commanche Court - 4-0-5-2-13 (24) / **0.37** / **-0.83** - sp 9/4

PaddyPower.com Newlands Chase - Naas

21st February - g2 - 2m - 5yo+

Dosage Strength

★★★★

Year	Horse	DP	tot	DI	CD	Run sty	Field Size	Gng
2009	Carthalawn	4-6-18-0-0	28	2.11	0.50	hu	5	sft
2008	Maralan	4-2-6-6-2	20	0.82	0.00	hu	7	gs
2007	Nickname	2-1-8-3-0	14	1.00	0.14	hu	5	hvy
2006	Sir Oj	3-0-5-0-0	8	2.20	0.75	cp	9	sft
2005	Central House	2-1-8-4-5	20	0.54	-0.45	fr	4	sft
2004	Strong Run	5-3-6-0-0	14	3.67	0.93	fr	4	gs
2003	Arctic Copper	4-6-7-0-7	24	1.29	0.00	cp	8	gs
2002	Knife Edge	1-4-15-2-0	22	1.32	0.18	cp	7	hvy
2001	Moscow Express	3-1-8-4-0	16	1.00	0.19	hu	7	gs
2000	His Song	5-1-8-4-0	18	1.25	0.39	cp	6	sft
1999	Papillon	0-1-4-1-6	12	0.33	-1.00	cp	6	sft
1998	Opera Hat	3-3-6-0-0	12	3.00	0.75	fr	5	gs
1997	Opera Hat	3-3-6-0-0	12	3.00	0.75	fr	7	sft
1996	Opera Hat	3-3-6-0-0	12	3.00	0.75	fr	5	gs

DP

14/14 had 8 points or more in their Dosage Profile
13/14 had 12 points or more in their Dosage Profile

DI

12/14 had a DI of 0.82 and above
9/14 had a DI of 1.25 and above
1/14 had a DI above 3.00
Majority Range : 1.00 to 3.00 - 71% of winners

CD

12/14 had a CD of 0.00 and above
10/14 had a CD of 0.14 and above
1/14 had a CD above 0.75
Majority Range : 0.00 to 0.75 - 79% of winners

Average

DI 1.75 / CD 0.28

Running Style

fr-5 / cp-5 / hu-4 - No advantage to any running style in the Newlands Chase although front runners have only won 2 of the last 11 renewals.

Summary

The Newlands Chase is an excellent race for Dosage strong individuals as all 14 runnings have been won by horses with 8 points or more in their Profile. This 2 mile-Grade 2 chase is also well suited to horses with a Dosage that is leaning on the speed side with 12/14 winners having a DI of 0.82 and above and 12/14 winners having a CD of 0.00 and above. These stats can be narrowed more to highlight the strength of speed horses in this race with 9/14 having a DI of 1.25 and above and 10/14 having a CD of 0.14 and above. The Dosage Profile figures also highlight the dominance of speed horses here with 13/14 winners having at least 1 point in the Brilliant section of their profile.

Notable Defeats

'09 Mansony - **1-1-4-0-0 (6)** / 2.00 / 0.50 - sp 6/4
'08 Don't Be Bitin - 2-0-10-1-3 (16) / **0.78** / **-0.19** - sp 9/2
'98 Jeffell - **2-3-1-0-0 (6)** / 11.00 / 1.17 - sp 5/2

Dovecot Novices' Hurdle - Kempton

27th February - cl1 g2 - 2m - 4yo+

Dosage Strength

★★★★★

Year	Horse	DP	tot	DI	CD	Run sty	Field Size	Gng
2009	Trenchant	8-0-6-0-0	14	3.67	1.14	cp	8	gs
2008	Pigeon Island	6-1-17-2-0	26	1.48	0.42	hu	9	gd
2007	Shatabdi	1-0-2-9-8	20	0.11	-1.15	cp	5	sft
2003	Puntal	1-0-7-5-7	20	0.29	-0.85	fr	6	gd
2002	Hitman	3-1-9-5-0	18	0.89	0.11	fr	10	gs
2001	St Pirran	5-0-11-0-0	16	1.91	0.63	cp	9	gs
2000	Hariymi	8-5-13-2-0	28	2.29	0.68	cp	4	sft
1999	Premier Generation	2-0-6-0-0	8	1.67	0.50	cp	6	sft
1998	Buddy Marvel	3-3-3-0-3	12	1.67	0.25	fr	6	gf
1997	San Martino	4-5-10-3-0	22	1.75	0.45	hu	7	gd
1996	Kimanicky	4-2-5-1-0	12	2.43	0.75	cp	8	sft
1995	Balanak	2-2-15-4-3	26	0.79	-0.15	cp	9	hvy
1994	Jazilah	4-3-3-4-2	16	1.13	0.19	hu	10	sft

DP

13/13 had 8 points or more in their Dosage Profile
10/13 had 14 points or more in their Dosage Profile

DI

11/13 had a DI of 0.79 and above
9/13 had a DI of 1.13 and above
8/13 had a DI of 1.48 and above
Majority Range : 0.79 to 2.43 - 77% of winners

CD

11/13 had a CD of -0.15 and above
10/13 had a CD of 0.11 and above
8/13 had a CD of 0.25 and above
Majority Range : -0.15 to 0.75 - 77% of winners

Average

DI 1.54 / CD 0.23

Running Style

fr-3 / cp-7 / hu-3 - Close to pace runners hold the best record with 7 winners. Hold up runners have only won once in the past 9 runnings.

Summary

This sharp 2 miles around Kempton Park's hurdle course is ideal for a speed based novice. 11/13 winners had a DI of 0.79 and above being narrowed to 9/13 with a DI of 1.13 and above. CD ratings follow a similar path with 11/13 having a rating of -0.15 and above, again being narrowed to 10/13 with a CD of 0.11 and above. Only 2 horse have achieved success with heavily stamina based Dosage ratings, Puntal in 2003 and Shatabdi in 2007. Strengthening the Dosage score of this race even more is the DP totals which indicate that all 13 winners were classed as Dosage strong and 10/13 winners had 14 or more points in their profile.

Notable Defeats

'08 I'msingingtheblues - **0-0-6-0-0 (6)** / 1.00 / 0.00 - sp 11/2
'07 Buster Hyvonen - 2-2-6-4-2 (16) / **0.78** / **-0.13** - sp 7/4
'07 Oslot - **1-1-2-0-0 (4)** / 3.00 / 0.75 - sp 9/4
'02 Sossus Vlei - 1-0-1-0-6 (8) / **0.23** / **-1.25** - sp 4/1
'99 Prominent Profile - 3-5-2-0-0 (10) / **9.00** / **1.10** - sp 11/8

Dosage Fact

Apart from 1993 winner Roll A Dollar every other winner since 1988 was classed as Dosage strong.

Pendil Novices' Chase - Kempton

27th February - cl1 g2 - 2m4f - 5yo+

Dosage Strength

★★★

Year	Horse	DP	tot	DI	CD	Run sty	Field Size	Gng
2009	Herecomesthetruth	0-1-1-4-2	8	0.23	-0.88	fr	4	gd
2008	Oslot	~~1-1-2-0-0~~	4	~~3.00~~	~~0.75~~	cp	5	gd
2007	Natal	2-1-4-3-0	10	1.00	0.20	cp	7	sft
2005	Limerick Boy	3-3-14-0-0	20	1.86	0.45	cp	7	sft
2004	Calling Brave	2-2-18-0-0	22	1.44	0.27	fr	5	gd
2003	Hand Inn Hand	4-1-10-2-5	22	0.83	-0.14	fr	8	gd
2002	Golden Goal	2-4-5-1-0	12	2.43	0.58	hu	5	gd
2001	Crocadee	0-0-2-8-4	14	0.08	-1.14	fr	6	gd
2000	Serenus	4-5-24-6-1	40	1.11	0.13	cp	4	gs
1999	Makounji	2-0-8-4-4	18	0.50	-0.44	cp	4	sft
1998	Stormy Passage	4-3-13-4-2	26	1.08	0.12	cp	4	gf
1997	Land Afar	4-2-5-4-3	18	0.89	0.00	hu	6	gd
1996	Draborgie	2-0-2-4-0	8	0.60	0.00	fr	4	sft
1995	Brief Gale	5-3-4-0-0	12	5.00	1.08	hu	7	hvy
1994	Monsieur Lecure	4-0-14-0-4	22	1.00	0.00	fr	4	sft

DP

14/15 had 8 points or more in their Dosage Profile
11/15 had 12 points or more in their Dosage Profile

DI

12/14 had a DI of 1.86 and below
10/14 had a DI of 1.11 and below
Majority Range : 0.50 to 1.86 - 71% of winners

CD

12/14 had a CD of -0.44 and above
10/14 had a CD of 0.00 and above
1/14 had a CD of 0.58 and above
Majority Range : -0.44 to 0.45 - 71% of winners

Average

DI 1.29 / CD 0.02

Running Style

fr-6 / cp-6 / hu-3 - Hold up horses come off worst in the Pendil Novices' Chase with 3 wins, their recent record is even poorer with only 1 victory in the past 11 renewals.

Summary

Dosage ratings in the middle ranges fair best in this novice chase run over the intermediate distance of 2m4f. CD ratings highlight this fact best with 9/14 winners having a rating of between -0.44 and 0.45. DI ratings also point to well balanced runners with 9/14 falling between 0.50 and 1.86. Only once has the Pendil Novices' Chase been run on heavy ground and this produced the winner (Brief Gale) who's Dosage rating was the most wrong. As with other forms of race study heavy ground can throw up some surprise results. 2008 winner Oslot was the only horse that was classed as Dosage weak, every other winner held 8 points or more in their profile. Looking at Dosage Profiles provides another stat to work with as every winner bar Herecomesthetruth in '09 and Crocadee in '01 had at least 2 points in the Brilliant section of their Dosage.

Notable Defeats

'09 Ouzbeck - **1-0-1-0-0 (2)** / 3.00 / 1.00 -sp 15/8
'08 Hobbs Hill - 2-1-8-6-7 (24) / **0.41** / **-0.63** - sp 8/13
'05 Duncliffe - 3-6-5-0-0 (14) / **4.60** / **0.86** - sp 7/4
'03 Scots Grey - 1-0-8-6-7 (22) / **0.29** / **-0.82** - sp 9/4

Racing Post Chase - Kempton

27th February - cl1 g3 hcp - 3m - 5yo+

Dosage Strength

★★★★

Year	Horse	DP	tot	DI	CD	Run sty	Field Size	Gng
2009	Nacarat	0-2-6-0-2	10	1.00	-0.20	fr	20	gd
2008	Gungadu	4-0-5-3-0	12	1.18	0.42	cp	15	gd
2007	Simon	1-0-8-7-0	16	0.45	-0.31	hu	10	sft
2005	Farmer Jack	3-1-10-3-5	22	0.69	-0.27	cp	16	sft
2004	Marlborough	3-3-4-0-0	10	4.00	0.90	hu	11	gd
2003	La Landiere	3-3-8-0-2	16	1.67	0.31	cp	14	gd
2002	Gunther Mcbride	1-0-7-6-0	14	0.47	-0.29	cp	14	gd
2001	Young Spartacus	0-2-8-4-0	14	0.75	-0.14	hu	15	gd
2000	Gloria Victis	2-0-0-8-2	12	0.20	-0.67	fr	13	gs
1999	Dr Leunt	12-5-10-5-4	36	1.57	0.44	fr	8	sft
1998	Super Tactics	~~2-0-2-0-0~~	4	~~3.00~~	~~1.00~~	cp	7	gf
1997	Mudahim	5-5-10-4-0	24	1.67	0.46	cp	9	gd
1996	Rough Quest	0-0-6-8-6	20	0.18	-1.00	hu	9	sft
1995	Val D'Alene	2-0-0-8-2	12	0.20	-0.67	hu	9	hvy
1994	Antonin	~~0-0-2-0-2~~	4	~~0.33~~	~~-1.00~~	cp	16	sft

DP

13/15 had 10 points or more in their Dosage Profile
12/15 had between 10 and 24 points in their Dosage Profile

DI

12/13 had a DI of 1.67 and below
9/13 had a DI of 1.18 and below
0/13 had a DI below 0.18
Majority Range : 0.18 to 1.18 - 69% of winners

CD

12/13 had a CD of 0.46 and below
8/13 had a CD of -0.14 and below
1/13 had a CD below -0.67
Majority Range : -0.31 to 0.46 - 69% of winners

Average

DI 1.08 / CD -0.08

Running Style

fr-3 / cp-7 / hu-5 - Until Nacarat's wide margin victory in last years renewal front runners had drawn a blank for 7 years. Close to pace runners have had most success although hold up runners are not far behind.

Summary

Another 3 mile chase around Kempton that puts to rest the theory of this being an easy 3 miles. Only 2004 winner Marlborough can be classed as a speedy Dosage winner as every other winner had a DI of 1.67 and below and a CD of 0.46 and below. These ranges can be narrowed much further with 9/13 winners having a DI of 1.18 and below and 8/13 having a CD of -0.14 and below. Winners do not carry bundles of stamina however as only Rough Quest in 1996 won with a CD below -0.67. Rough Quest was also the only winner to have zero points in either the Brilliant or Intermediate section of their Dosage Profile - at least 2 points of inherited speed was found in every other of the 12 winners profiles. 13/15 winners were classed as Dosage strong, including the last 10 winners.

Notable Defeats

'09 Big Fella Thanks - 5-1-4-0-0 (10) / **4.00** / **1.10** - sp 7/2
'07 Lucifer Bleu - **0-0-3-1-0 (4)** / 0.60 / -0.25 - sp 15/8
'05 Colonel Frank - 6-2-6-2-0 (16) / **2.20** / **0.75** - sp 4/1
'02 Lord Of The River - 2-3-10-0-0 (16) / **2.20** / **0.56** - sp 7/2
'99 Mr Strong Gale - 3-3-4-0-0 (10) / **4.00** / **0.90** - sp 7/2

Adonis Juvenile Novices' Hurdle - Kempton

27th February - cl1 g2 - 2m - 4yo

Dosage Strength

★★★★

Year	Horse	DP	tot	DI	CD	Run sty	Field Size	Gng
2009	Hebridean	4-2-8-8-0	22	0.83	0.09	hu	7	gs
2008	Binocular	6-0-8-2-0	16	1.67	0.63	hu	11	gd
2007	Punjabi	2-5-16-1-2	26	1.36	0.15	fr	6	sft
2005	Penzance	1-0-8-5-0	14	0.56	-0.21	cp	8	sft
2004	Trouble At Bay	3-1-13-3-4	24	0.78	-0.17	hu	9	gd
2003	Well Chief	6-1-9-2-0	18	1.77	0.61	hu	7	gd
2002	Giocomo	2-16-6-0-0	24	7.00	0.83	cp	14	gd
2001	Bilboa	3-0-4-8-7	22	0.29	-0.73	cp	8	gs
2000	Snow Drop	6-2-4-0-0	12	5.00	1.17	hu	7	sft
1999	Katarino	0-0-7-1-0	8	0.78	-0.13	cp	6	sft
1998	Fataliste	~~3-0-1-2-0~~	6	~~1.40~~	~~0.67~~	fr	5	gf
1997	L'Opera	3-3-9-5-0	20	1.11	0.20	cp	10	gd
1996	Zabadi	6-1-11-4-0	22	1.32	0.41	hu	9	sft
1995	Greenback	4-0-0-0-4	8	1.00	0.00	fr	7	hvy
1994	Mysilv	6-2-2-8-6	24	0.60	-0.25	fr	3	sft

DP

14/15 had 8 points or more in their Dosage Profile
10/15 had 16 points or more in their Dosage Profile

DI

13/14 had a DI of 0.56 and above
11/14 had a DI of 0.78 and above
2/14 had a DI above 1.77
Majority Range : 0.56 to 1.77 - 79% of winners

CD

13/14 had a CD of -0.25 and above
9/14 had a CD of 0.00 and above
2/14 had a CD above 0.63
Majority Range : -0.25 to 0.41 - 64% of winners

Average

DI 1.72 / CD 0.19

Running Style

fr-4 / cp-5 / hu-6 - Not much between running styles here with hold up runners just prevailing with 6 victories.

Summary

Not a race for stamina heavy runners with only 2001 winner Bilboa having a DI below 0.56 and a CD below -0.25. 11/14 winners had a DI of 0.78 and above with 9/14 winners having a CD of 0.00 and above. '02 winner Giocomo and '00 winner Snow Drop had vast amounts of speed in their Dosage but this is unusual for a winner of the Adonis Juvenile Hurdle with most winners falling below the 1.77 DI mark and the 0.63 CD mark. DP totals point towards Dosage strong juveniles with only '98 winner Fataliste having less than 8 points in his profile. The Dosage Profiles highlight the need for at least the minimum amount of inherited speed as only '99 winner Katarino had zero points in the Brilliant column of his profile.

Notable Defeats

'07 Poquelin - 5-0-5-0-0 (10) / **3.00** / **1.00** - sp 9/4
'04 Mondul - **0-0-0-0-0 (0)** / inf / inf - sp 11/4
'03 East Tycoon - 5-0-6-1-0 (12) / **2.00** / **0.75** - sp 9/4
'97 Kerawi - 6-1-15-0-0 (22) / **1.93** / 0.59 - sp 6/4
'96 Ocean Hawk - 5-2-9-0-0 (16) / **2.56** / **0.75** - sp 5/2

Dosage Fact

This race has proven an excellent trial for the Triumph Hurdle at the Cheltenham festival with numerous winners of this race going on to win or place in the juvenile showpiece in March. This is no surprise as the CD averages are almost identical; 0.19 in the Adonis and 0.18 in the Triumph.

Eider Chase - Newcastle

27th February - cl2 hcp - 4m1f - 5yo+

Dosage Strength

★★★★★

Year	Horse	DP	tot	DI	CD	Run sty	Field Size	Gng
2009	Merigo	1-1-8-0-0	10	1.50	0.30	cp	13	hvy
2008	Comply Or Die	2-0-6-4-0	12	0.71	0.00	cp	18	gs
2007	Nil Desperandum	0-0-7-7-0	14	0.33	-0.50	hu	16	hvy
2006	Philson Run	2-0-7-3-0	12	0.85	0.08	hu	17	hvy
2004	Tyneandthyneagain	0-1-6-15-4	26	0.18	-0.85	cp	20	gd
2002	This Is Serious	3-0-1-4-2	10	0.54	-0.20	hu	15	sft
2001	Narrow Water	1-3-2-0-6	12	0.71	-0.58	cp	12	hvy
2000	Scotton Green	2-0-3-0-11	16	0.28	-1.13	cp	16	hvy
1999	Hollybank Buck	2-3-7-2-4	18	0.89	-0.17	hu	15	gs
1998	Domaine De Pron	1-1-12-0-2	16	1.00	-0.06	cp	11	gd
1997	Seven Towers	~~0-0-2-0-0~~	2	~~1.00~~	~~0.00~~	hu	12	gd
1996	Killeshin	11-3-7-1-0	22	3.89	1.09	hu	15	gs
1995	Willsford	2-2-0-0-18	22	0.22	-1.36	fr	10	gs

DP

12/13 had 10 points or more in their Dosage Profile
11/13 had between 10 and 22 points in their Dosage Profile

DI

10/12 had a DI of 1.00 and below
8/12 had a DI of 0.85 and below
1/12 had a DI above 1.50
Majority Range : 0.18 to 1.00 - 83% of winners

CD

10/12 had a CD of 0.08 and below
8/12 had a CD of -0.06 and below
Majority Range : -0.85 to 0.08 - 67% of winners

Average

DI 0.93 / CD -0.28

Running Style

fr-1 / cp-6 / hu-6 - Horses attempting to make all in the Eider do so at their own peril as only Willsford in 1995 has managed the feat in the past 13 runnings. Close to pace runners and hold up horses share 6 wins a piece.

Summary

This stamina test over Newcastle's galloping-testing track throws up no surprises when it comes to Dosage ratings. This race had been dominated by stamina heavy Dosage horses, with 10/12 having a DI of 1.00 and below and 10/12 having a CD of 0.08 and below. These ranges can be narrowed again as 8/12 had a DI of 0.85 and below and a CD of -0.06 and below. A factor in keeping these Dosage ratings pointing towards the stamina side must be the ground conditions at Gosforth Park as when soft is in the going description conditions can become incredibly testing, especially over 4m1f. DP totals point towards stoutly bred individuals with 12/13 having 10 points or more in their Profile.

Notable Defeats

'04 Harlov - 6-3-10-7-0 (26) / **1.17** / **0.31** - sp 11/2
'01 Murt's Man - 4-0-8-0-0 (12) / **2.00** / **0.67** - sp 6/1
'00 Cherokee Boy - 3-2-2-1-0 (8) / **3.00** / **0.88** - sp 5/1

Dosage Fact

The front running Willsford did not use a speedy Dosage to front run his way to glory but rather a very heavily stamina biased profile. A CD of -1.36 is one of the lowest winning CD ratings you will find in this book.

National Spirit Hurdle - Fontwell

28th February - cl1 g2 - 2m4f - 4yo+

Dosage Strength

★★★

Year	Horse	DP	tot	DI	CD	Run sty	Field Size	Gng
2009	Lough Derg	~~0-0-3-2-1~~	6	~~0.33~~	~~-0.67~~	fr	7	gd
2008	Lough Derg	~~0-0-3-2-1~~	6	~~0.33~~	~~-0.67~~	cp	8	gd
2007	United	3-3-10-0-0	16	2.20	0.56	fr	5	sft
2006	My Way De Solzen	1-2-9-3-5	20	0.60	-0.45	fr	6	hvy
2005	Blue Canyon	5-1-15-6-7	34	0.66	-0.26	hu	8	gs
2004	Starzaan	3-4-13-6-4	30	0.82	-0.13	cp	9	gd
2003	Classified	~~2-2-0-0-0~~	4	~~inf~~	~~1.50~~	hu	7	gs
2002	Rouble	3-1-7-4-3	18	0.71	-0.17	fr	5	sft
2001	Baracouda	2-3-8-1-2	16	1.29	0.13	hu	10	gs
2000	Male-Ana-Mou	3-2-1-0-16	22	0.33	-1.09	hu	4	gs

DP

7/10 had 16 points or more in their Dosage Profile

DI

6/7 had a DI of 1.29 and below
5/7 had a DI of 0.82 and below
0/7 had a DI above 2.20
Majority Range : 0.33 to 1.29 - 86% of winners

CD

6/7 had a CD of 0.13 and below
5/7 had a CD of -0.13 and below
1/7 had a CD below -0.45
Majority Range : -0.45 to 0.13 - 71% of winners

Average

DI 0.94 / CD -0.20

Running Style

fr-4 / cp-2 / hu-4 - Not much too choose between the running styles in the National Spirit Hurdle. Close to pace runners just come off worst with only the 2 victories.

Summary

With 3 of the 10 winners being classed as Dosage weak, horses with less than 8 points in their profile must come into consideration in future renewals. The 7 Dosage strong winners do add their own mini trend with all of them having 16 points or more in their profile. DI and CD ratings point in the direction of stamina based runners with 6/7 having a DI of 1.29 and below and a CD of 0.13 and below. These figures can be narrowed a touch with 5/7 having a CD of -0.13 and below and the same number having a CD of -0.13 and below. The one winner to have a rating higher than this was the front running mare United who took the 2007 renewal.

Notable Defeats

'09 Pierrot Lunaire - 3-4-12-1-2 (22) / **1.44** / **0.23** - sp 100/30
'06 Turtle Soup - 5-0-9-2-0 (16) / **1.46** / **0.50** - sp 9/2
'05 Big Moment - 11-3-9-0-1 (24) / **3.36** / **0.96** - sp 7/4
'04 Quazar - 6-2-11-1-0 (20) / 2.08 / 0.65 - sp 9/2
'03 Stromness - 10-5-19-0-0 (34) / **2.58** / **0.74** - sp 4/1

Gold Cup Handicap Chase - Newbury

6th March - cl1 g3 hcp - 2m4f - 5yo+

Dosage Strength

Year	Horse	DP	tot	DI	CD	Run sty	Field Size	Gng
2009	New Little Bric	2-3-9-2-2	18	1.12	0.06	cp	15	gd
2008	Natal	2-1-4-3-0	10	1.00	0.20	cp	10	gs
2007	Madison Du Berlais	~~0-0-3-1-0~~	4	~~0.60~~	~~-0.25~~	hu	11	sft
2006=	Cornish Sett	5-1-6-6-0	18	1.00	0.28	cp	15	gf
2006=	Horus	0-5-5-5-1	16	0.88	-0.13	fr	15	gf
2005	Supreme Prince	4-2-2-4-4	16	0.78	-0.13	cp	15	gs
2004	Isio	3-3-10-6-0	22	1.00	0.14	cp	15	gd
2003	Clan Royal	0-0-2-10-2	14	0.08	-1.00	cp	7	sft
2002	Stormhill Stag	4-3-1-8-6	22	0.52	-0.41	cp	8	gs
2000	Shepherds Rest	5-3-6-4-0	18	1.57	0.50	cp	5	sft
1999	Ashwell Boy	3-3-4-2-0	12	2.00	0.58	hu	4	sft
1998	Easy Buck	2-6-4-0-0	12	5.00	0.83	fr	2	hvy
1997	Too Plush	4-0-10-2-0	16	1.29	0.38	hu	5	gs

DP

12/13 had 10 points or more in their Dosage Profile
10/13 had between 10 and 18 points in their Dosage Profile

DI

10/12 had a DI of 0.78 and above
8/12 had a DI of 1.00 and above
1/12 had a DI above 2.00
Majority Range : **0.52 to 1.57 - 75% of winners**

CD

11/12 had a CD of -0.41 and above
10/12 had a CD of -0.13 and above
1/12 had a CD above 0.58
Majority Range : **-0.13 to 0.58 - 75% of winners**

Average

DI 1.35 / CD 0.11

Running Style

fr-2 / cp-8 / hu-3 - A strong race for close to pace runners with 8 victories, all of those 8 coming in the last 10 runnings. Front runners actually have an even poorer record than shown as '98 winner Easy Buck only had 1 opponent.

Summary

A race where stamina based runners have struggled with only 2/12 having a DI below 0.78 and a CD below -0.13. If we ignore Easy Bucks win in 1998, where he only had 1 opponent, then no winner had a DI above 2.00 or a CD above 0.58. In fact the trends suggest this mid distance handicap is best suited to horses with well balanced Dosage figures with 75% of winners falling between DI 0.52 and 1.57 and CD -0.13 and 0.58. High class Madison Du Berlais is the only winner to have less than 8 points in his Dosage Profile with every other winner being classed as Dosage strong.

Notable Defeats

'09 The Package - 2-0-11-4-5 (22) / **0.52** / **-0.45** - sp 11/4
'07 Flying Enterprise - 3-1-12-6-4 (26) / **0.63** / **-0.27** - sp 11/4
'07 Nozic - 1-1-8-2-4 (16) / **0.60** / **-0.44** - sp 7/2
'05 Buckby Lane - **1-0-1-4-0 (6)** / 0.33 / -0.33 - sp 100/30
'04 Exit Swinger - 4-4-6-0-0 (14) / **3.67** / **0.86** - sp 5/1

NH' Novices Handicap Hurdle Final - Sandown

13th March - cl1 g3 hcp - 2m4f - 4-7yo

Dosage Strength

★★★★

Year	Horse	DP	tot	DI	CD	Run sty	Field Size	Gng
2009	Big Eared Fran	5-4-15-3-1	28	1.43	0.32	hu	18	gd
2008	Beshabar	3-2-7-1-1	14	1.55	0.36	cp	17	gd
2007	Albertas Run	5-1-6-6-0	18	1.00	0.28	cp	16	hvy
2006	Killaghy Castle	0-0-5-3-0	8	0.45	-0.38	hu	17	sft
2005	Julius Caesar	8-1-29-8-0	46	1.04	0.20	hu	18	gs
2004	Control Man	0-0-5-7-0	12	0.26	-0.58	cp	16	sft
2003	Tana River	2-0-8-0-0	10	1.50	0.40	hu	12	hvy
2002	Latimers Place	2-2-8-4-0	16	1.00	0.13	hu	17	gs
2000	Direct Access	~~0-0-0-0-0~~	0	~~inf~~	~~inf~~	cp	15	hvy
1999	Errand Boy	2-1-5-1-11	20	0.38	-0.90	cp	13	gd
1998	Lordberniebouffant	2-0-1-5-4	12	0.26	-0.75	cp	11	sft
1997	Montroe	~~0-0-0-4-0~~	4	~~0.00~~	~~-1.00~~	fr	16	sft

DP

10/12 had 8 points or more in their Dosage Profile
8/12 had 12 points or more in their Dosage Profile

DI

10/10 had a DI of 1.55 and below
6/10 had a DI between 1.00 and 1.55
0/10 had a DI between 0.46 and 0.99
Majority Range : 1.00 to 1.55 - 60% of winners

CD

10/10 had a CD of 0.40 and below
6/10 had a CD between 0.13 and 0.40
0/10 had a CD between -0.37 and 0.12
Majority Range : -0.38 to 0.40 - 70% of winners

Average

DI 0.89 / CD -0.09

Running Style

fr-1 / cp-6 / hu-5 - Front running horses struggle in this novice hurdle with only the 1 winner, Montroe in 1997. Close to pace runners just shade it with 6 wins to hold up horses 5 wins.

Summary

A terrible race for horses with vast quantities of speed in their Dosage as 10/10 winners had a DI of 1.55 and below and 10/10 had a CD of 0.40 and below. This is another race that has 'gapping' stats although it is questionable how strong these are and it is better to keep an eye on them rather than relying heavily on them. 2000 winner Direct Access and 1997 winner Montroe were the only 2 winners with less than 8 points in their profile, every other winner was classed as Dosage strong.

Notable Defeats

'09 Quartz De Thaix - **0-0-3-1-2 (6)** / 0.33 / -0.83 - sp 5/1
'08 Gansey - **1-1-2-2-0 (6)** / 1.00 / 0.17 - sp 7/2
'07 Otto Des Pictons - **0-0-0-2-0 (2)** / 0.00 / -1.00 - sp 5/1
'06 Tokala - 10-1-13-0-0 (24) / **2.69** / **0.88** - sp 9/2
'04 Accipiter - 4-0-12-0-0 (16) / **1.67** / **0.50** - sp 11/2

Imperial Cup - Sandown

13th March - cl1 Lst hcp - 2m - 4yo+

Dosage Strength

★★★★

Year	Horse	DP	tot	DI	CD	Run sty	Field Size	Gng
2009	Dave's Dream	1-1-3-2-5	12	0.41	-0.75	cp	19	gd
2008	Ashkazar	7-1-23-9-2	42	0.87	0.05	fr	22	gd
2007	Gaspara	2-2-5-1-2	12	1.18	0.08	cp	17	hvy
2006	Victram	~~3-0-3-0-0~~	6	~~3.00~~	~~1.00~~	hu	21	sft
2005	Medison	0-0-8-0-0	8	1.00	0.00	hu	19	gs
2004	Scorned	5-2-13-2-0	22	1.59	0.45	cp	23	sft
2003	Korelo	2-0-9-5-0	16	0.68	-0.06	hu	17	hvy
2002	Polar Red	4-0-18-0-0	22	1.44	0.36	hu	16	gs
2001	Ibal	~~2-0-4-0-0~~	6	~~0.50~~	~~0.00~~	cp	23	hvy
2000	Magic Combination	7-1-10-6-0	24	1.18	0.38	hu	18	gd
1999	Regency Rake	3-1-3-8-5	20	0.38	-0.55	hu	9	sft
1998	Blowing Wind	5-2-7-4-4	22	0.91	0.00	hu	15	sft
1997	Calito Brigante	4-3-15-2-0	24	1.53	0.38	hu	18	gd
1996	Amancio	8-6-15-0-7	36	1.48	0.22	fr	11	sft
1995	Collier Bay	4-8-20-0-0	32	2.20	0.50	cp	10	sft

DP

13/15 had 8 points or more in their Dosage Profile
9/15 had 20 points or more in their Dosage Profile

DI

12/13 had a DI of 1.59 and below
10/13 had a DI of 1.48 and below
2/13 had a DI below 0.68
Majority Range : 0.68 to 1.59 - 77% of winners

CD

11/13 had a CD of -0.06 and above
10/13 had a CD of 0.00 and above
0/13 had a CD above 0.50
Majority Range : -0.06 to 0.50 - 85% of winners

Average

DI 1.14 / CD 0.08

Running Style

fr-2 / cp-5 / hu-8 - Horses coming from of the pace have the best record in the Imperial Cup with 8 winners, the fast pace generated by the large fields playing right into their hands. Front runners have struggled in recent years with only Ashkazar winning from the front in the past 13 renewals.

Summary

This 2 mile handicap suits horses with a well balanced Dosage profile. Speed horses are the most disadvantaged with 0/13 having a CD above 0.50 and only 1/13 having a DI above 1.59. Stamina horses have won this race in recent times although they too are at a disadvantage around Sandown Park's 2 mile hurdle course. If the 2 winners that were heavily stamina influenced are ignored a very strong CD majority range is left with 85% of winners falling between -0.06 and 0.50. Last years winner Dave's Dream was a big Dosage buster being the heaviest stamina based winner of the past 15 years. When a horse such as this comes along and breaks a strong Dosage trend with a convincing victory it can be worthwhile putting this horse in your notebook as a horse to follow in the future.

Notable Defeats

'09 Seven Is My Number - 4-1-9-0-0 (14) / **2.11** / **0.64** - sp 7/2
'09 Numide - 3-5-7-1-0 (16) / 2.56 / 0.63 - sp - 5/1
'99 Dr Jazz - 1-0-6-2-1 (10) / **0.67** / **-0.20** - sp 2/1
'97 Doctoor - 6-8-9-1-2 (26) / **2.47** / **0.58** - sp 3/1
'96 Kingsfold Pet - 8-0-2-0-2 (12) / **3.00** / **1.00** - sp 4/1

Supreme Novice Hurdle - Cheltenham

16th March - cl1 g1 - 2m 110yds - 4yo+

Dosage Strength

Year	Horse	DP	tot	DI	CD	Run sty	Field Size	Gng
2009	Go Native	0-0-2-4-10	16	0.07	-1.50	hu	20	gs
2008	Captain Cee Bee	4-1-8-1-0	14	1.80	0.57	cp	22	gs
2007	Ebaziyan	4-1-10-6-3	24	0.71	-0.13	hu	22	sft
2006	Noland	7-6-19-0-0	32	2.37	0.63	cp	20	gs
2005	Arcalis	2-2-16-0-0	20	1.50	0.30	hu	20	gd
2004	Brave Inca	0-1-7-9-9	26	0.21	-1.00	cp	19	gd
2003	Back In Front	3-3-14-4-2	26	1.00	0.04	cp	19	gd
2002	Like-A-Butterfly	3-2-4-0-7	16	0.78	-0.38	cp	28	gs
2000	Sausalito Bay	3-1-11-5-2	22	0.76	-0.09	fr	15	gd
1999	Hors La Loi III	~~2-0-0-4-0~~	6	~~0.50~~	~~0.00~~	cp	20	gs
1998	French Ballerina	7-1-19-8-5	40	0.78	-0.08	cp	30	gd
1997	Shadow Leader	2-1-16-4-1	24	0.85	-0.04	hu	29	gd
1996	In Defence	6-3-3-1-1	14	3.00	0.86	fr	27	gs
1995	Tourist Attraction	2-2-1-7-0	12	0.60	-0.08	cp	20	sft
1994	Arctic Kinsman	1-4-7-10-0	22	0.63	-0.18	cp	18	gs

DP

14/15 had 12 or more points in their Dosage Profile
11/15 had 16 or more points in their dosage profile

DI

12/14 had a DI of 1.80 and below
11/14 had a DI of 1.50 and below
10/14 had a DI of 1.00 and below
2/14 had a DI below 0.60
Majority Range : 0.60 to 1.80 - 71% of winners

CD

11/14 had a CD of 0.30 and below
10/14 had a CD of 0.04 and below
2/14 had a CD below -0.38.
Majority Range : -0.38 to 0.30 - 64% of winners

Average

DI 1.08 / CD -0.08

Running Style

fr-2 / cp-9 / hu-4 - Sitting close to the pace has reaped most rewards in the festival opener with 9 victories. In Defence won the race from the front with the fastest dosage rating of the past fifteen winners.

Summary

A two mile novice championship race where a large field and a fast pace are normally assured, a speedy dosage winner is not, however, assured. Not the easiest race to assess using dosage as winners cover a large range, however it is possibly best to concentrate on winners that have a slightly less speedy Dosage orientation. 10/14 winners had a DI of 1.00 and below and 10/14 had a CD of 0.04 and below. This is not to say that the Supreme Novices' is ideal for stamina based runners as only last years winner Go Native and the irrepressible Brave Inca have had CD ratings below -0.38.

Notable Defeats

'08 Muirhead - 3-3-5-0-1 (12) / **2.43** / **0.58** - sp 8/1
'05 Marcel - **2-0-0-0-0 (2)** / inf / 2.00 - sp 13/2
'05 My Way De Solzen - 1-2-9-3-5 (20) / **0.60** / **-0.45** - sp 8/1
'04 Albuhera - 5-3-10-0-0 (18) / **2.60** / **0.72** - sp 5/1
'00 Youlneverwalkalone - 3-2-4-2-7 (18) / 0.64 / **-0.44** - sp 5/4

Dosage Fact

Both Brave Inca and Go Native (by far and away the most stamina heavy winners) won their race's by the short distance of a neck.

Arkle Challenge Trophy - Cheltenham

16th March - cl1 g1 - 2m - 5yo+

Dosage Strength

Year	Horse	DP	tot	DI	CD	Run sty	Field Size	Gng
2009	Forpadydeplasterer	5-1-8-4-0	18	1.25	0.39	cp	17	gs
2008	Tidal Bay	3-2-4-2-1	12	1.40	0.33	cp	14	gs
2007	My Way De Solzen	1-2-9-3-5	20	0.60	-0.45	cp	13	sft
2006	Voy Por Ustedes	1-0-6-1-4	12	0.50	-0.58	cp	10	gs
2005	Contraband	2-4-18-2-0	26	1.36	0.23	hu	19	gd
2004	Well Chief	6-1-9-2-0	18	1.77	0.61	hu	16	gd
2003	Azertyuiop	2-0-2-8-2	14	0.27	-0.57	cp	9	gd
2002	Moscow Flyer	3-1-6-4-0	14	1.00	0.21	hu	12	gs
2000	Tiutchev	2-0-16-0-2	20	1.00	0.00	hu	12	gd
1999	Flagship Uberalles	6-1-7-4-0	18	1.40	0.50	cp	14	gs
1998	Champleve	1-0-4-8-1	14	0.27	-0.57	cp	16	gd
1997	Or Royal	~~0-0-1-0-1~~	2	~~0.33~~	~~-1.00~~	cp	9	gd
1996	Ventana Canyon	1-1-13-5-4	24	0.55	-0.42	cp	16	gs
1995	Klairon Davis	4-4-0-0-0	8	inf	1.50	hu	11	sft
1994	Nakir	3-0-3-2-0	8	1.29	0.50	cp	10	gs

DP

14/15 had 8 points or more in their dosage profile
11/15 had 12 points or more in their dosage profile

DI

13/14 had a DI of 1.77 and below
12/14 had a DI of 1.40 and below
0/14 had a DI below 0.27
Majority Range : 0.50 to 1.40 - 71% of winners

CD

12/14 had a CD of 0.50 and below
10/14 had a CD of 0.39 and below
0/14 had a CD below -0.58
Majority Range : -0.58 to 0.50 - 86% of winners

Average

DI 0.97 / CD 0.12

Running Style

fr-0 / cp-10 / hu-5 - With 0/15 renewals going to front runners it's safe to say you don't want to be making the pace in the Arkle. Close to pace runners have had the most success with 10 winners.

Summary

Slightly surprising that with this being a two mile novice championship race there is only one runner with a DI above 1.77, 1995 winner Klairon Davis. In fact if we remove Klairon Davis and Well Chief from calculations then every winner of the past fifteen years had a DI of 1.40 and below and a CD of 0.50 and below, suggesting speed alone is not enough to win an Arkle. Stamina alone will also not win an Arkle as all winners had at least 1 point in the brilliant section of their Dosage Profile showing that at least the smallest influence of pure speed is required to succeed in the Arkle. DP totals point towards the Dosage strong with only '97 winner Or Royal classed as Dosage weak.

Notable Defeats

'09 Tatenen - 3-1-7-1-0 (12) / **1.67** / 0.50 - sp 4/1
'08 Noland - 7-6-19-0-0 (32) / **2.37** / **0.63** - sp 7/4
'05 War Of Attrition - 0-1-3-8-4 (16) / **0.19** / **-0.94** - sp 11/4
'00 Decoupage - 2-1-6-9-14 / **0.23** / **-1.00** - sp 7/4

Dosage Fact

Or Royal apart, the last horse to have less than 8 Dosage Points was the 1975 winner Broncho II.

Champion Hurdle - Cheltenham

16th March - cl1 g1 - 2m 110yds - 4yo+

Dosage Strength

★★★★

Year	Horse	DP	tot	DI	CD	Run sty	Field Size	Gng
2009	Punjabi	2-5-16-1-2	26	1.36	0.15	cp	23	gs
2008	Katchit	1-2-5-3-1	12	0.85	-0.08	cp	15	gs
2007	Sublimity	9-1-12-4-0	26	1.60	0.58	hu	10	sft
2006	Brave Inca	0-1-7-9-9	26	0.21	-1.00	cp	18	gs
2005	Hardy Eustace	4-2-6-0-2	14	1.80	0.43	fr	14	gd
2004	Hardy Eustace	4-2-6-0-2	14	1.80	0.43	fr	9	gd
2003	Rooster Booster	6-6-6-4-2	24	1.67	0.42	hu	17	gd
2002	Hors La Loi III	~~2-0-0-4-0~~	6	~~0.50~~	~~0.00~~	hu	15	gs
2000	Istabraq	11-9-26-10-0	56	1.43	0.38	cp	12	gd
1999	Istabraq	11-9-26-10-0	56	1.43	0.38	cp	14	gs
1998	Istabraq	11-9-26-10-0	56	1.43	0.38	cp	18	gd
1997	Make A Stand	6-0-4-0-2	12	2.00	0.67	fr	21	gd
1996	Collier Bay	4-8-20-0-0	32	2.00	0.50	cp	16	gs
1995	Alderbrook	2-0-5-0-11	18	0.33	-1.00	hu	14	sft
1994	Flakey Dove	~~2-0-2-0-0~~	4	~~3.00~~	~~1.00~~	hu	15	gs

DP

13/15 had 12 points or more in their Dosage Profile
9/15 had 18 points or more in their Dosage Profile

DI

11/13 had a DI of 0.85 and above
10/13 had a DI of 1.36 and above
0/13 had a DI above 2.00
Majority Range : 1.36 to 2.00 - 77% of winners

CD

11/13 had a CD of -0.08 and above
9/13 had a CD of 0.38 and above
0/13 had a CD above 0.67
Majority Range : 0.38 to 0.67 - 69% of winners

Average

DI 1.38 / CD 0.17

Running Style

fr-3 / cp-7 / hu-5 - Close to pace runners hold a slight advantage with 7 victories. Both front runners, Hardy Eustace (twice) & Make A Stand, had the two highest DI ratings at 1.80 & 2.00.

Summary

Apart from Alderbrook (who's victory came in the soft) and the dosage defying Brave Inca, all winners had a CD of -0.08 and above and a DI of 0.85 and above. These stats can be narrowed slightly with 10/13 winners having a DI of 1.36 and above and 9/13 winners having a CD of 0.38 and above. Looking a bit closer however we can also see that no winner had a DI above 2.00 or a CD above 0.67 suggesting true speedsters struggle to get home in the Champion Hurdle. A CD figure on the plus side mixed with a DI above 1.35 would be the best starting point when looking for future champion hurdlers.

Notable Defeats

'07 Detroit City - 11-3-14-0-0 (28) / **3.00** / **0.89** - sp 6/4
'04 Rigmarole - 10-5-23-0-0 (38) / **2.30** / **0.66** - sp 4/1
'02 Landing Light - 3-3-19-13-10 (48) / **0.48** / **-0.50** - sp 100/30
'95 Large Action - 2-0-14-0-4 (20) / **0.82** / **-0.20** - sp 4/1

Dosage Fact

Since 1980 only 2 horses have had a DI above 2.00 - Gaye Brief in 1983 (DI 2.08) and Kribensis in 1990 (DI 4.00).

Trophy Handicap Chase - Cheltenham

13th March - cl1 g3 hcp - 3m 110yds - 5yo+

Dosage Strength

★★★

Year	Horse	DP	tot	DI	CD	Run sty	Field Size	Gng
2009	Wichita Lineman	4-0-11-5-2	22	0.76	-0.05	cp	21	gs
2008	An Accordion	5-4-7-5-1	22	1.32	0.32	cp	14	gs
2007	Joes Edge	4-2-5-5-4	20	0.74	-0.15	hu	23	gs
2006	Dun Doire	3-5-5-0-1	14	3.00	0.64	hu	21	gs
2005	Kelami	0-0-8-0-0	8	1.00	0.00	cp	20	gd
2004	Fork Lightning	~~0-1-1-0-0~~	2	~~3.00~~	~~0.50~~	hu	11	gd
2003	Youlneverwalkalone	3-2-4-2-7	18	0.64	-0.44	hu	18	gd
2002	Frenchman's Creek	~~0-0-0-0-2~~	2	~~0.00~~	~~-2.00~~	hu	23	gs
2000	Marlborough	3-3-4-0-0	10	4.00	0.90	hu	12	gd
1999	Betty's Boy	~~2-0-0-0-0~~	2	~~inf~~	~~2.00~~	hu	18	gs
1998	Unguided Missile	9-0-7-0-2	18	2.27	0.78	fr	13	gd
1997	Flyers Nap	3-6-9-2-6	26	1.08	-0.08	hu	21	gd
1996	Maamur	9-7-14-0-0	30	3.29	0.83	cp	10	gs
1995	Rough Quest	0-0-6-8-6	20	0.18	-1.00	hu	16	sft
1994	Antonin	~~0-0-2-0-2~~	4	~~0.33~~	~~-1.00~~	hu	11	gs

DP

11/15 had 8 points or more in their Dosage Profile
9/15 had 14 points or more in their Dosage Profile

DI

10/11 had DI of 0.64 and above
9/11 had a DI of 0.74 and above
0/11 had a DI between 1.33 and 2.26
Majority Range : 1.00 to 4.00 - 64% of winners

CD

9/11 had a CD of -0.15 and above
7/11 had a DI of -0.05 and above
0/11 had a DI between 0.01 and 0.31
Majority Range : -0.15 to 0.90 - 82% of winners

Average

DI 1.66 / CD 0.16

Running Style

fr-1 / cp-4 / hu-10 - Held up out the back is the place to be in this handicap chase with 10/15 taking up this position. Only one front runner has made the winners enclosure - Unguided Missile in 1998.

Summary

A muddling race to access using dosage but we can narrow the winning profile down slightly. With only two winners having a DI below -0.15 we can see that even though this race is run over 3m+, mass reserves of stamina are not essential. CD figures show that only one winner had a DI below 0.64, the other ten winners range from 0.64 all the way up to 4.00. Rough Quest stands out as the slowest winner based on dosage and his race was the only renewal that was run on going softer than good to soft. DP totals muddy the water even more with 4 winners being classed as Dosage weak, though the last 5 winners did have 8 points or more in their profile.

Notable Defeats

'05 Iris Bleu - 0-0-4-6-2 (12) / **0.20** / **-0.83** - sp 11/2
'00 Spendid - 5-5-0-2-0 (12) / **5.00** / **1.08** - sp 5/1
'99 Kadou Nonantais - 1-0-4-3-6 (14) / **0.27** / **-0.93** - sp 4/1

Ballymore Properties Novice Hurdle - Cheltenham

17th March - cl1 g1 - 2m 5f - 4yo+

Dosage Strength

★★★★

Year	Horse	DP	tot	DI	CD	Run sty	Field Size	Gng
2009	Mikael D'Haguenet	~~0-0-5-1-0~~	6	~~0.71~~	~~-0.17~~	hu	14	gs
2008	Fiveforthree	~~0-0-3-2-1~~	6	~~0.33~~	~~-0.83~~	hu	15	gs
2007	Massini's Maguire	5-1-8-6-0	20	1.00	0.25	fr	15	gs
2006	Nicanor	4-3-10-9-0	26	0.86	0.08	hu	17	gd
2005	No Refuge	5-0-13-2-8	28	0.70	-0.29	hu	20	gd
2004	Fundamentalist	4-2-2-4-4-	16	0.78	-0.13	cp	15	gd
2003	Hardy Eustace	4-2-6-0-2	14	1.80	0.43	cp	19	gd
2002	Galileo	4-3-4-2-1	14	1.80	0.50	hu	27	gs
2000	Monsignor	2-9-11-0-0	22	3.00	0.59	hu	14	gd
1999	Barton	4-3-8-5-0	20	1.22	0.30	hu	18	gs
1998	French Holly	4-16-13-11-6	50	1.13	0.02	cp	18	gd
1997	Istabraq	11-9-26-10-0	56	1.43	0.38	hu	17	gf
1996	Urubande	2-2-12-0-0	16	1.67	0.38	fr	24	gs
1995	Putty Road	1-4-13-0-2	20	1.35	0.10	cp	21	sft
1994	Danoli	2-2-12-0-4	20	1.00	-0.10	hu	23	gs

DP

13/15 had 14 points or more in their Dosage Profile
9/15 had 20 points or more in their Dosage Profile

DI

13/13 had a DI of 0.70 and above
12/13 had a DI of 1.80 and below
10/13 had a DI of 1.00 and above
Majority Range : 0.70 to 1.80 - 92% of winners

CD

13/13 had a CD of -0.29 and above
10/13 had a CD of 0.02 and above
0/13 had a CD above 0.59 or below -0.29
Majority Range : -0.13 to 0.59 - 92% of winners

Average

DI 1.36 / CD 0.19

Running Style

fr-2 / cp-4 / hu-9 - Horses coming from the back account for most winners in the Ballymore Properties Hurdle with 9 victories. Front runners have only taken 1 of the last 12 renewals.

Summary

It is best to concentrate on horses with a CD on the plus side as only 3 winners in the past 15 years have won this race with a minus CD figure and none of these winners had a CD below -0.29. Even modern day greats such as Denman and Inglis Drever could not overcome this stat. Monsignor is the only winner with a DI above 1.80 so horses with an even higher DI rating are likely to struggle to win this novice event. The majority ranges highlighted a very strong, incorporating 92% of previous winners and make an excellent starting point for future handicapping of this Grade 1 novice race. Until the last two renewals all winners had 14 or more points in their Dosage Profile making this a race for a dosage strong individual. With the last two only having 6 points each is this about to change?

Notable Defeats

'09 Diamond Harry - 7-3-7-0-1 (18) / **3.00** / **0.83** - sp 4/1
'06 Denman - 0-1-1-6-2 (10) / **0.18** / **-0.90** - sp 11/10
'04 Inglis Drever - 3-0-22-15-2 (42) / **0.50** / **-0.31** - sp 7/4
'03 Pizarro - 1-1-1-5-2 (10) / **0.33** / **-0.60** - sp 2/1

Dosage Fact

Both horses with less than 8 DP's were trained by Willie Mullins.

Royal & Sun Alliance Novice Chase - Cheltenham

17th March - cl1 g1 - 3m 1110yds - 5yo+

Dosage Strength

★★★★

Year	Horse	DP	tot	DI	CD	Run sty	Field Size	Gng
2009	Cooldine	0-0-5-3-0	8	0.45	-0.38	cp	15	gs
2008	Albertas Run	5-1-6-6-0	18	1.00	0.28	hu	11	gs
2007	Denman	0-1-1-6-2	10	0.18	-0.90	cp	17	gs
2006	Star De Mohaison	4-1-5-4-2	16	0.88	0.06	cp	15	gd
2005	Trabolgan	3-0-1-4-0	8	0.78	0.25	cp	9	gd
2004	Rule Supreme	4-1-3-4-4	16	0.68	-0.19	hu	10	gd
2003	One Knight	~~0-0-0-0-0~~	0	~~inf~~	~~inf~~	fr	9	gd
2002	Hussard Collonges	0-0-6-4-0	10	0.43	-0.40	cp	19	gs
2000	Lord Noelie	3-3-6-2-0	14	1.80	0.50	cp	9	gd
1999	Looks Like Trouble	1-4-5-2-0	12	1.67	0.33	cp	14	gs
1998	Florida Pearl	0-0-4-8-6	18	0.13	-1.11	hu	10	gd
1997	Hanakham	2-0-6-0-6	14	0.56	-0.57	hu	14	gf
1996	Nahthen Lad	2-1-6-9-4	22	0.38	-0.55	hu	12	gs
1995	Brief Gale	5-3-4-0-0	12	5.00	1.08	hu	13	sft
1994	Monsieur Le Cure	4-0-14-0-4	22	1.00	0.00	hu	18	gs

DP

14/15 had 8 points or more in their Dosage Profile
10/15 had 12 points or more in their Dosage Profile

DI

13/14 had a DI of 1.80 and below
11/14 had a DI of 1.00 and below
9/14 had a DI of 0.88 and below
Majority Range : 0.13 to 1.00 - 79% of winners

CD

12/14 had a CD of 0.33 and below
9/14 had a CD of 0.06 and below
1/14 had a CD above 0.50
Majority Range : -0.57 to 0.33 - 71% of winners

Average

DI 1.07 / CD -0.11

Running Style

fr-1 / cp-7 / hu-7 - Close to place runners and hold up horses share the honours here. One Knight was the only runner that managed to hold on from the front.

Summary

With only the front running One Knight succeeding with less than 8 Dosage points in his profile this is another race to concentrate on Dosage strong animals. Speed based horses have struggled in recent renewals of the RSA Chase with 11 from 14 winners having a DI of 1.00 and below and 9 from 14 winners having a CD of 0.06 and below, proving that it is stamina that is needed to take this top novice event. The demanding Cheltenham circuit with its testing uphill finish definitely has a part to play in the poor showing of speed horses. 8 of the last 9 winners (excluding the dosage weak One Knight) had a DI of 1.00 and below suggesting that speed is becoming even less important in this 3 mile novice event.

Notable Defeats

'08 Pomme Tiepy - **0-0-0-2-0 (2)** / 0.00 / -1.00 - sp 9/2
'06 The Listener - **0-1-1-0-0 (2)** / 3.00 / 0.50 - sp 6/1
'03 Jair Du Cochet - **0-0-1-1-0 (2)** / 0.33 / -0.50 - sp 4/1
'00 Native Upmanship - 5-0-9-0-0 (14) / **2.11** / **0.71** - sp 7/2

Dosage Fact

All 6 finishers in the 2009 renewal had a DI of 1.00 or below.

Queen Mother Champion Chase - Cheltenham

17th March - cl1 g1 - 2m - 5yo+

Dosage Strength

★★★

Year	Horse	DP	tot	DI	CD	Run sty	Field Size	Gng
2009	Master Minded	4-1-7-2-0	14	1.55	0.50	cp	12	gs
2008	Master Minded	4-1-7-2-0	14	1.55	0.50	cp	8	gs
2007	Voy Por Ustedes	1-0-6-1-4	12	0.50	-0.58	cp	10	gs
2006	Newmill	~~0-0-4-2-0~~	6	~~0.50~~	~~-0.33~~	fr	12	gd
2005	Moscow Flyer	3-1-6-4-0	14	1.00	0.21	cp	8	gd
2004	Azertyuiop	2-0-2-8-2	14	0.27	-0.57	hu	8	gd
2003	Moscow Flyer	3-1-6-4-0	14	1.00	0.21	cp	11	gd
2002	Flagship Uberalles	6-1-7-4-0	18	1.40	0.50	hu	12	gs
2000	Edredon Bleu	~~0-0-0-2-0~~	2	~~0.00~~	~~-1.00~~	fr	9	gd
1999	Call Equiname	14-4-2-0-0	20	19.00	1.60	cp	13	gs
1998	One man	~~1-0-4-1-0~~	6	~~1.00~~	~~0.17~~	fr	8	gd
1997	Martha's Son	3-6-5-0-0	14	4.60	0.86	hu	6	gf
1996	Klairon Davis	4-4-0-0-0	8	inf	1.50	hu	7	gs
1995	Viking Flagship	6-1-7-2-2	18	1.40	0.39	cp	10	sft
1994	Viking Flagship	6-1-7-2-2	18	1.40	0.39	cp	8	gs

DP

12/15 had 8 points or more in their Dosage Profile
11/15 had between 12 and 20 points in their Dosage Profile

DI

10/12 had a DI of 1.00 and above
7/12 had a DI between 1.00 and 1.55
0/12 had a DI between 1.56 and 4.59
Majority Range : 0.50 to 1.55 - 67% of winners

CD

10/12 had a CD of 0.21 and above
8/12 has a CD between 0.21 and 0.86
0/12 had a CD between 0.51 and 0.85
Majority Range : 0.21 to 0.86 - 67% of winners

Average

DI 1.47 / CD 0.46

Running Style

fr-3 / cp-8 / hu-4 - Close to pace runners hold the advantage in the Queen Mother Champion Chase with 8 victories. Hold up runners have only won 1 of the last 7 renewals.

Summary

A slightly odd race as far as dosage is concerned with nothing between 1.56 to 4.59 on the DI side and nothing between 0.51 and 0.85 on the CD side. Why this trend occurs is a mystery but the facts are there for all to see. Although Azertyuiop and Voy Por Ustedes had negative CD ratings and DI ratings under 0.50 every other winner had a CD above 0.20 and DI above 1.00. Looking closer, all winners apart from the previously mentioned had points in both the Brilliant section and Intermediate section of their dosage profile highlighting that inherited speed is the key in the Champion Chase. Three winners have won this race with less than 8 points in their profile although none of the Dosage strong winners could be classed as Dosage heavy as no winner had more than 20 points in their profile.

Notable Defeats

'08 Tamarinbleu - 1-3-10-6-0 (20) / **0.82** / **-0.05** - sp 7/2
'08 Twist Magic - 1-0-11-8-2 (22) / **0.42** / **-0.45** - sp 5/1
'06 Kauto Star - 2-2-6-10-2 (22) / **0.47** / **-0.36** - sp 2/1
'98 Ask Tom - 3-3-4-2-0 (12) / **2.00** / **0.58** - sp 5/2
'97 Strong Promise - 4-5-3-2-0 (16) / **2.56** / **0.69** - sp 5/2

Dosage Fact

Interestingly, the 3 winners that won the race from the front in the past 15 years all had less than 8 points in their dosage profile.

Coral Cup - Cheltenham

17th March - cl1 g3 hcp hurdle - 2m5f - 4yo+

Dosage Strength

Year	Horse	DP	tot	DI	CD	Run sty	Field Size	Gng
2009	Ninetieth Minute	2-0-6-6-2	16	0.45	-0.38	hu	27	gs
2008	Naiad Du Misselot	~~0-0-0-0-0~~	0	~~inf~~	~~inf~~	hu	24	gs
2007	Burntoak Boy	7-3-9-0-1	20	2.64	0.75	hu	28	gs
2006	Sky's The Limit	1-1-6-2-0	10	1.00	0.10	hu	30	gd
2005	Idole First	4-2-7-4-1	18	1.12	0.22	cp	29	gd
2004	Monkerhostin	3-3-6-3-1	16	1.29	0.25	hu	27	gd
2003	Xenophon	1-1-6-2-0	10	1.00	0.10	cp	27	gd
2002	Ilnamar	~~0-0-0-4-0~~	4	~~0.00~~	~~-1.00~~	cp	27	gs
2000	What's Up Boys	6-1-3-4-4	18	0.89	0.06	cp	26	gd
1999	Khayrawani	8-4-14-14-0	40	0.90	0.15	hu	30	gs
1998	Top Cees	6-3-20-5-8	42	0.83	-0.14	hu	21	gd
1997	Big Stand	4-0-0-4-0	8	1.00	0.50	hu	28	gf
1996	Trainglot	7-3-8-0-0	18	3.50	0.94	hu	20	gs
1995	Chance Coffey	0-0-2-10-2	14	0.08	-1.00	hu	30	sft
1994	Time For A Run	7-0-11-0-2	20	1.67	0.50	hu	30	gs

DP

13/15 had 8 points or more in their Dosage Profile
12/15 had 10 points or more in their Dosage Profile

DI

11/13 had a DI of 1.67 and below
10/13 had a DI of 1.29 and below
1/13 had a DI below 0.45
Majority Range : 0.45 to 1.29 - 69% of winners

CD

11/13 had a CD of 0.50 and below
9/13 had a CD 0.25 and below
1/13 had a CD below -0.38
Majority Range : -0.38 to 0.50 - 77& of winners

Average

DI 1.26 / CD 0.16

Running Style

fr-0 / cp-4 / hu-11 - A clear advantage to being held up out the back in the Coral Cup with 11/15 hold up runners scoring. Another poor race for front runners with 0/15 taking the honours.

Summary

Horses that have a well balanced Dosage rating are the ideal sorts for this middle distance handicap hurdle. Stamina horses struggle to make an impact with only 3 winners having a negative CD rating and only 1/13 having a CD below -0.38. This competitive handicap is also not ideal for horses with speed based ratings as 11/13 winners had a DI of 1.67 and below and a CD of 0.50 and below. '08 winner Naiad Du Misselot & '02 winner Ilnamar are the only 2 Dosage weak winners, every other winner holding 8 points or more in their profile. The Dosage Profiles themselves highlight that only the stamina heavy Chance Coffey failed to have any points in the Brilliant section of his profile.

Notable Defeats

'07 Copesale lad - 2-0-1-4-5 (12) / **0.26** / **-0.83** - sp 6/1
'05 Distant Prospect - 12-5-11-0-0 (26) / **3.73** / **1.04** - sp 100/30
'00 Ross Moff - 0-1-8-13-4 (26) / **0.24** / **-0.77** - sp 15/2

National Hunt Chase - Cheltenham

17th March - cl2 hcp Chase - 4m - 5yo+

Dosage Strength

★★★★

Year	Horse	DP	tot	DI	CD	Run sty	Field Size	Gng
2009	Tricky Trickster	3-1-6-8-4	22	0.47	-0.41	hu	19	gs
2008	Old Benny	4-0-8-6-0	18	0.80	0.11	hu	20	gs
2007	Butlers Cabin	6-2-10-6-0	24	1.18	0.33	hu	19	gs
2006	Hot Weld	4-1-3-0-0	8	4.33	1.13	fr	22	gd
2005	Another Rum	3-4-5-4-0	16	1.46	0.38	cp	20	gd
2004	Native Emperor	3-0-7-4-2	16	0.68	-0.13	hu	22	gd
2003	Sudden Shock	4-4-10-10-0	28	0.87	0.07	hu	24	gd
2002	Rith Dubh	8-0-10-0-2	20	1.86	0.60	hu	26	gs
2000	Relaxation	5-0-5-0-2	12	1.67	0.50	cp	21	gd
1999	Dee Jay Dee	2-3-3-2-0	10	1.86	0.50	hu	21	gs
1998	Wandering Light	4-2-2-4-2	14	1.00	0.14	hu	24	gd
1997	Flimsy Truth	6-0-2-10-0	18	0.64	0.11	fr	28	gf
1996	Loving Around	4-0-4-0-0	8	3.00	1.00	cp	22	gs
1995	Front Line	7-3-6-0-4	20	1.86	0.45	hu	25	sft
1994	Christmas Gorse	3-0-11-6-0	20	0.74	0.00	hu	19	gs

DP

15/15 had 8 points or more in their Dosage Profile
12/15 had 12 points or more in their Dosage profile

DI

14/15 had a DI of 0.64 and above
11/15 had a DI of 0.80 and above
2/15 had a DI above 1.86
Majority Range : 0.64 to 1.86 - 80% of winners

CD

14/15 had a CD of -0.13 and above
13/15 had a CD of 0.00 and above
2/15 had a CD above 0.60
Majority Range : 0.00 to 0.60 - 73% of winners

Average

DI 1.49 / CD 0.32

Running Style

fr-2 / cp-3 / hu-10 - This marathon chase is best suited to hold up runners with the 4 miles giving them ample time to get into a challenging position. 10/15 hold up runners have won here with front runners and close to pace winners few and far between.

Summary

This amateur riders race has grown in stature in recent years and has been attracting some above average entrants. The DP totals back up this sentiment with all 15 winners being classed as Dosage strong. This marathon chase is the longest distance of any race at the festival, however, stamina based runners are noticeable in their absence. 14/15 winners had a DI of 0.64 and above and 14/15 winners had a CD of -0.13 and above. This can be narrowed again with 11/15 winners having a DI of 0.80 and above and 13/15 winners having a CD of 0.00 and above. Dosage Profiles highlight the call for speed over stamina with every winner having at least 2 points in the Brilliant section of their profile and only 6 winners having any points in the Professional section. Last years winner Tricky Trickster had the most stamina biased Dosage of any winner but he was also one of the most impressive winners and could be one to watch out for in some of the larger staying handicaps.

Notable Defeats

'09 Coe - 0-1-3-4-2 (10) / **0.33** / **-0.70** - sp 15/2
'07 Nine De Sivola - 0-0-6-2-0 (8) / **0.60** / **-0.26** - sp 11/2
'06 Far From Trouble - 0-1-6-11-4 (22) / **0.22** / **-0.82** - sp 7/2
'06 Basilea Star - **2-0-4-0-0 (6)** / 2.00 / 0.67 - sp 5/1
'05 Keepatem - 5-0-7-0-0 (12) / **2.43** / **0.83** - 9/2

Champion Bumper - Cheltenham

17th March - cl1 g1 - 2m 110yds - 4 - 6yo

Dosage Strength

Year	Horse	DP	tot	DI	CD	Run sty	Field Size	Gng
2009	Dunguib	1-3-8-4-2	18	0.80	-0.17	hu	24	gs
2008	Cousin Vinny	1-2-16-1-0	20	1.22	0.15	cp	23	gs
2007	Cork All Star	9-3-22-0-0	34	2.09	0.62	cp	24	gs
2006	Hairy Molly	0-0-5-9-6	20	0.14	-1.05	cp	23	gd
2005	Missed That	1-0-4-6-1	12	0.33	-0.50	cp	24	gd
2004	Total Enjoyment	5-2-4-2-1	14	1.80	0.57	cp	24	gd
2003	Liberman	4-1-14-1-0	20	1.50	0.40	cp	25	gd
2002	Pizarro	1-1-1-5-2	10	0.33	-0.60	hu	23	gs
2000	Joe Cullen	~~2-0-0-2-0~~	4	~~1.00~~	~~0.50~~	hu	17	gd
1999	Monsignor	2-9-11-0-0	22	3.00	0.59	cp	25	gs
1998	Alexander Banquet	0-1-6-7-0	14	0.40	-0.43	cp	25	gd
1997	Florida Pearl	0-0-4-8-6	18	0.13	-1.11	cp	25	gf
1996	Wither or Which	6-0-2-4-2	14	1.00	0.29	cp	24	gs
1995	Dato Star	5-1-7-4-1	18	1.12	0.28	cp	21	sft
1994	Mucklemeg	4-3-5-0-0	12	3.80	0.92	hu	25	gs

DP

14/15 had 10 points or more in their Dosage Profile
11/15 had 14 points or more in their Dosage Profile

DI

12/14 had a DI of 2.09 and below
11/14 had a DI of 1.80 and below
10/14 had a DI of 1.50 and below
Majority Range : 0.33 to 1.80 - 64% of winners

CD

13/14 had a CD of 0.62 and below
10/14 had a CD of 0.40 and below
2/14 had a CD below -0.60
Majority Range : -0.60 to 0.62 - 79% of winners

Average

DI 1.26 / CD 0.00

Running Style

fr-0 / cp-11 / hu-4 - Front runners are at a massive disadvantage here with 0/15 managing to lead from pillar to post. Close to the pace is the place to be with a massive 11/15 taking the spoils.

Summary

Not a race that's easy to narrow down using dosage. The strongest trend available comes from the DP totals with 14/15 winners classed as Dosage strong, only 2000 winner Joe Cullen had less than 10 points in his profile. Horses with an extremely fast Dosage rating look to be at a minor disadvantage with only 1994 winner Mucklemeg and 1999 winner Monsignor having a DI above 2.09. It is difficult to confidently rule out any particular Dosage group of horses in this Grade 1 bumper race so when handicapping in the future it may be best not to rely on Dosage to heavily.

Notable Defeats

'06 Equus Maximus 4-3-6-0-1 (14) / **2.50** / **0.64** - sp 5/2
'00 Inca - 5-0-7-0-0 (12) / **2.43** / **0.83** - sp 2/1
'98 Joe Mac - **0-0-1-5-0 (6)** / 0.09 / -0.83 - sp 6/4

Pertemps Final Hurdle - Cheltenham

18th March - cl1 Lst hcp Hurdle - 3m - 5yo+

Dosage Strength

Year	Horse	DP	tot	DI	CD	Run sty	Field Size	Gng
2009	Kayf Aramis	2-0-10-4-0	16	0.78	0.00	cp	22	gs
2008	Ballyfitz	3-0-3-10-2	18	0.33	-0.44	cp	24	gs
2007	Oscar park	4-0-8-8-2	22	0.57	-0.18	hu	24	gs
2006	Kadoun	5-3-5-5-4	22	0.91	0.00	cp	24	gd
2005	Oulart	3-1-3-1-6	14	0.65	-0.43	cp	22	gd
2004	Creon	4-0-8-4-0	16	1.00	0.25	hu	24	gd
2003	Inching closer	7-1-4-1-1	14	2.50	0.86	hu	24	gd
2002	Freetown	8-3-12-5-8	36	0.89	-0.06	cp	24	gs
2000	Rubhahunish	3-1-8-2-4	18	0.80	-0.17	cp	24	gd
1999	Generosa	5-6-8-4-1	24	1.67	0.42	hu	24	gs
1998	Unsinkable Boxer	4-0-0-8-10	22	0.22	-0.91	hu	24	gd
1997	Pharanear	6-0-0-0-2	8	3.00	1.00	hu	24	gd
1996	Great Easeby	8-1-12-9-6	36	0.71	-0.11	hu	24	gs
1995	Miracale Man	2-0-0-4-4	10	0.25	-0.80	hu	23	sft
1994	Tindari	5-4-13-0-0	22	2.38	0.64	hu	32	gs

DP

15/15 had 8 points or more in their Dosage Profile
13/15 had 14 points or more in their Dosage Profile

DI

12/15 had a DI of 1.67 and below
11/15 had a DI of 1.00 and below
Majority Range : 0.22 to 1.00 - 73% of winners

CD

11/15 had a CD of 0.25 and below
10/15 had a CD of 0.00 and below
2/15 had a CD below -0.44
Majority Range : -0.44 to 0.25 - 60% of winners

Average

DI 1.11 / CD 0.00

Running Style

fr-0 / cp-6 / hu-9 - The figures show this is a graveyard for front runners. Out the back is the place to be although close to pace runners more than hold their own.

Summary

The Dosage ratings for the Pertemps cover a wide range, however, there are still stats available to narrow the field slightly. The strongest Dosage stat involves the DP totals with all 15 winners holding 8 points or more in their profile and 13/15 holding 14 points or more in their profile. A DI rating of 1.67 and below is preferable as only 3/15 had a rating above this. To narrow the range further we can see that 11/15 had a DI of 1.00 or below and given that this is a 3 mile handicap round Cheltenham's demanding track this comes as no surprise. With CD figures ranging from 1.00 down to -0.91 it is difficult to give negatives to any range however the figures suggest it is best to concentrate on runners with a CD of 0.25 and below as with 11/15 previous winners. Although the race average may not suggest it, this race is suited to runners with a Dosage leaning towards stamina.

Notable Defeats

'08 Miko De Beauchene - **0-0-0-0-0 (0) /** inf / inf - sp 7/1
'06 Olaso - 3-3-3-0-1 (10) / **3.00** / **0.70** - sp 6/1
'05 Ravenswood - 6-1-11-2-0 (20) / 1.67 / **0.55** - sp 7/2
'04 Keepatem - 5-0-7-0-0 (12) / **2.43** / **0.83** - sp 4/1

Ryanair Chase - Cheltenham

18th March - cl1 g1 - 2m5f - 5yo+

Dosage Strength

Year	Horse	DP	tot	DI	CD	Run sty	Field Size	Gng
2009	Imperial Commander	3-2-4-2-1	12	1.40	0.33	cp	10	gs
2008	Our Vic	2-0-9-5-0	16	0.68	-0.06	fr	9	gs
2007	Taranis	~~0-0-6-0-0~~	6	~~1.00~~	~~0.00~~	cp	9	gs
2006	Fondmort	2-0-2-4-0	8	0.60	0.00	cp	11	gd
2005	Thisthatandtother	1-2-13-0-0	16	1.46	0.25	cp	12	gd

DP

4/5 had 8 points or more in their Dosage Profile
4/5 had between 8 and 16 points in their Dosage Profile

DI

4/4 had a DI of between 0.60 and 1.46
Majority Range : 0.60 to 1.46 - 100% of winners

CD

4/4 had a CD of -0.06 and above
3/4 had a CD of 0.00 and above
Majority Range : -0.06 to 0.33 - 100% of winners

Average

DI 1.04 / CD 0.13

Running Style

fr-1 / cp-4 / hu-0 - No Hold up runner has taken the honours yet and only one horse has won from the front so it looks best to run close to pace if you want to win the Ryanair Chase.

Summary

Very early days yet but this Grade 1 race is already starting to show a dosage bias. Stamina based horses have struggled in this race and it looks like the emphasis is very much on speed rather than stamina over this 2m5f trip. Given that horse's of Voy Por Ustedes and Monet's Garden calibre were beaten in this race I expect the trend of negative CD horses and horses with less than 8 dosage points struggling in this race to continue. Our Vic did win this race (2008) with a CD just on the negative side but he was also beaten in this race on the 4 other occasions it has been run. The majority ranges above are the best starting point when looking for future winners of this race.

Notable Defeats

'09 Voy Por Ustedes - 1-0-6-1-4 (12) / **0.50** / **-0.58** - sp 4/5
'07 Monets Garden - **0-0-0-2-0 (2)** / 0.00 / -1.00 - sp 7/4

Dosage Fact

The first 3 home in the 2005 & 2006 runnings all fell within the majority ranges identified above.

World Hurdle - Cheltenham

18th March - cl1 g1 - 3m - 4yo+

Dosage Strength

★★★★

Year	Horse	DP	tot	DI	CD	Run sty	Field Size	Gng
2009	Big Bucks	1-0-4-3-2	10	0.43	-0.50	hu	14	gs
2008	Inglis Drever	3-0-22-15-2	42	0.50	-0.31	hu	17	gs
2007	Inglis Drever	3-0-22-15-2	42	0.50	-0.31	hu	14	gs
2006	My Way De Solzen	1-2-9-3-5	20	0.60	-0.45	cp	20	gd
2005	Inglis Drever	3-0-22-15-2	42	0.50	-0.31	hu	12	gd
2004	Iris's Gift	5-0-2-1-0	8	3.00	1.13	cp	10	gd
2003	Baracouda	2-3-8-1-2	16	1.29	0.13	hu	11	gd
2002	Baracouda	2-3-8-1-2	16	1.29	0.13	hu	16	gd
2000	Bacchanal	4-7-16-1-0	28	2.11	0.50	cp	10	gf
1999	Anzum	0-1-6-0-13	20	0.25	-1.25	hu	12	gs
1998	Princeful	2-0-6-4-2	14	0.56	-0.29	hu	9	gd
1997	Karshi	5-3-6-6-4	24	0.85	-0.04	cp	17	gd
1996	Cyborgo	~~2-0-0-4-0~~	6	~~0.50~~	~~0.00~~	fr	19	gd
1995	Dorans Pride	~~2-0-2-0-2~~	6	~~1.00~~	~~0.00~~	cp	11	sft
1994	Balasani	4-4-0-12-6	26	0.44	-0.46	hu	14	gd

DP

13/15 had 8 points or more in their Dosage Profile
10/15 had 16 points or more in their Dosage Profile

DI

11/13 had a DI of 1.29 and below
9/13 had a DI of 0.85 and below
Majority Range : 0.43 to 1.29 - 77% of winners

CD

11/13 had a CD of 0.13 and below
10/13 had a CD between -0.50 and 0.13
9/13 had a CD of -0.04 and below
Majority Range : -0.50 to 0.13 - 77% of winners

Average

DI 0.95 / CD -0.16

Running Style

fr-1 / cp-5 / hu-9 - Hold up runners take the honours here. They have a good 15 year record and have also won 8 of the last 10 runnings.

Summary

A strong dosage race where stamina is definitely the call. No surprises that the average for this stayers championship race is leaning on the stamina side as 3 miles around Prestbury Park over hurdles is a gruelling test. 11 of the 13 winners had a DI of 1.29 and below and a CD of 0.13 and below. Furthermore, 9 of that 11 had a DI of 0.85 and below and a CD of -0.04 and below. The 2 winners that fell out with these ranges (the high class pair of Bacchanal and Iris's Gift) both were hot on the heels of the front runners throughout the race, this links in with their speedy dosage ratings. Although Cyborgo and Dorans Pride both won with less than 8 points in their Dosage Profile the last 12 winners have all been Dosage strong.

Notable Defeats

'09 Kasbah Bliss - 4-0-6-2-0 (12) / **1.40** / **0.50** - sp 10/11
'09 Punchestowns - 2-1-9-0-0 (12) / **1.67** / **0.42** - sp 100/30
'07 Mighty Man - 7-2-6-0-1 (16) / **3.00** / **0.88** - sp 100/30
'03 Limestone Lad - 3-3-2-2-2 (12) / **1.40** / **0.25** - sp 9/4
'98 Ocean Hawk - 5-2-9-0-0 (16) / **2.56** / **0.75** - sp 5/1

Dosage Fact

The last 7 runners-up all had a CD on the plus side.

Freddie Williams Plate - Cheltenham

18th March - cl1 g3 hcp - 2m5f - 5yo+

Dosage Strength

★★★

Year	Horse	DP	tot	DI	CD	Run sty	Field Size	Gng
2009	Something Wells	2-0-9-5-2	18	0.57	-0.28	cp	23	gs
2008	Mister Mcgoldrick	8-2-6-3-1	20	1.86	0.65	cp	22	gs
2007	Idole First	4-2-7-4-1	18	1.12	0.22	cp	23	gs
2006	Non So	1-9-2-2-0	14	3.67	0.64	cp	24	gd
2005	Liberthine	1-0-5-4-0	10	0.54	-0.20	hu	22	gd
2004	Tikram	15-9-18-1-1	44	3.00	0.82	hu	16	gd
2003	Young Spartcus	0-2-8-4-0	14	0.75	-0.14	hu	19	gd
2002	Blowing Wind	5-2-7-4-4	22	0.91	0.00	hu	21	gs
2000	Dark Stranger	4-3-1-0-4	12	1.67	0.25	cp	18	gd
1999	Majadou	1-0-6-5-0	12	0.50	-0.25	cp	18	gs
1998	Super Coin	1-0-6-5-0	12	0.50	-0.25	hu	14	gd
1997	Terao	2-0-4-4-2	12	0.50	-0.33	cp	21	gf
1996	Old Bridge	2-0-6-8-6	22	0.29	-0.73	cp	13	gs
1995	Kadi	5-5-10-0-0	20	3.00	0.75	hu	12	sft
1994	Elfast	4-0-0-4-2	10	0.67	0.00	hu	18	gs

DP

15/15 had 10 points or more in their Dosage Profile
14/15 had between 10 and 22 points in their Dosage Profile

DI

12/15 had a DI of 1.86 and below
10/15 had a DI of 1.12 and below
1/15 had a DI below 0.29
Majority Range : 0.50 to 1.12 - 60% of winners

CD

12/15 had a CD of 0.25 and below
9/15 had a CD of 0.00 and below
1/15 had a CD below -0.33
Majority Range : -0.33 to 0.25 - 67% of winners

Average

DI 1.30 / CD 0.08

Running Style

fr-0 / cp-8 / hu-7 - Front runners are to be avoided with 0/15 hitting the mark. Close to pace runners just shade it over hold up runners with 8 wins to 7.

Summary

Not a race to rely to strongly on dosage however it does throw up a few angles. The Freddie Williams Plate (formerly know as the Racing Post Plate) has been an excellent race for dosage strong animals with no winner in the past 15 years having less than 10 points in their profile. 12/15 winners had a DI of 1.86 and below and a CD of 0.25 and below. Horses with stamina heavy Dosage ratings have struggled in this race as only Old Bridge in 1996 had a CD below -0.33 and a DI below 0.50. Plenty of winners have, however, had a touch of stamina in their dosage with 8/15 having a CD of 0.00 or below. Three winners held a DI rating of 3.00 and above however none of these speedsters front ran, in fact 2 of them (Tikram & Kadi) came from a held up position.

Notable Defeats

'08 Bible Lord - 1-9-8-0-0 (18) / **3.50** / 0.61 - sp 6/1
'08 Gwanako - **2-0-2-2-0 (6)** / 1.00 / 0.33 - sp 9/1
'07 Opera Mundi - **0-0-3-3-0 (6)** / 0.33 / 0.50 - sp 7/2
'04 Iznogoud - 2-0-1-5-2 (10) / **0.33** / **-0.50** - sp 9/2

Kim Muir Challenge Cup - Cheltenham

18th March - cl2 hcp - 3m 110yds - 5yo+

Dosage Strength

★★★★

Year	Horse	DP	tot	DI	CD	Run sty	Field Size	Gng
2009	Character Building	5-1-6-4-0	16	1.29	0.44	hu	24	gs
2008	High Chimes	1-0-14-0-1	16	1.00	0.00	hu	24	gs
2007	Cloudy Lane	2-1-13-4-0	20	0.90	0.05	cp	24	gs
2006	You're Special	11-4-15-8-4	42	1.15	0.24	cp	21	gd
2005	Juveigneur	2-2-5-3-0	12	1.18	0.25	cp	24	gd
2004	Maximize	8-6-0-2-0	16	7.00	1.25	hu	22	gd
2003	Royal Predica	0-2-10-0-2	14	1.00	-0.14	hu	23	gd
2002	The Bushkeeper	3-0-5-4-0	12	0.85	0.17	hu	23	gs
2000	Honey Mount	15-6-16-5-8	50	1.38	0.30	hu	23	gd
1999	Celtic Giant	1-0-11-6-2	20	0.48	-0.40	cp	22	gs
1998	In Truth	13-2-11-2-0	28	2.73	0.93	fr	14	gd
1997	King Lucifer	~~2-0-0-4-0~~	6	~~0.50~~	~~0.00~~	cp	11	gd
1996	Stop The Waller	~~0-0-3-0-1~~	4	~~0.60~~	~~-0.50~~	cp	22	gs
1995	Flyers Nap	3-6-9-2-6	26	1.08	-0.08	hu	16	sft
1994	Fighting Words	~~2-0-0-4-0~~	6	~~0.50~~	~~0.00~~	hu	15	gs

DP

12/15 had 12 points or more in their Dosage Profile
9/15 had 16 points or more in their Dosage Profile

DI

11/12 had a DI of 0.85 and above
9/12 had a DI of 1.00 and above
2/12 had a DI above 1.38
Majority Range : 0.85 to 1.38 - 75% of winners

CD

12/12 had a CD of -0.40 and above
11/12 had a CD of -0.14 and above
2/12 had a CD above 0.44
Majority Range : -0.14 to 0.44 - 75% of winners

Average

DI 1.67 / CD 0.25

Running Style

fr-1 / cp-6 / hu-8 - Another festival race that is a graveyard for front runners with only 1998 winner In Truth managing to hold on from the front. Hold up horse have the best record with 8 winners.

Summary

A race that has been attracting better quality horses in recent times and one that gives strong dosage angles to work with. Although 3 winners were classed as Dosage weak the past 11 winners were all Dosage strong, highlighting the improved quality of this race. As far as Dosage ratings are concerned the winners of this amateur riders race have been leaning towards the speed side with 12/12 winners having a CD of -0.40 and above and 11/12 having a DI of 0.85 and above. These stats can be narrowed still with 11/12 having a CD of -0.14 and above and 9/12 having a DI of 1.00 and above. Only 2 horses have won with a DI above 1.38 or a CD above 0.44 as horses with vast quantities of speed tend to struggle to get home over this extended 3 miles.

Notable Defeats

'09 Shouldhavehadthat - 1-8-3-0-0 (12) / **7.00** / **0.83** - sp 6/1
'08 My Immortal - 2-3-5-2-0 (12) / **1.67** / 0.42 - sp 7/1
'06 Parsons Legacy - 4-5-10-0-1 (20) / **2.33** / **0.55** - sp 7/1
'05 Oh Be The Hokey - 3-1-8-0-0 (12) / **2.00** / **0.58** - sp 9/2

Triumph Hurdle - Cheltenham

19th March - cl1 g1 - 2m1f - 4yo

Dosage Strength

★★★

Year	Horse	DP	tot	DI	CD	Run sty	Field Size	Gng
2009	Zaynar	5-1-6-3-1	16	1.29	0.38	hu	18	gs
2008	Celestial Halo	3-0-16-4-5	28	0.65	-0.29	fr	14	gs
2007	Katchit	1-2-5-3-1	12	0.85	-0.08	cp	23	gs
2006	Detroit City	11-3-14-0-0	28	3.00	0.89	cp	17	gd
2005	Penzance	1-0-8-5-0	14	0.56	-0.21	cp	23	gd
2004	Made In Japan	7-1-11-5-2	26	1.08	0.23	hu	23	gd
2003	Spectroscope	3-2-14-5-0	24	1.00	0.13	cp	27	gd
2002	Scolardy	2-2-8-0-0	12	2.00	0.50	cp	28	gd
2000	Snow Drop	6-2-4-0-0	12	5.00	1.17	cp	28	gd
1999	Katarino	0-0-7-1-0	8	0.78	-0.13	cp	23	gs
1998	Upgrade	9-1-10-2-0	22	2.14	0.77	fr	25	gd
1997	Commanche Court	4-0-5-2-13	24	0.37	-0.83	hu	28	gd
1996	Paddys Return	3-0-5-8-2	18	0.44	-0.33	hu	29	gd
1995	Kissair	8-1-3-4-0	16	1.91	0.81	cp	26	sft
1994	Mysilv	6-2-2-8-6	24	0.60	-0.25	fr	28	gd

DP

15/15 had 8 points or more in their Dosage Profile
14/15 had 12 points or more in their Dosage Profile

DI

12/15 had a DI of 2.00 and below
10/15 had a DI of 1.29 and below
0/15 had a DI below 0.37
Majority Range : 0.37 to 1.29 - 67% of winners

CD

14/15 had a CD of -0.33 and above
10/15 had a CD of -0.13 and above
1/15 had a CD above 0.89
Majority Range : -0.33 to 0.50 - 67% of winners

Average

DI 1.44 / CD 0.18

Running Style

fr-3 / cp-8 / hu-4 - Front runners fair slightly better here than other Cheltenham Festival races but it is still the close to pace runners that come out on top with 8 winners.

Summary

First thing to look for is a horse with at least 8 points in its dosage profile as no winner in the past 15 years was classed as Dosage weak. DI ratings show that only 2 winners have had a rating above 2.14 - the majority of winners (10/15) had a DI of 1.29 and below. Only 1 winner had a CD below -0.33 with stamina heavy horses struggling to get competitive in the Triumph Hurdle. Above -0.33, however, the CD figures do cover a fairly extensive range but it is possibly best to concentrate on the -0.33 to 0.50 range as only the talented Detroit City fell outside this range in the past 8 years.

Notable Defeats

'08 Franchoek - 6-1-11-0-0 (18) / **2.27** / 0.72 - sp evens
'03 Golden Cross - 8-2-12-0-0 (22) / **2.67** / **0.82** - sp 11/2
'02 Giocomo - 2-16-6-0-0 (24) / **7.00** / **0.83** - sp 7/1

Dosage Fact

The last winner to have less than 8 points in its Dosage Profile was Shiny Copper in 1982.

Cheltenham Gold Cup - Cheltenham

19th March - cl1 g1 - 3m2f - 5yo+

Dosage Strength

★★★★

Year	Horse	DP	tot	DI	CD	Run sty	Field Size	Gng
2009	Kauto Star	2-2-6-10-2	22	0.47	-0.36	cp	16	gs
2008	Denman	0-1-1-6-2	10	0.18	-0.90	cp	12	gs
2007	Kauto Star	2-2-6-10-2	22	0.47	-0.36	hu	18	gs
2006	War of Attrition	0-1-3-8-4	16	0.19	-0.94	cp	22	gd
2005	Kicking King	2-0-8-8-2	20	0.43	-0.40	hu	15	gd
2004	Best Mate	1-1-10-5-1	18	0.64	-0.22	cp	10	gd
2003	Best Mate	1-1-10-5-1	18	0.64	-0.22	hu	15	gd
2002	Best Mate	1-1-10-5-1	18	0.64	-0.22	hu	18	gd
2000	Looks Like Trouble	1-4-5-2-0	12	1.67	0.33	cp	12	gf
1999	See More Business	0-0-3-6-1	10	0.18	-0.80	cp	12	gs
1998	Cool Dawn	2-2-8-0-0	12	2.00	0.50	fr	17	gd
1997	Mr Mulligan	2-3-7-4-2	18	0.89	-0.06	cp	14	gd
1996	Imperial Call	3-3-4-0-2	12	2.00	0.42	hu	10	gd
1995	Master Oats	9-0-3-2-0	14	3.00	1.14	cp	15	sft
1994	The Fellow	0-0-4-4-2	10	0.25	-0.80	cp	15	gd

DP

15/15 had 8 points or more in their Dosage Profile
15/15 had between 10 & 22 points in their Dosage Profile

DI

14/15 had a DI of 2.00 and below
11/15 had a DI of 0.89 and below
0/15 had a DI above 3.00
Majority Range : 0.18 to 0.89 - 73% of winners

CD

14/15 had a CD of 0.50 and below
11/15 had a CD of -0.06 and below
0/15 had a CD below -0.94
Majority Range : -0.94 to -0.06 - 73% of winners

Average

DI 0.91 / CD -0.19

Running Style

fr-1 / cp-9 / hu-5 - With stamina being the percentage call it is no surprise to see only the 1 front running winner. Close to pace runners having taken 9 of the past 15 Cheltenham Gold Cups.

Summary

With every winner holding 8 or more points in their Dosage Profile the blue riband of jumps racing is not for a dosage weak animal. The Gold Cup requires a horse to have a dosage that is leaning on the stamina side. The past 10 runnings have only seen 1 horse with a CD above -0.22 (Looks Like Trouble, who's victory came on good to firm) suggesting the race is becoming even more of a stamina test than in previous years. Horses that run close to the pace and have a dosage on the stamina side are ideally suited to the rigours of this race. If the winner is to win the race from the front they will need the required 'speedy' dosage rating so that they are able to burn their opponents off from the front, similar to Cool Dawn in the 1998 renewal. Alternatively, a stamina heavy horse such as Denman was able to take up the running from half-way and utilise his dosage rating to grind his opponents into submission.

Notable Defeats

'05 Celestial Gold - **1-1-0-2-0 (4)** / 1.00 / 0.25 - sp 9/2
'99 Florida Pearl - 0-0-4-8-6 (18) / **0.13** / **-1.11** - sp 5/2
'98 Dorans Pride - **2-0-2-0-2 (6)** / 1.00 / 0.00 - sp 9/4
'96 One Man - **1-0-4-1-0 (6)** / 1.00 / 0.17 -sp 11/8

Dosage Fact

The last winner to have less than 8 points in their DP was Nortons Coin who was a 100-1 winner in the 1992 renewal.

Vincent O'Brien County Hurdle - Cheltenham

19th March - cl1 g3 hcp - 2m1f - 5yo+

Dosage Strength

★★★★

Year	Horse	DP	tot	DI	CD	Run sty	Field Size	Gng
2009	American Trilogy	2-2-7-0-1	12	1.67	0.33	hu	27	gs
2008	Silver Jaro	2-0-10-2-0	14	1.00	0.14	hu	22	gs
2007	Pedrobob	4-0-8-10-4	26	0.44	-0.38	cp	28	gs
2006	Desert Quest	11-1-20-12-4	48	0.85	0.06	hu	29	gd
2005	Fontanesi	5-1-20-8-4	38	0.73	-0.13	hu	30	gd
2004	Sporazene	6-7-18-3-4	38	1.38	0.21	hu	23	gd
2003	Spirit leader	6-3-3-4-4	20	1.11	0.15	hu	28	gd
2002	Rooster Booster	6-6-6-4-2	24	1.67	0.42	hu	21	gd
2000	Master Tern	2-3-5-8-0	18	0.71	-0.06	hu	21	gf
1999	Sir Talbot	2-2-4-1-11	20	0.43	-0.85	cp	28	gs
1998	Blowing Wind	5-2-7-4-4	22	0.91	0.00	hu	27	gd
1997	Barna Boy	2-7-7-0-2	18	2.27	0.39	hu	20	gd
1996	Star Rage	6-1-9-0-2	18	1.77	0.50	cp	28	gd
1995	Home Counties	2-3-5-0-16	26	0.41	-0.96	hu	23	sft
1994	Dizzy	~~2-0-0-0-0~~	2	~~inf~~	~~2.00~~	cp	24	gd

DP

14/15 had 12 points or more in their Dosage Profile
12/15 had 18 points or more in their Dosage Profile

DI

14/14 had a DI of 2.27 and below
13/14 had a DI of 1.77 and below
10/14 had a DI of 1.38 and below
Majority Range : 0.41 to 1.67 - 86% of winners

CD

14/14 had a CD of 0.50 and below
10/14 had a CD of 0.21 and below
2/14 had a CD below -0.38
Majority Range : -0.38 to 0.42 - 79% of winners

Average

DI 1.10 / CD -0.01

Running Style

fr-0 / cp-4 / hu-11 - Another tough race for front runners with the pace setters drawing a blank in the County Hurdle. Hold up horses hold a strong hand here with 11 victories including 8 of the last 9 runnings.

Summary

The Vincent O'Brien County Hurdle has been a solid race for Dosage strong animals with only 1994 winner Dizzy having less than 12 points in her profile. This handicap hurdle has actually been won by some very stoutly bred individuals with 12/15 having 18 points or more in their profile. DI ratings show that speedy individuals have struggled in the big fields of this 2m1f hurdle with only '97 winner Barna Boy having a DI above 1.77. 10/14 winners had a DI of 1.38 and below with the same number having a CD of 0.21 and below. Horses with stamina heavy Dosage ratings have also faired relatively poorly with only 2 winners being classes as stamina heavy. Both the winners with CD ratings below -0.38, Master Tern & Silver Jaro, won their races with some cut in the ground. Looking into the Dosage Profiles show that every winner had at least 2 points in the Brilliant section of their profile and only the aforementioned Master Tern and Silver Jaro failed to score at least 1 point in the Professional section of their profile.

Notable Defeats

'09 Dave's Dream - 1-1-3-2-5 (12) / **0.41** / **-0.75** - sp 7/2
'08 Wanango - 7-1-2-1-1 (12) / **3.00** / **1.00** - sp 6/1
'07 Fair Along - **1-0-1-0-0 (2)** / 3.00 / 1.00 - sp 3/1
'99 Decoupage - 2-1-6-9-14 (32) / **0.23** / **-1.00 -** sp 100/30

Johnny Henderson Grand Annual Chase - Cheltenham

19th March - cl1 g3 hcp - 2m 110yds - 5yo+

Dosage Strength

Year	Horse	DP	tot	DI	CD	Run sty	Field Size	Gng
2009	Oh Crick	4-0-4-2-0	10	1.50	0.60	hu	18	gs
2008	Tiger Cry	2-0-5-3-0	10	0.82	0.10	hu	17	gs
2007	Andreas	4-0-8-2-0	14	1.33	0.43	hu	23	gs
2006	Greenhope	6-12-0-0-0	18	inf	1.33	fr	23	gd
2005	Fota Island	4-1-1-4-4	14	0.65	-0.21	cp	24	gd
2004	St Pirran	5-0-11-0-0	16	1.91	0.63	hu	21	gd
2003	Palarshan	1-1-10-4-4	20	0.54	-0.45	hu	21	gd
2002	Fadoudal Du Cochet	1-0-4-5-2	12	0.33	-0.58	cp	18	gd
2000	Samakaan	7-1-10-2-6	26	1.00	0.04	hu	16	gf
1999	Space Trucker	4-2-10-8-0	24	0.85	0.08	hu	15	gs
1998	Edredon Bleu	~~0-0-0-2-0~~	2	~~0.00~~	~~-1.00~~	fr	17	gd
1997	Uncle Ernie	4-0-4-6-4	18	0.50	-0.33	hu	16	gd
1996	Kibreet	11-2-11-0-0	24	3.36	1.00	cp	13	gd
1995	Sound Reveille	0-2-4-10-6	22	0.22	-0.91	fr	8	sft
1994	Snitton Lane	6-3-2-1-0	12	5.00	1.17	hu	17	gd

DP

14/15 had 10 points or more in their Dosage Profile
10/15 had 14 points or more in their Dosage Profile

DI

11/14 had a DI of 1.91 and below
8/14 had a DI of 1.00 and below
Majority Range : 0.50 to 1.50 - 57% of winners

CD

11/14 had a CD of 0.63 and below
8/14 had a CD of 0.10 and below
1/14 had a CD below -0.58
Majority Range : -0.45 to 0.63 - 64% of winners

Average

DI 1.39 / CD 0.21

Running Style

fr-3 / cp-3 / hu-9 - Hold up runners have taken the majority of runnings with 9 winners. Front runners have only taken 1 of the past 10 renewals.

Summary

A difficult race for Dosage analysis with winning ratings spanning a fairly wide range. DP totals offer the strongest trend with 14/15 winners having 10 points or more in their Dosage Profile. Only future Queen Mother champion Edredon Bleu defied this statistic. As is to be expected this 2 mile handicap chase is not littered with stamina winners as only Sound Reveille in 1995 had a CD below -0.58. Sound Reveille was also the only winner to fail to have any points in the Brilliant section of their Dosage Profile, highlighting the importance of inherited speed in the Grand Annual Chase.

Notable Defeats

'09 Poquelin - 5-0-5-0-0 (10) / **3.00** / **1.00** - sp 3/1
'03 Ross Moff - 0-1-8-13-4 (26) / **0.24** / **-0.77** - sp 6/1
'95 Around The Horn - 15-1-4-0-0 (20) / **9.00** / **1.55** - sp 7/2

Midlands National - Uttoxeter

20th March - cl1 Lst hcp - 4m1f 110yds - 5yo+

Dosage Strength

Year	Horse	DP	tot	DI	CD	Run sty	Field Size	Gng
2009	Russian Trigger	0-1-4-5-10	20	0.18	-1.20	hu	15	sft
2008	Himalayan Trail	~~1-0-1-4-0~~	6	~~0.33~~	~~-0.33~~	hu	16	gs
2007	Baron Windrush	0-0-3-4-7	14	0.12	-1.29	cp	18	sft
2006	GVA Ireland	0-1-6-1-0	8	1.00	0.00	cp	18	hvy
2005	Philson Run	2-0-7-3-0	12	0.85	0.08	hu	18	gs
2003	Intelligent	4-4-3-0-1	12	3.80	0.83	hu	17	sft
2002	The Bunny Boiler	4-1-3-2-0	10	1.86	0.70	hu	14	hvy
2000	Ackzo	2-2-3-0-11	18	0.44	-0.89	hu	6	gd
1999	Young Kenny	1-0-8-0-11	20	0.33	-1.00	cp	14	gs
1998	Miss Orchestra	2-1-3-0-2	8	1.29	0.13	cp	13	gd
1997	Seven Towers	~~0-0-2-0-0~~	2	~~1.00~~	~~0.00~~	hu	10	gd
1996	Another Excuse	9-6-1-0-6	22	2.38	0.55	hu	17	gd
1995	Lucky Lane	2-2-2-0-4	10	1.00	-0.20	cp	10	sft
1994	Glenbrook D'or	4-2-0-4-2	12	1.00	0.17	hu	15	sft

DP

12/14 had 8 points or more in their Dosage Profile
9/14 had between 10 and 20 points in their Dosage Profile

DI

9/12 had a DI of 1.29 and below
8/12 had a DI of 1.00 and below
1/12 had a DI above 2.38
Majority Range : 0.33 to 1.29 - 58% of winners

CD

9/12 had a CD of 0.17 and below
7/12 had a CD of 0.08 and below
0/12 had a CD between -0.88 and -0.21
Majority Range : -1.29 to 0.17 - 75% of winners

Average

DI 1.19 / CD -0.18

Running Style

fr-0 / cp-5 / hu-9 - 4m1f around Uttoxeter's galloping track has proven too much for front running horses with 0/14 renewals going to the pace setters. Hold up horses having taken the prize on most occasions.

Summary

As is to be expected in a marathon chase run over an extended 4m1f the Dosage ratings tip the scale in favour of stamina based horses. 9/12 winners had a DI of 1.29 and below which can be narrowed slightly as 8/12 had a DI of 1.00 and below. CD ratings also highlight stamina sorts with 9/12 having a CD of 0.17 and below which is narrowed to 7/12 winners having a CD of 0.08 and below. A 'gapping' stat does appear in the CD ratings with 0/12 having a rating between -0.88 and -0.21, however this is more than likely an aberration, though it is a trend that should be kept in mind when handicapping future races. DP totals point towards the Dosage strong with 12 winners having 8 or more points in their profile.

Notable Defeats

'09 Kilcrea Asla - 4-2-6-8-2 (22) / 0.69 / **-0.09** - sp 11/2
'08 Arnold Layne - **0-1-1-0-0 (2)** / 3.00 / 0.50 - sp 13/2
'07 Ladalko - **0-0-1-1-0 (2)** / 0.33 / -0.50 - sp 13/2
'05 D'Argent - **0-1-1-0-0 (2)** / 3.00 / 0.50 - sp 5/1
'03 Coole Spirit - 3-5-5-0-1 (12) / **2.43** / **0.58** - sp 4/1

Festival Novices' Hurdle - Fairyhouse

4th - 7th April - g2 - 2m4f - 4yo+

Dosage Strength

★★★

Year	Horse	DP	tot	DI	CD	Run sty	Field Size	Gng
2009	Oscar Dan Dan	2-0-8-8-2	20	0.43	-0.40	cp	10	gd
2008	Cooldine	0-0-5-3-0	8	0.45	-0.38	cp	9	gs
2007	Aitmatov	1-0-9-3-5	18	0.44	-0.61	hu	8	gd
2006	Vic Venturi	2-1-8-4-1	16	0.78	-0.06	hu	9	gs
2005	Sher Beau	~~1-0-3-2-0~~	6	~~0.71~~	~~0.00~~	cp	7	sft
2004	Sadlers Wings	4-1-20-13-2	40	0.60	-0.20	cp	11	gs
2003	Pay It Forward	1-1-2-3-1	8	0.60	-0.25	cp	7	gf
2002	Thari	11-5-16-4-0	36	2.00	0.64	hu	8	gs
2001	Risk Accessor	3-3-7-0-15	28	0.51	-0.75	cp	6	gs
2000	Boley Lad	~~0-2-2-2-0~~	6	~~1.00~~	~~0.00~~	hu	9	gs
1999	Winter Garden	10-1-7-6-0	24	1.53	0.63	hu	5	gs
1998	Verrazano Bridge	5-0-7-7-0	12	2.43	0.83	hu	5	gd
1997	Moscow Express	3-1-8-4-0	16	1.00	0.19	hu	6	gf
1996	Macallister	5-3-4-0-0	12	5.00	1.08	cp	9	gd
1995	Major Rumpus	1-3-2-2-2	10	1.00	-0.10	hu	8	gf

DP

13/15 had 8 points or more in their Dosage profile
10/15 had 12 points or more in their Dosage profile

DI

10/13 had a DI of 1.53 and below
9/13 had a DI of 1.00 and below
0/13 had a DI below 0.43
Majority Range : 0.43 to 1.00 - 69% of winners

CD

9/13 had a CD of 0.19 and below
8/13 had a CD of -0.06 and below
0/13 had a CD below -0.75
Majority Range : -0.75 to 0.19 - 69% of winners

Average

DI 1.29 / CD 0.05

Running Style

fr-0 / cp-7 / hu-8 - Any front runner attempting this race is up against it as the pace setters have drawn a blank in the last 15 renewals. Close to pace runners and hold up horses are evenly matched with the latter just shading it with 8 victories.

Summary

This 2m4f novice's hurdle sways very much in favour of the stamina heavy animal. 9 of the 13 winners had a DI of 1.00 and below and the same number had a CD of 0.19 and below. To highlight the dominance of the stamina influenced runners even more the stats show that 8/13 had a CD of -0.06 and below with 7 of the last 8 Dosage strong winners having a negative CD rating. Before steaming into any old stamina based horse in future, be aware that no winner had a CD below -0.75. Dosage strong winners come to the fore in this Grade 2 novice race with only 2005 winner Sher Beau and 2000 winner Boley Lad having less than 8 points in their Dosage profile.

Notable Defeats

'09 Roberto Goldback - 3-4-13-0-0 (20) / **2.08** / 0.50 - sp 2/1
'05 Our Ben - 0-2-4-6-2 (14) / **0.40** / -0.57 - sp 2/1
'03 Khetaam - 13-4-11-2-0 (30) / **3.00** / **0.93** - sp even
'02 One Night Out - **0-0-2-4-0 (6)** / 0.20 / -0.67 - sp 2/1

Powers Gold Cup - Fairyhouse

4th - 7th April - g1 - 2m4f - 5yo+

Dosage Strength

Year	Horse	DP	tot	DI	CD	Run sty	Field Size	Gng
2009	Aran Concerto	1-4-5-2-0	12	1.67	0.33	cp	8	gd
2008	Conna Castle	2-0-5-1-0	8	1.29	0.38	hu	4	gs
2007	One Cool Cookie	3-1-6-4-2	16	0.78	-0.06	fr	11	gd
2006	Justified	3-6-6-0-1	16	3.00	0.63	fr	8	gs
2005	Like-A-Butterfly	3-2-4-0-7	16	0.78	-0.38	cp	13	sft
2004	Hi Cloy	5-0-5-0-0	10	3.00	1.00	hu	6	gs
2003	Thari	11-5-16-4-0	36	2.00	0.64	cp	3	gd
2002	Big And Bold	2-3-4-0-1	10	2.33	0.50	cp	11	gs
2001	Sackville	2-1-5-2-2	12	0.85	-0.08	cp	9	gd
2000	Native Upmanship	5-0-9-0-0	14	2.11	0.71	fr	5	sft
1999	Rince Ri	3-0-3-0-2	8	1.29	0.25	cp	14	gs
1998	Delphi Lodge	3-1-8-2-4	18	0.80	-0.17	hu	11	gs
1997	Dorans Pride	~~2-0-2-0-2~~	6	~~1.00~~	~~0.00~~	cp	6	gf
1996	Love The Lord	3-9-8-0-0	20	4.00	0.75	hu	5	gd
1995	Strong Platinum	3-3-4-4-2	16	1.00	0.06	cp	9	gf

DP

14/15 had 8 points or more in their Dosage Profile
13/15 had between 8 and 20 points in their Dosage Profile

DI

14/14 had a DI of 0.78 and above
10/14 had a DI of 1.00 and above
9/14 had a DI of 1.29 and above
Majority Range : **0.78 to 2.33 - 79% of winners**

CD

14/14 had a CD of -0.38 and above
12/14 had a CD of -0.08 and above
1/14 had a CD above 0.75
Majority Range : **-0.08 to 0.64 - 64% of winners**

Average

DI 1.78 / CD 0.33

Running Style

fr-3 / cp-8 / hu-4 - Close to pace runners have the best record in this novice chase with 8 victories. Although only having 3 wins to their name front runners have actually taken 2 of the last 4 renewals.

Summary

The Powers Gold Cup favours horses with plenty of speed in their Dosage. 14/14 winners had a DI of 0.78 and above, being narrowed to 10/14 with a DI of 1.00 and above. CD ratings follow the same pattern with 14/14 having a CD of -0.38 and above, being narrowed again to 10/14 with a CD of 0.06 and above. DP totals highlight the advantage of being Dosage strong with every winner, except the constant thorn in the side of Dosage Dorans Pride, having 8 points or more in their profile. The Dosage Profiles themselves also tell of the need for speed with every winner having at least 1 point in the Brilliant section of their profile, the majority actually having 3 points or more.

Notable Defeats

'08 Big Zeb - 4-0-8-8-2 (22) / **0.57** / **-0.18** - sp evens
'06 Missed That - 1-0-4-6-1 (12) / **0.33** / **-0.50** - sp 4/1
'05 Carrigeen Victor - 2-0-6-6-0 (14) / **0.56** / **-0.14** - sp 9/2
'04 Kicking King - 2-0-8-8-2 (20) / **0.43** / **-0.40** - sp 9/4
'99 Micko's Dream - 2-1-7-2-4 (16) / **0.68** / **-0.31** - sp 4/1

Irish Grand National - Fairyhouse

5th April - Grade A hcp - 3m5f - 5yo+

Dosage Strength

Year	Horse	DP	tot	DI	CD	Run sty	Field Size	Gng
2009	Niche Market	1-2-3-4-2	12	0.60	-0.33	hu	28	gd
2008	Hear The Echo	1-2-5-0-0	8	2.20	0.50	hu	23	gs
2007	Butlers Cabin	6-2-10-6-0	24	1.18	0.33	hu	29	gd
2006	Point Barrow	3-3-2-2-2	12	1.40	0.25	hu	26	gd
2005	Numbersixvalverde	2-0-0-6-2	10	0.25	-0.60	hu	26	sft
2004	Granit D'Estruval	2-0-2-8-2	14	0.27	-0.57	cp	28	gs
2003	Timbera	3-0-8-0-13	24	0.41	-0.83	cp	21	gd
2002	The Bunny Boiler	4-1-3-2-0	10	1.86	0.70	hu	17	gs
2001	Davids Lad	0-0-4-0-4	8	0.33	-1.00	hu	19	gd
2000	Commanche Court	4-0-5-2-13	24	0.37	-0.83	hu	24	gs
1999	Glebe Lad	2-0-2-4-2	10	0.43	-0.40	hu	18	gs
1998	Bobbyjo	5-1-4-6-4	20	0.67	-0.15	hu	22	gs
1997	Mudahim	5-5-10-4-0	24	1.67	0.46	hu	20	gd
1996	Feathered Gale	3-3-4-4-2	16	1.00	0.06	hu	17	gd
1995	Flashing Steel	7-7-4-2-0	20	4.00	0.95	cp	18	gd

DP

15/15 had 8 points or more in their Dosage Profile
13/15 had between 10 and 24 points in their Dosage Profile

DI

13/15 had a DI of 1.86 and below
11/15 had a DI of 1.40 and below
10/15 had a DI of 1.18 and below
Majority Range : 0.25 to 1.18 - 67% of winners

CD

11/15 had a CD of 0.33 and below
9/15 had a CD of 0.06 and below
Majority Range : -1.00 to 0.25 - 67% of winners

Average

DI 1.11 / CD -0.10

Running Style

fr-0 / cp-3 / hu-12 - A strong bias at play here with 80% of winners being held up during the race. Front runners have an abysmal record with 0/15 renewals going the way of horses attempting to make all from the front.

Summary

The strongest Dosage pointer in the Irish National comes in the way of DP totals, with all 15 winners holding 8 points or more in their profile. CD ratings have a slight bias towards stamina with 9/15 having a CD of 0.06 or below. A similar picture is painted on the DI side with 9/15 having a DI of 1.00 and below. Generally there is a fairly even spread of the Dosage figures and not the heavy bias towards stamina you may expect from a national. The ground conditions are likely to have a bearing on this with only the 2005 running being run on ground worse than good to soft. Interestingly only Davids Lad failed to score any points in the Brilliant section of his Dosage Profile, every other winner had at least 1 point of inherited speed.

Notable Defeats

'08 Royal County Star - 4-0-4-0-0 (8) / **3.00** / **1.00** - sp 6/1
'06 Dun Doire - 3-5-5-0-1 (14) / **3.00** / **0.64** - sp 9/2
'02 Rathbawn Prince - 3-4-4-0-1 (12) / **3.00** / 0.67 - sp 13/2

Dosage Fact

Desert Orchid was the last horse to front run his way to glory when taking the 1989 renewal.

Dunboyne Novices' Hurdle - Fairyhouse

4th - 7th April - g2 - 2m - 4yo+

Dosage Strength

Year	Horse	DP	tot	DI	CD	Run sty	Field Size	Gng
2009	Kempes	2-5-14-5-0	26	1.17	0.15	cp	7	gd
2008	Jered	0-1-3-4-2	10	0.33	-0.70	hu	6	gs
2007	De Valira	5-2-12-4-1	24	1.18	0.25	cp	8	gf
2006	Glenfinn Captain	0-0-1-0-7	8	0.07	-1.75	fr	4	gs
2005	Justified	3-6-6-0-1	16	3.00	0.63	cp	11	sft
2004	Royal Alphabet	5-0-7-4-0	16	1.13	0.38	hu	9	gs
2003	Glenhaven Nugget	4-1-2-4-5	16	0.60	-0.31	cp	5	gf
2002	Scottish Memories	3-0-3-4-2	12	0.60	-0.17	hu	11	gs
2001	Ned Kelly	5-0-7-0-0	12	2.43	0.83	cp	5	gd
2000	Ross Moff	0-1-8-13-4	26	0.24	-0.77	fr	6	gs
1999	Cardinal Hill	3-1-12-4-2	22	0.83	-0.05	cp	6	gs
1998	Unarmed	2-0-5-3-0	10	0.82	0.10	hu	7	gs
1997	Gazalani	3-0-7-8-0	18	0.57	-0.11	cp	7	gd
1996	CastleKellyLeader	6-1-1-4-4	16	0.88	0.06	fr	4	gd
1995	Hotel Minella	4-3-9-0-2	18	1.77	0.39	hu	6	gd

DP

15/15 had 8 points or more in their Dosage Profile
12/15 had 12 points or more in their Dosage Profile

DI

12/15 had a DI of 1.18 and below
9/15 had a DI of 0.88 and below
0/15 had a DI below 0.24
Majority Range : 0.24 to 1.18 - 73% of winners

CD

13/15 had a CD of 0.39 and below
11/15 had a CD of 0.25 and below
9/15 had a CD of 0.10 and below
Majority Range : -0.31 to 0.39 - 67% of winners

Average

DI 1.04 / CD -0.07

Running Style

fr-3 / cp-7 / hu-5 - Close to pace runners get the call here with 7 victories against their name. Front runners have only won 1 of the last 9 renewals.

Summary

Speedily bred runners are noticeable by their absence in this 2 mile novice hurdle with a majority of winners leaning on the stamina side. 12/15 had a DI of 1.18 and below and 13/15 winners had a CD of 0.39 and below. Both these ranges can be narrowed still with 9/15 winners having a DI of 0.88 and below and 11/15 winners having a CD of 0.25 and below. These statistics are slightly surprising as the ground cannot be offered up as an excuse for the poor showing of speed heavy runners as only once has the going been described as worse than good to soft. DP totals offer up a solid trend with all 15 winners being classed as Dosage strong, 12 of those 15 having 12 points or more in their Dosage profile.

Notable Defeats

'09 Donna's Palm - 4-1-5-0-2 (12) / **1.67** / **0.42** - sp 4/1
'08 Made In Taipan - 3-2-2-1-0 (8) / **3.00** / **0.88** - sp 3/1
'07 Sizing Europe - 2-2-6-0-0 (10) / **2.33** / **0.60** - sp 4/1
'06 Jazz Messenger - 4-0-2-1-1 (8) / **1.67** / **0.63** - sp 11/8
'01 Joe Cullen - **2-0-0-2-0 (4)** / 1.00 / 0.50 - sp 3/1

Liverpool (Long Distance) Hurdle - Aintree

8th April - cl1 g1 - 3m 110yds - 4yo+

Dosage Strength

Year	Horse	DP	tot	DI	CD	Run sty	Field Size	Gng
2009	Big Bucks	1-0-4-3-2	10	0.43	-0.50	hu	10	gd
2008	Blazing Bailey	3-0-16-2-9	30	0.58	-0.47	hu	11	gd
2007	Mighty Man	7-2-6-0-1	16	3.00	0.88	cp	6	gd
2006	Mighty Man	7-2-6-0-1	16	3.00	0.88	cp	12	gd
2005	Monet's Garden	0-0-0-2-0	2	0.00	-1.00	hu	9	gs
2004	Iris's Gift	5-0-2-1-0	8	3.00	1.13	fr	8	gd

DP

5/6 had a 8 points or more in their Dosage Profile
4/6 had 10 points or more in their Dosage Profile

DI

3/5 had a DI of 3.00
2/5 had a DI of 0.58 and below
Majority Range : N/A

CD

3/5 had a CD of 0.88 and above
2/5 had a CD of -0.47 and below
Majority Range : N/A

Average

DI 2.00 / CD 0.38

Running Style

fr-1 / cp-2 / hu-3 - Hold up runners have the early advantage in this Aintree version of the stayers hurdle. Only Iris's Gift has taken the race front the front.

Summary

Not much to analyse with only 6 runnings of the Liverpool Hurdle being run, a race that used to be held at Ascot before 2004 when it was called the Long Distance Hurdle. 6 runnings have produced 5 Dosage strong winners with only the course specialist Monet's Garden defying this stat. DI ratings show a mixed return with 3 winners (2 horses) having a DI of exactly 3.00 and 2 winners having a DI of 0.58 and below. CD trends follow the same pattern with 3 winners having a CD of 0.88 and above and the other 2 winners having a CD of -0.47 and -0.50. Looking at the stats available it may be best concentrating on slightly speedier individuals as the flat track and general good ground available at this meeting should play to their strengths here more than it would at Cheltenham.

Notable Defeats

'08 Millenium Royal - **2-0-4-0-0 (6)** / 2.00 / 0.67 - sp 15/2
'04 Sh Boom - 0-1-4-0-7 (12) / **0.33** / **-1.08** - sp 5/1

Dosage Fact

The 2 horses that finished in second spot to the stamina based pair of Big Bucks and Blazing Bailey both had speed orientated Dosage ratings - '09 runner up Mighty Man with DI 3.00 & CD 0.88 and '08 runner up Faasel with DI 2.24 & CD 0.68.

Bowl Chase - Aintree

8th April - cl1 g1 - 3m1f - 5yo+

Dosage Strength

Year	Horse	DP	tot	DI	CD	Run sty	Field Size	Gng
2009	Madison Du Berlais	~~0-0-3-1-0~~	4	~~0.60~~	~~-0.25~~	fr	10	gd
2008	Our Vic	2-0-9-5-0	16	0.68	-0.06	fr	5	gd
2007	Exotic Dancer	4-4-10-3-1	22	1.44	0.32	hu	5	gd
2006	Celestial Gold	~~1-1-0-2-0~~	4	~~1.00~~	~~0.25~~	hu	9	gd
2005	Grey Abbey	2-1-4-4-1	12	0.71	-0.08	fr	8	gs
2004	Tiutchev	2-0-16-0-2	20	1.00	0.00	cp	8	gd
2003	First Gold	2-0-0-4-2	8	0.33	-0.50	fr	7	gd
2002	Florida Pearl	0-0-4-8-6	18	0.13	-1.11	cp	6	gd
2001	First Gold	2-0-0-4-2	8	0.33	-0.50	fr	7	sft
2000	See More Business	0-0-3-6-1	10	0.18	-0.80	fr	4	gd
1999	Macgeorge	8-6-0-2-0	16	7.00	1.25	cp	5	gs
1998	Escartefigue	2-2-16-0-0	20	1.50	0.30	cp	8	gs
1997	Barton Bank	4-2-6-8-2	22	0.69	-0.09	fr	5	gd
1996	Scotton Banks	1-2-5-4-0	12	0.85	0.00	fr	6	gd
1995	Merry Gale	5-3-4-0-2	14	2.50	0.64	hu	6	gd

DP

13/15 had 8 points or more in their Dosage Profile
10/15 had 12 points or more in their Dosage Profile

DI

11/13 had a DI of 1.50 and below
9/13 had a DI of 1.00 and below
Majority Range : **0.33 to 1.50 - 69% of winners**

CD

11/13 had a CD of 0.32 and below
9/13 had a CD of 0.00 and below
1/13 had a CD below -0.80
Majority Range : **-0.50 to 0.32 - 69% of winners**

Average

DI 1.33 / CD -0.05

Running Style

fr-8 / cp-4 / hu-3 - A race for a front runner although it is a stamina based front runner rather than a speedy type, with all front runners having a DI of 0.85 and below.

Summary

Although 2 of the last 4 runnings have gone to Dosage weak animals this is another race to concentrate on the Dosage strong. 13/15 winners had 8 points or more in their Dosage profile with 10/15 having 12 points or more. Whilst Aintree is a flat track and the ground has only once ridden worse than good to soft this 3m1f race still favours horses with Dosage ratings that hint at stamina influences. 9/13 winners had a DI of 1.00 and below with the same number having a CD of 0.00 and below. The Dosage averages are artificially high with the inclusion of 1999 winner Macgeorge's extremely speedy figures. If he were to be removed from analysis the Dosage averages would be a much more realistic DI 0.86 and CD -0.16.

Notable Defeats

'05 Thisthatandtother - 1-2-13-0-0 (16) / **1.46** / **0.25** - sp 5/1
'02 Lord Noelie - 3-3-6-2-0 (14) / **1.80** / **0.50** - sp 2/1
'01 Legal Right - 9-6-21-1-3 (40) / **1.76** / **0.43** - sp 4/1

Dosage Fact

The 2 horses with less than 8 Dosage points were both trained by a Pipe. Celestial Gold by Martin Pipe and Madison Du Berlais by son David Pipe.

4yo Novices' Hurdle - Aintree

8th April - cl1 g1 - 2m 110yds - 4yo

Dosage Strength

★★★★

Year	Horse	DP	tot	DI	CD	Run sty	Field Size	Gng
2009	Walkon	1-1-3-3-0	8	0.78	0.00	cp	13	gd
2008	Binocular	6-0-8-2-0	16	1.67	0.63	cp	10	gd
2007	Katchit	1-2-5-3-1	12	0.85	-0.08	cp	12	gd
2006	Detroit City	11-3-14-0-0	28	3.00	0.89	cp	13	gd
2005	Faasel	10-7-13-4-0	34	2.24	0.68	hu	12	gs
2004	Al Eile	5-4-14-0-5	28	1.33	0.14	cp	18	gd
2003	Le Duc	2-1-9-0-2	14	1.15	0.07	hu	19	gd
2002	Quazar	6-2-11-1-0	20	2.08	0.65	cp	17	gd
2001	Bilboa	3-0-4-8-7	22	0.29	-0.73	hu	14	sft
2000	Lord Brex	1-4-10-1-0	16	1.67	0.31	hu	12	gd
1999	Hors La Loi III	~~2-0-0-4-0~~	6	~~0.50~~	~~0.00~~	cp	6	gs
1998	Deep Water	5-4-7-4-4	24	1.09	0.08	hu	14	gd
1997	Quakers Field	~~1-1-0-2-2~~	6	~~0.50~~	~~-0.50~~	hu	12	gd
1996	Zabadi	6-1-11-4-0	22	1.32	0.41	hu	11	gd

DP

12/14 had 8 points or more in their Dosage Profile
11/14 had 12 points or more in their Dosage Profile

DI

11/12 had a DI of 0.78 and above
9/12 had a DI of 1.09 and above
1/12 had a DI above 2.24
Majority Range : 0.78 to 1.67 - 67% of winners

CD

11/12 had a CD of -0.08 and above
10/12 had a CD of 0.00 and above
1/12 had a CD above 0.68
Majority Range : 0.00 to 0.68 - 75% of winners

Average

DI 1.46 / CD 0.25

Running Style

fr-0 / cp-7 / hu-7 - Unexpectedly a poor race for front runners. No pace setter has been able to make use of Aintree's sharp track with 0/14 renewals going their way. Hold up horses and close to pace horses share the honours.

Summary

Stamina based horses struggle to make an impact in this juvenile novices' hurdle with only the French bred Bilboa winning with a DI below 0.78 and a CD below -0.08. Her stamina based Dosage rating was taken into play by the soft underfoot conditions. 11/12 winners had a DI of 0.78 and above and a CD of -0.08 and above but this speed bias is highlighted even further with 9/12 having a DI of 1.09 and above and 10/12 having a CD of 0.00 and above. Only Detroit City has succeeded in the race with a DI above 2.24 and a CD above 0.68 so any extra fast runners must have a huge class advantage before they can be considered for this race. There have been 2 winners with less than 8 points in their Dosage Profile, however the last 10 winners have all been Dosage strong. The dominance of speed in this race is highlighted once again with all winners having at least 1 point in the Brilliant section of their Dosage Profile.

Notable Defeats

'08 Celestial Halo - 3-0-16-4-5 (28) / **0.65** / **-0.29 -** sp 7/4
'06 Afsoun - 3-0-10-3-2 (18) / **0.80** / **-0.06 -** sp 7/2
'06 Fair Along - **1-0-1-0-0 (2)** / 3.00 / 1.00 - sp 9/2
'01 Azertyuiop - 2-0-2-8-2 (14) / **0.27** / **-0.57 -** sp 5/2

Dosage Fact

The last horse to have 0 points in the Brilliant section of their Dosage Profile was 1992 winner Salwan, with his Dosage rating of 0-0-10-0-0 (10) / 1.00 / 0.00.

Foxhunters Chase - Aintree

8th April - cl2 - 2m5f - 6yo+

Dosage Strength

★★★

Year	Horse	DP	tot	DI	CD	Run sty	Field Size	Gng
2009	Trust Fund	4-2-5-0-3	14	1.55	0.29	hu	29	gd
2008	Christy Beamish	2-2-4-0-0	8	3.00	0.75	cp	19	gs
2007	Scots Grey	1-0-8-6-7	22	0.29	-0.82	fr	27	gd
2006	Katarino	0-0-7-1-0	8	0.78	-0.13	cp	30	gd
2005	Katarino	0-0-7-1-0	8	0.78	-0.13	hu	30	sft
2004	Forest Gunner	9-0-1-0-0	10	19.00	1.80	hu	25	gd
2003	Divet Hill	13-3-5-2-1	24	3.36	1.04	fr	21	gd
2002	Torduff Express	2-2-13-8-1	26	0.68	-0.15	cp	30	gd
2001	Gunner Welburn	5-0-1-1-1	8	2.20	0.88	cp	27	sft
2000	Bells Life	6-0-12-0-4	22	1.20	0.18	cp	26	gd
1999	Elegant Lord	3-3-2-0-0	8	7.00	1.13	fr	23	gs
1998	Cavalero	~~0-0-0-0-6~~	6	~~0.00~~	~~-2.00~~	cp	30	sft
1997	Blue Cheek	4-3-9-0-0	16	2.56	0.69	cp	14	gd

DP

12/13 had 8 points or more in their Dosage Profile
8/13 had between 8 and 16 points in their Dosage Profile

DI

10/12 had a DI of 0.78 and above
8/12 had a DI of 1.20 and above
7/12 had a DI of 1.55 and above
Majority Range : 0.68 to 3.00 - 67% of winners

CD

11/12 had a CD of -0.15 and above
8/12 had a CD of 0.18 and above
7/12 had a CD of 0.29 and above
Majority Range : -0.15 to 0.88 - 67% of winners

Average

DI 3.53 / CD 0.46

Running Style

fr-3 / cp-7 / hu-3 - Sitting close to the pace over the national fences has proven the most effective strategy with 7 winners. Front runners and hold up runners share 3 winners each.

Summary

Not a race for stamina heavy runners with only Scots Grey in 2007 having a DI below 0.68 and a CD below -0.15. This is the strongest statistic to bear in mind when handicapping future races as ratings above this become very patchy, ranging from -0.15 all the way up to 1.80 on the CD side. DP totals highlight the strength of Dosage strong winners in this race with 12/13 having 8 points or more in their profile, the last 11 winners all passing this statistic. A surprising statistic this race throws up is the relatively large number of winners with speed heavy Dosage ratings. Six of the twelve winners had a DI of 2.20 and above and a CD of 0.69 and above. This may indicate that it is more important to have speed over the 2m5f trip when tackling the national fences rather the stamina attributes usually associated with the unique obstacles.

Notable Defeats

'08 Where Now - **2-0-2-0-0 (4)** / 1.00 / 0.50 - sp 8/1
'07 Drombeag - 1-2-1-5-3 (12) / **0.41** / **-0.58** - sp 6/1
'07 Le Passing - **1-1-4-0-0 (6)** / 2.00 / 0.50 - sp 6/1
'05 Cobreces - 1-2-11-3-3 (20) / 0.74 / **-0.25** - sp 15/2

Dosage Fact

The freakishly speedily bred Forest Gunner was followed home in 2nd place in the 2004 renewal by the equally speedily bred Sikander A Azam who had a Dosage rating of 7-3-4-0-0 (14) / 6.00 / 1.21.

Mersey Novices' Hurdle - Aintree

8th April - cl1 g2 - 2m4f - 4yo+

Dosage Strength

★★★★

Year	Horse	DP	tot	DI	CD	Run sty	Field Size	Gng
2009	Bouggler	5-1-9-3-2	20	1.11	0.20	cp	17	gs
2008	Elusive Dream	12-0-24-14-4	54	0.80	0.04	cp	8	gd
2007	Tidal Bay	3-2-4-2-1	12	1.40	0.33	cp	10	gd
2006	Natal	2-1-4-3-0	10	1.00	0.20	hu	11	gd
2005	Turpin Green	0-1-4-5-2	12	0.33	-0.67	hu	9	gs
2004	Garde Champetre	4-3-12-9-2	30	0.76	-0.07	cp	13	gd
2003	Leinster	4-1-1-4-4	14	0.65	-0.21	cp	15	gd
2002	Classified	~~2-2-0-0-0~~	4	~~inf~~	~~1.50~~	hu	12	gd
2001	Montalcino	4-3-15-0-4	26	1.26	0.12	hu	6	sft
2000	Best Mate	1-1-10-5-1	18	0.64	-0.22	fr	5	gd
1999	Barton	4-3-8-5-0	20	1.22	0.30	cp	6	gd
1998	Promalee	4-4-2-2-0	12	3.00	0.83	cp	12	sft
1997	Sanmartino	4-5-10-3-0	22	1.75	0.45	hu	10	gd

DP

12/13 had 10 points or more in their Dosage profile
11/13 had 12 points or more in their Dosage Profile

DI

11/12 had a DI of 0.64 and above
8/12 had a DI of 0.80 and above
2/12 had a DI above 1.40
Majority Range : 0.64 to 1.40 - 75% of winners

CD

11/12 had a CD of -0.22 and above
9/12 had a CD of -0.07 and above
1/12 had a CD above 0.45
Majority Range : -0.22 to 0.45 - 83% of winners

Average

DI 1.16 / CD 0.11

Running Style

fr-1 / cp-7 / hu-5 - Not a race for a front running sort with only the great Best Mate managing to take the race from the front. Close to pace runners have a slightly better record than hold up horses with 7 wins to 5.

Summary

This Grade 2 novice hurdle run over the intermediate trip of 2m4f is best suited to a well balanced individual with a well balanced Dosage Profile. 11/12 winners had a DI of 0.64 and above but only 2 winners had a rating above 1.40. CD ratings take the same route with 11/12 having a CD of -0.22 and above but only 1/12 having a CD of 0.45 and above. DP totals point to a stoutly bred individual with 12/13 having 10 points or more in their profile, only the Martin Pipe trained Classified having a Dosage weak profile. The Dosage Profiles highlight the need for inherited speed with only 2005 winner Turpin Green having 0 points in the Brilliant section of his Dosage Profile.

Notable Defeats

'09 Cape Tribulation - 3-3-13-2-13 (34) / **0.58** / **-0.56** - sp 3/1
'08 Franchoek - 6-1-11-0-0 (18) / **2.27** / **0.72** - sp 9/4
'06 Blazing Bailey - 3-0-16-2-9 (30) / **0.58** / **-0.47** - sp 7/2
'06 Beuna Vista - 2-0-17-17-2 (38) / **0.38** / **-0.45** - sp 4/1

Red Rum Handicap Chase - Aintree

8th April - cl1 g3 hcp - 2m - 5yo+

Dosage Strength

Year	Horse	DP	tot	DI	CD	Run sty	Field Size	Gng
2009	Oh Crick	4-0-4-2-0	10	1.50	0.60	hu	17	gd
2008	Stan	~~2-1-3-0-0~~	6	~~3.00~~	~~0.83~~	cp	18	gd
2007	Bambi De L'orme	2-1-5-0-6	14	0.65	-0.50	hu	15	gd
2006	Jacks Craic	5-5-6-0-0	16	4.33	0.94	hu	16	gd
2005	Fota Island	4-1-1-4-4	14	0.65	-0.21	hu	15	gs
2004	Tidour	6-2-1-3-0	12	2.43	0.92	hu	14	gd
2003	Golden Alpha	6-4-5-1-0	16	3.57	0.94	fr	16	gd
2002	Dark n Sharp	4-1-5-0-0	10	3.00	0.90	hu	15	gd
2001	Aghawadda Gold	2-0-0-4-2	8	0.33	-0.50	fr	12	sft
2000	Jungli	3-0-5-0-0	8	2.20	0.75	fr	7	gd
1999	Flying Instructor	0-0-0-4-4	8	0.00	-1.50	cp	7	gd
1998	Jeffell	~~2-3-1-0-0~~	6	~~11.00~~	~~1.17~~	fr	5	sft
1997	Down the Fell	1-2-1-6-0	10	0.54	-0.20	cp	10	gd
1996	Arctic Kinsman	1-4-7-10-0	22	0.63	-0.18	cp	10	gd
1995	Coulton	4-2-5-0-1	12	2.43	0.67	hu	12	gf

DP

13/15 had 8 points or more in their Dosage Profile
12/15 had between 8 and 16 points in their Dosage Profile

DI

11/13 had a DI of 0.54 and above
7/13 had a DI of 1.50 and above
0/13 had a DI between 0.64 and 1.49
Majority Range : 1.50 to 4.33 - 54% of winners

CD

10/13 had a CD of -0.21 and above
7/13 had a CD of 0.60 and above
0/13 had a CD between -0.17 and 0.59
Majority Range : 0.60 to 0.94 - 54% of winners

Average

DI 1.71 / CD 0.20

Running Style

fr-4 / cp-4 / hu-7 - Hold up horses come out on top here with 7 victories. Front runners have only won 1 of the previous 8 renewals.

Summary

This 2 mile handicap chase, named in honour of the triple Grand National hero Red Rum, has been won by some extremely fast individuals. 7/13 winners had a DI of 1.50 and above and a CD of 0.60 and above, with the DI trend being narrowed slightly to 6/12 winners having a rating of 2.20 and above. However, this is another race that has developed a 'gapping' trend, hinting that horses with a mid range Dosage rating struggle to get competitive in this handicap. 0/13 winners had a DI between 0.64 and 1.49 or a CD between -0.17 and 0.59. The Dosage Profiles advise that inherited speed is an important factor in this race with only '99 winner Flying Instructor failing to score any points in the Brilliant section of his profile.

Notable Defeats

'08 Leslingtaylor - 4-4-16-3-5 (32) / **1.00** / **-0.03** - sp 11/2
'08 Lennon - 1-0-6-5-2 (14) / **0.40** / **-0.50** - sp 5/1
'06 Andreas - 4-0-8-2-0 (14) / **1.33** / **0.43** - sp 7/2
'02 Ichi Beau - 0-0-2-10-6 (18) / **0.06** / **-1.22** - sp 6/1
'00 Samakaan - 7-1-10-2-6 (26) / **1.00** / **0.04** - sp 10/11

Mildmay Novices' Chase - Aintree

9th April - cl1 g2 - 3m1f - 5yo+

Dosage Strength

★★★★

Year	Horse	DP	tot	DI	CD	Run sty	Field Size	Gng
2009	Killyglen	0-1-3-4-2	10	0.33	-0.70	cp	9	gd
2008	Big Bucks	1-0-4-3-2	10	0.43	-0.50	hu	8	gd
2007	Aces Four	2-0-4-2-0	8	1.00	0.25	cp	10	gd
2006	Star De Mohaison	4-1-5-4-2	16	0.88	0.06	cp	15	gd
2005	Like-A-Butterfly	3-2-4-0-7	16	0.78	-0.38	hu	10	gd
2004	Simply Supreme	4-1-1-8-4	18	0.44	-0.39	cp	11	gd
2003	Irish Hussar	4-1-1-4-4	14	0.65	-0.21	fr	9	gd
2002	Barton	4-3-8-5-0	20	1.22	0.30	hu	9	gd
2001	Whats Up Boys	6-1-3-4-4	18	0.89	0.06	cp	7	sft
2000	High Game	3-2-4-0-13	22	0.47	-0.82	cp	8	gd
1999	Spendid	5-5-0-2-0	12	5.00	1.08	hu	7	gd
1998	Boss Doyle	2-0-6-0-2	10	1.00	0.00	cp	8	sft
1997	Cyborgo	~~2-0-0-4-0~~	6	~~0.50~~	~~0.00~~	cp	7	gd
1996	Addington Boy	5-3-2-0-2	12	3.00	0.75	cp	7	gd

DP

13/14 had 8 points or more in their Dosage Profile
12/14 had between 10 and 22 points in their Dosage Profile

DI

11/13 had a DI of 1.22 and below
10/13 has a DI of 1.00 and below
0/13 had a DI below 0.33
Majority Range : 0.33 to 1.22 - 85% of winners

CD

11/13 had a CD of 0.30 and below
9/13 had a CD of 0.06 and below
Majority Range : -0.50 to 0.30 - 69% of winners

Average

DI 1.24 / CD -0.04

Running Style

fr-1 / cp-9 / hu-4 - Front runners are to be avoided in this staying novice chase with only Irish Hussar taking it from the front. Close to pace runners have a comfortable advantage in this race with 9 winners.

Summary

Horses holding a large stock of speed in their Dosage have not enjoyed the test this race has presented them with in recent years. 11/13 winners had a DI of 1.22 and below and a CD of 0.30 and below, being narrowed further with 10/13 having a CD of 1.00 and below and 9/13 having a CD of 0.06 and below. Although speed orientated horses have struggled every winner bar last years victor Killyglen had points in the Brilliant section of their profile. This highlights that even the smallest inherited speed attribute is an advantage when looking to negotiate Aintree's sharp-flat Mildmay course. DP totals point towards the Dosage strong with only 1997 winner Cyborgo having less than 8 points in his profile.

Notable Defeats

'09 Herecomesthetruth - 0-1-1-4-2 (8) / **0.23** / **-0.88** - sp 3/1
'07 Turko - 3-4-7-4-0 (18) / **1.40** / **0.33** - sp 4/1
'04 Royal Emperor - **0-0-2-0-0 (2)** / 1.00 / 0.00 - sp 5/2
'01 Shotgun Willy - 3-1-10-0-0 (14) / **1.80** / **0.50** - sp 4/4

Dosage Fact

Every winner from 1989 until 1995 had a CD rating of 0.00 and below, adding to the poor record of speed based horses.

Sefton Novices' Hurdle - Aintree

9th April - cl1 g1 - 3m110yds - 4yo+

Dosage Strength

Year	Horse	DP	tot	DI	CD	Run sty	Field Size	Gng
2009	Ogee	3-1-6-4-0	14	1.00	0.21	cp	15	gd
2008	Pettifour	4-1-3-4-4	16	0.68	-0.19	fr	13	gd
2007	Chief Dan George	3-3-6-2-0	14	1.80	0.50	hu	10	gd
2006	Black Jack Ketchum	4-0-6-10-2	22	0.47	-0.27	hu	11	gs
2005	Asian Maze	3-2-1-2-0	8	2.20	0.75	fr	17	gd
2004	Accipiter	4-0-12-0-0	16	1.67	0.50	hu	13	gd
2003	Iris's Gift	5-0-2-1-0	8	3.00	1.13	hu	9	gd
2002	Stromness	10-5-19-0-0	34	2.58	0.74	hu	15	gd
2001	Garruth	0-1-6-9-4	20	0.25	-0.80	cp	13	sft
2000	Sackville	2-1-5-2-2	12	0.85	-0.08	hu	17	gd
1999	King's Road	~~2-0-0-4-0~~	6	~~0.50~~	~~0.00~~	fr	15	gd
1998	Unsinkable Boxer	4-0-0-8-10	22	0.22	-0.91	hu	12	sft
1997	Forest Ivory	3-9-8-0-0	20	4.00	0.75	hu	12	gd

DP

12/13 had 8 points or more in their Dosage Profile
10/13 had 12 points or more in their Dosage Profile

DI

10/12 had a DI of 0.47 and above
8/12 had a DI of 0.85 and above
Majority Range : 0.22 to 1.80 - 67% of winners

CD

10/12 had a CD of -0.27 and above
7/12 had a DI of 0.21 and above
1/12 had a CD above 0.75
Majority Range : -0.27 to 0.50 - 50%

Average

DI 1.56 / CD 0.19

Running Style

fr-3 / cp-2 / hu-8 - Hold up horses have taken the most renewals of the Sefton Novices' hurdle with 8 hitting the mark. Close to pace runners have a surprisingly poor recent record with only 1 scoring in the past 8.

Summary

This staying novice event does not produce the amount of stamina winners one would expect for a 3m1f hurdle race. Only Garruth in 2001 and Unsinkable Boxer in 1998 had a DI below 0.47 and a CD below -0.27. 10/12 winners had a DI of 0.47 and above and a CD of -0.27 and above. The most surprising angle this races highlights is the fine record of horses with a CD of 0.50 and above, with 5 of the last 8 renewals going the way of these speedy Dosage types. Once again this is a race dominated by the Dosage strong with 12/13 having 8 points or more in their profile.

Notable Defeats

'09 Weapon's Amnesty - 1-1-4-6-2 (14) / **0.40** / **-0.50** - sp 7/2
'07 Silverburn - 0-1-1-6-2 (10) / **0.18** / **-0.90** - sp 4/1
'03 Pizarro - 1-1-1-5-2 (10) / **0.33** / **-0.60** - sp 5/1
'01 Hindiana - 2-0-0-8-2 (12) / **0.20** / **-0.67** - sp 7/4
'00 Bindaree - 1-1-3-4-1 (10) / 0.54 / **-0.30** - sp 4/1

Melling Chase - Aintree

9th April - cl1 g1 - 2m4f - 5yo+

Dosage Strength

★★★★

Year	Horse	DP	tot	DI	CD	Run sty	Field Size	Gng
2009	Voy Por Ustedes	1-0-6-1-4	12	0.50	-0.58	cp	10	gd
2008	Voy Por Ustedes	1-0-6-1-4	12	0.50	-0.58	hu	6	gd
2007	Monets Garden	~~0-0-0-2-0~~	2	~~0.00~~	~~-1.00~~	cp	6	gd
2006	Hi Cloy	5-0-5-0-0	10	3.00	1.00	cp	11	gd
2005	Moscow Flyer	3-1-6-4-0	14	1.00	0.21	cp	6	gd
2004	Moscow Flyer	3-1-6-4-0	14	1.00	0.21	cp	7	gd
2003	Native Upmanship	5-0-9-0-0	14	2.11	0.71	hu	6	gd
2002	Native Upmanship	5-0-9-0-0	14	2.11	0.71	hu	8	gd
2001	Fadalko	2-0-5-5-0	12	0.60	-0.08	cp	7	sft
2000	Direct Route	3-3-4-2-0	12	2.00	0.58	hu	5	gd
1999	Direct Route	3-3-4-2-0	12	2.00	0.58	hu	6	gd
1998	Opera Hat	3-3-6-0-0	12	3.00	0.75	fr	5	sft
1997	Martha's Son	3-6-5-0-0	14	4.60	0.86	hu	4	gd

DP

12/13 had 10 points or more in their Dosage Profile
11/13 had 12 or 14 points in their Dosage Profile

DI

12/12 had a DI of 0.50 and above
9/12 had a DI of 1.00 and above
7/12 had a DI of 2.00 and above
Majority Range : 1.00 to 3.00 - 67% of winners

CD

10/12 had a CD of -0.08 and above
9/12 had a CD of 0.21 and above
7/12 had a CD of 0.58 and above
Majority Range : 0.21 to 1.00 - 75% of winners

Average

DI 1.87 / CD 0.36

Running Style

fr-1 / cp-6 / hu-6 - Although favouring speedier animals only 1 winner has taken the race from the front. Close to pace and hold up horses share the spoils here.

Summary

Good ground and an easy track allow the speedier types to dominate in this middle distance chase. Apart from the exceptionally talented Voy Por Ustedes and the soft ground winner Fadalko every Melling Chase victor had a DI of 1.00 and above and a CD of 0.21 and above. Looking at the Dosage Profiles again shows the importance of speed in this race - Dosage busting Voy Por Ustedes was the only winner to have gained any points in the Professional column. DP totals favour Dosage strong individuals with only course specialist Monet's Garden having less than 10 points. Although the last 3 results have gone against the grain Voy Por Ustedes only just held on from the "Dosage correct" Schindlers Hunt in the '09 renewal and I expect the stats to come back in line in future renewals.

Notable Defeats

'07 Taranis - **0-0-6-0-0 (6)** / 1.00 / 0.00 - sp 5/1
'03 Edredon Bleu - **0-0-0-2-0 (2)** / 0.00 / -1.00 - sp 5/1
'98 Or Royal - **0-0-1-0-1 (2)** / 0.33 / -1.00 - sp 5/2

Top Novices' Hurdle - Aintree

10th April - cl1 g2 - 2m110yds - 4yo+

Dosage Strength

★★★★

Year	Horse	DP	tot	DI	CD	Run sty	Field Size	Gng
2009	El Dancer	2-0-8-6-0	16	0.60	-0.13	cp	11	gd
2008	Pierrot Lunaire	3-4-12-1-2	22	1.44	0.23	cp	14	gd
2007	Blythe Knight	11-1-12-2-2	28	1.80	0.61	hu	8	gd
2006	Straw Bear	5-1-6-4-4	20	0.82	-0.05	hu	16	gs
2005	Mighty Man	7-2-6-0-1	16	3.00	0.88	hu	7	gd
2004	Royal Shakespeare	5-1-6-6-0	18	1.00	0.28	hu	12	gd
2003	Limerick Boy	3-3-14-0-0	20	1.86	0.45	hu	12	gd
2002	In Contrast	3-0-5-2-0	10	1.22	0.40	cp	11	gd
2001	Ilico II	~~1-3-2-0-0~~	6	~~5.00~~	~~0.83~~	cp	15	sft
2000	Phardante Flyer	1-0-8-0-1	10	1.00	0.00	cp	13	gd
1999	Joe Mac	~~0-0-1-5-0~~	6	~~0.09~~	~~-0.83~~	hu	9	gs
1998	Fataliste	~~3-0-1-2-0~~	6	~~1.40~~	~~0.67~~	fr	10	gd
1997	Midnight Legend	6-4-8-2-0	20	2.33	0.70	cp	9	gd
1996	Tragic Hero	4-1-16-2-1	24	1.18	0.21	hu	15	gd

DP

11/14 had 10 points or more in their Dosage Profile
9/14 had 16 points or more in their Dosage Profile

DI

11/11 had a DI of 0.60 and above
9/11 had a DI of 1.00 and above
2/11 had a DI above 1.86
Majority Range : 0.60 to 1.86 - 82% winners

CD

11/11 had a CD of -0.13 and above
9/11 had a CD of 0.00 and above
8/11 had a CD of 0.21 and above
Majority Range : -0.13 to 0.45 - 73%

Average

DI 1.48 / CD 0.33

Running Style

fr-1 / cp-6 / hu-7 - Front runners have drawn a blank in this race since Fataliste provided them with their only victory in 1998. Hold up horses just shade it over close to pace runners with 7 wins to 6.

Summary

This extended 2 mile novice hurdle is no place for the stamina heavy with 0/13 having a DI below 0.60 or a CD below -0.13. DI and CD ratings highlight the speed leanings of this race with 9/11 having a DI of 1.00 and above and 8/11 having a CD of 0.21 and above. Dosage Profiles indicate the need for inherited speed with every winner having at least 1 point in the Brilliant section of their profile. Runners with vast amounts of speed in their Dosage have however struggled in this novice event with only 2 horses having taken this race with a DI rating above 1.86, Midnight Legend in 1997 and course specialist Mighty Man in 2005.

Notable Defeats

'09 Somersby - 2-0-4-2-4 (12) / **0.50** / **-0.50** - sp 9/2
'03 Glenhaven Nugget - 4-1-2-4-5 (16) / **0.60** / **-0.31** - sp 7/2
'02 Westender - 2-0-17-13-2 (34) / **0.45** / **-0.38** - sp 5/4
'01 Dark Shell - 1-1-6-6-12 (26) / **0.24** / **-1.04** - sp 5/2

Maghull Novices' Chase - Aintree

10th April - cl1 g1 - 2m - 5yo+

Dosage Strength

★★★★

Year	Horse	DP	tot	DI	CD	Run sty	Field Size	Gng
2009	Kalahari King	4-0-8-4-0	16	1.00	0.25	hu	7	gs
2008	Tidal Bay	3-2-4-2-1	12	1.40	0.33	cp	8	gd
2007	Twist Magic	1-0-11-8-2	22	0.42	-0.45	hu	6	gd
2006	Foreman	~~1-0-3-1-1~~	6	~~0.71~~	~~-0.17~~	cp	7	gs
2005	Ashley Brook	4-0-5-1-2	12	1.18	0.25	fr	10	gd
2004	Well Chief	6-1-9-2-0	18	1.77	0.61	hu	10	gd
2003	Le Roi Miguel	3-1-4-2-0	10	1.50	0.50	cp	5	gd
2002	Armaturk	2-0-6-4-2	14	0.56	-0.29	fr	5	gd
2001	Ballinclay King	0-0-8-0-6	14	0.40	-0.86	cp	7	hvy
2000	Cenkos	6-0-2-2-0	10	2.33	1.00	cp	6	gd
1999	Flagship Uberalles	6-1-7-4-0	18	1.40	0.50	cp	7	gs
1998	Direct Route	3-3-4-2-0	12	2.00	0.58	hu	6	gd
1997	Squire Silk	2-4-6-4-0	16	1.29	0.25	hu	6	gd
1996	Ask Tom	3-3-4-2-0	12	2.00	0.58	cp	10	gd
1995	Morceli	5-1-8-2-2	18	1.25	0.28	fr	7	gd

DP

14/15 had 10 or more points in their Dosage Profile
13/15 had between 10 and 18 points in their Dosage Profile

DI

11/14 had a DI of 1.00 and above
9/14 had a DI of 1.25 and above
0.14 had a DI below 0.40
Majority Range : 1.29 to 2.00 - 71% of winners

CD

11/14 had a CD of 0.25 and above
1/14 had a CD above 0.61
1/14 had a CD below -0.45
Majority Range : 0.25 to 0.61 - 71% of winners

Average

DI 1.32 / CD 0.25

Running Style

fr-3 / cp-7 / hu-5 - Close to pace runners just take the honours here with 7 victories. Front runners come off worst with 3 winners.

Summary

Some of the top 2 milers of recent times have taken this Grade 1 novice chase and the Dosage figures highlight speed as being the key to this race. 11/14 had a DI of 1.00 and above and a CD of 0.25 and above with the DI range being narrowed further to 9/14 with a rating of 1.25 and above. Ballinclay King, who had the most stamina influenced rating, won his race on heavy going, the slower ground reducing the impact the speed orientated runners were able to have. Ballinclay king was also the only runner to have had 0 points in the Brilliant section of his profile - every other winner had at least 1 point. DP totals point heavily in the favour of Dosage strong animals with only the German bred Foreman winning with less than 10 points in his profile.

Notable Defeats

'08 Takeroc - **1-1-4-0-0 (6)** / 2.00 / 0.50 - sp 5/2
'07 Fair Along - **1-0-1-0-0 (2)** / 3.00 / 1.50 - sp 7/2
'06 Voy Por Ustedes - 1-0-6-1-4 (12) / **0.50** / **-0.58** - sp 10/11
'05 War Of Attrition - 0-1-3-8-4 (16) / **0.19** / **-0.94** - sp 11/4
'00 Decoupage - 2-1-6-9-14 (32) / **0.23** / **-1.00** - sp 6/4

Dosage Fact

Heavy ground winner Ballinclay King only just clung onto victory by a neck from the speedily bred Whitenzo. Whitenzo's Dosage figures were much more in line with what is usual for a Maghull Novice winner (5-3-15-0-1 (24) / 1.82 / 0.46) showing that even on rain softened ground the speedy horses remain competitive in this 2 miler.

Aintree Hurdle - Aintree

10th April - cl1 g1 - 2m4f - 4yo+

Dosage Strength

★★★★★

Year	Horse	DP	tot	DI	CD	Run sty	Field Size	Gng
2009	Solwhit	4-0-5-0-3	12	1.18	0.17	hu	16	gs
2008	Al Eile	5-4-14-0-5	28	1.33	0.14	cp	9	gd
2007	Al Eile	5-4-14-0-5	28	1.33	0.14	cp	11	gd
2006	Asian Maze	3-2-1-2-0	8	2.20	0.75	fr	9	gs
2005	Al Eile	5-4-14-0-5	28	1.33	0.14	hu	9	gd
2004	Rhinestone Cowboy	3-0-10-1-2	16	1.00	0.06	cp	11	gd
2003	Sacundai	8-0-17-2-7	34	0.94	0.00	hu	11	gd
2002	Ilnamar	~~0-0-0-4-0~~	4	~~0.00~~	~~-1.00~~	cp	14	gd
2001	Barton	4-3-8-5-0	20	1.22	0.30	cp	8	hvy
2000	Mister Morose	~~2-0-0-4-0~~	6	~~0.50~~	~~0.00~~	cp	10	gd
1999	Istabraq	11-9-26-10-0	56	1.43	0.38	hu	7	gd
1998	Pridwell	6-1-21-10-0	38	0.85	0.08	cp	6	sft
1997	Bimsey	0-0-16-0-2	18	0.80	-0.22	cp	7	gd

DP

11/13 had 8 points or more in their Dosage Profile
9/13 had 16 points or more in their Dosage Profile

DI

10/11 had a DI between 0.80 and 1.43
0/11 had a DI below 0.80 or above 2.20
Majority Range : 0.80 to 1.43 - 91% of winners

CD

9/11 had a CD between 0.00 and 0.38
0/11 had a CD below -0.22 or above 0.75
Majority Range : 0.00 to 0.38 - 82% of winners

Average

DI 1.24 / CD 0.18

Running Style

fr-1 / cp-8 / hu-4 - Sitting close to the pace pays handsomely here with 8 victories coming from the position. Front running mare Asian Maze was by far and away the fastest dosage winner.

Summary

This intermediate distance Grade 1 hurdle represents one of the strongest Dosage races on the National Hunt calendar. The last winner to have a negative CD rating was 1997 winner Bimsey - every winner since then has had a CD of 0.00 and above. Further still, only Asian Maze had a CD above 0.38. This leaves a strong CD range of 0.00 to 0.38. On the DI side, again taking out Asian Maze, every winner fell between 0.80 and 1.43. A very workable range on both fronts and a stat that even Best Mate, Inglis Drever, Detroit City and the usual Dosage buster Brave Inca could not overcome. Champion Hurdle and Stayers Hurdle winners have all struggled in this race and with such a small dosage range to work with it really is no surprise. DP totals highlight the Dosage strong, as only Ilnamar in 2002 and Mister Morose in 2000 had less than 8 points in their profile.

Notable Defeats

'09 Celestial Halo - 3-0-16-4-5 (28) / **0.65** / **-0.29** - sp 9/2
'07 Detroit City - 11-3-14-0-0 (28) / **3.00** / **0.89** - sp 7/4
'05 Inglis Drever - 3-0-22-15-2 (42) / **0.50** / **-0.31** - sp 9/4
'01 Best Mate - 1-1-10-5-1 (18) / **0.64** / **-0.22** - sp 3/1

Dosage Fact

Not only was Asian Maze the fastest Dosage winner she also won by the largest margin - 17 lengths.

Grand National Chase - Aintree

10 th April - cl1 g3 hcp - 4m4f - 6yo+

Dosage Strength

★★★★

Year	Horse	DP	tot	DI	CD	Run sty	Field Size	Gng
2009	Mon Mome	~~1-1-2-0-0~~	4	~~3.00~~	~~0.75~~	hu	40	gs
2008	Comply Or Die	2-0-6-4-0	12	0.71	0.00	cp	40	gd
2007	Silver Birch	2-0-4-8-6	20	0.25	-0.80	cp	40	gd
2006	Numbersixvalverde	2-0-0-6-2	10	0.25	-0.60	hu	40	gs
2005	Hedgehunter	8-3-8-2-7	28	1.15	0.11	cp	40	gs
2004	Amberleigh House	5-1-8-2-4	20	1.00	0.05	hu	39	gd
2003	Monty's Pass	3-4-6-0-7	20	1.00	-0.20	cp	40	gd
2002	Bindaree	1-1-3-4-1	10	0.54	-0.30	cp	40	gd
2001	Red Marauder	~~5-0-1-0-0~~	6	~~11.00~~	~~1.67~~	cp	40	hvy
2000	Papillon	0-1-4-1-6	12	0.33	-1.00	cp	40	gd
1999	Bobbyjo	5-1-4-6-4	20	0.67	-0.15	cp	32	gd
1998	Earth Summit	3-0-11-2-0	16	1.13	0.25	cp	37	sft
1997	Lord Gyllene	2-0-2-4-6	14	0.27	-0.86	fr	36	gd
1996	Rough Quest	0-0-6-8-6	20	0.18	-1.00	hu	27	gd
1995	Royal Athlete	~~0-0-0-0-0~~	0	~~inf~~	~~inf~~	hu	35	gd

DP

12/15 had 10 points or more in their Dosage Profile
9/15 had between 12 and 20 points in their Dosage Profile

DI

12/12 had a DI of 1.15 and below
10/12 had a DI of 1.00 and below
8/12 had a DI of 0.71 and below
Majority Range : 0.18 to 1.00 - 83% of winners

CD

12/12 had a CD of 0.25 and below
9/12 had a CD of 0.00 and below
Majority Range : -1.00 to 0.00 - 75% of winners

Average

DI 0.62 / CD -0.38

Running Style

fr-1 / cp-9 / hu-5 - Front runners struggle in the National with only Lord Gyllene making every post a winning one. Sitting close to the pace is the ideal position to win the national from, as with 9 of the last 15 winners.

Summary

Being the longest race on the calendar it comes as no surprise to see the winners enclosure dominated by stamina based horses. The majority of winners had a DI of 1.00 and below and a CD of 0.00 and below, dispelling the bizarre theory held amongst some of the racing crowd that the ideal horse for the National is a 2m/2m4f specialist. The hard facts of the matter are that speedsters do not get home around the gruelling 4m4f National course. DP totals indicate that it pays to side with Dosage strong animals as although 3 winners did win with less than 8 points in their DP they returned at SP's of 40/1, 33/1 and 100/1. Hedgehunter was arguably the classiest winner in the past 15 runnings, highlighted by the fact he held the most points in his Dosage Profile (28).

Notable Defeats

'09 Butler's Cabin - 6-2-10-6-0 (24) / **1.18** / **0.33** - sp 7/1
'07 Monkerhostin - 3-3-6-3-1 (16) / **1.29** / **0.25** - sp 8/1
'05 Forest Gunner - 9-0-1-0-0 (10) / **19.00** / **1.80** - sp 8/1
'03 Shotgun Willy - 3-1-10-0-0 (14) / **1.80** / **1.50** - sp 7/1

Dosage Fact

1990 winner Mr Frisk had by far the fastest Dosage rating of any winner in the past 25 years, 1-4-3-0-0 (8) / 4.33 / 0.75. This speed based Dosage combined with firm ground allowed him to beat the track record, which he still holds.

Aintree Champion Bumper - Aintree

10th April - cl1 g2 - 2m1f - 4-6yo

Dosage Strength

★★★

Year	Horse	DP	tot	DI	CD	Run sty	Field Size	Gng
2009	Sitting Tennant	3-12-12-6-1	34	1.62	0.29	cp	19	gs
2008	Honest John	6-4-16-2-0	28	1.80	0.50	hu	20	gd
2007	Theatrical Moment	3-2-15-1-1	22	1.32	0.23	cp	14	gd
2006	Pangbourne	4-0-4-0-0	8	3.00	1.00	cp	22	gs
2005	The Cool Guy	3-5-5-3-0	16	1.91	0.50	cp	22	gd
2004	Diamond Sal	1-2-14-0-5	22	0.83	-0.27	hu	15	gd
2003	Classic Native	3-0-5-0-0	8	2.20	0.75	hu	21	gd
2002	Kickham	4-3-4-5-4	20	0.82	-0.10	cp	20	gd
2001	The Bajan Bandit	3-0-4-0-13	20	0.33	-1.00	cp	17	hvy
2000	Quadco	3-0-8-0-11	22	0.47	-0.73	hu	19	gd
1999	King of the Castle	2-0-0-6-0	8	0.33	-0.25	hu	17	gd
1998	Kings Road	~~2-0-0-4-0~~	6	~~0.50~~	~~0.00~~	cp	12	sft
1996	Burn Out	4-3-19-2-0	28	1.43	0.32	hu	15	gd
1995	Dante's Cavalier	~~1-0-5-0-0~~	6	~~1.40~~	~~0.33~~	hu	14	gf
1994	Nahla	6-3-4-9-4	26	0.73	-0.08	hu	12	hvy

DP

13/15 had 8 points or more in their Dosage Profile
10/15 had 16 points or more in their Dosage profile

DI

10/13 had a DI of 0.73 and above
7/13 had a DI of 1.32 and above
1/13 had a DI above 2.20
Majority Range : 0.73 to 1.91 - 62% of winners

CD

11/13 had a CD of -0.27 and above
9/13 had a CD of -0.10 and above
2/13 had a CD above 0.50
Majority Range : -0.27 to 0.50 - 69% of winners

Average

DI 1.29 / CD 0.09

Running Style

fr-0 / cp-7 / hu-8 - Front runners have failed to score in the past 15 runnings of this Grade 2 bumper race. Hold up runners just shade it over close to pace runners with 8 wins although close to pace runners have won 4 of the last 5.

Summary

Judged on Dosage ratings the Aintree Champion Bumper is best suited to Dosage strong runners that have a well balanced Dosage Profile. 10/13 winners had a DI of 0.73 and above but only 1 of those winners, 2006 victor Pangbourne, had a rating above 2.20. Similarly, 11/13 winners had a CD of -0.27 and above but only 2 winners had a rating above 0.50. The Bajan Bandit, who had the most stamina influenced rating, won his race in the hock deep heavy ground oflthe 2001 meeting. Although not dominated by speed bred horses every winner had at least 1 point in the Brilliant section of their Dosage Profile with a majority of winners having 3 points or more.

Notable Defeats

'08 Cape Tribulation - 3-3-13-2-13 (34) / **0.58** / **-0.56** - sp 11/2
'06 Alfie Flits - 14-7-15-0-0 (36) / **3.80** / **0.97** - sp 9/4
'05 Noland - 7-6-19-0-0 (32) / **2.37** / **0.63** - sp 5/2
'03 John Oliver - 7-4-13-0-0 (24) / **2.69** / **0.75** - 3/1

Silver Trophy Chase - Cheltenham

14th April - cl1 g2 Lmtd hcp- 2m5f - 5yo+

Dosage Strength

Year	Horse	DP	tot	DI	CD	Run sty	Field Size	Gng
2009	Atouchbetweenacara	3-3-6-0-0	12	3.00	0.75	fr	9	gd
2008	Stan	~~2-1-3-0-0~~	6	~~3.00~~	~~0.83~~	cp	14	gs
2007	Nycteos	1-0-5-4-0	10	0.54	-0.20	fr	6	gd
2006	Our Vic	2-0-9-5-0	16	0.68	-0.06	fr	7	gd
2005	Quazar	6-2-11-1-0	20	2.08	0.65	cp	5	gd
2004	Seebald	8-3-12-7-0	30	1.31	0.40	cp	8	gf
2003	Poliantas	~~0-0-0-0-0~~	0	~~inf~~	~~inf~~	fr	7	gd
2002	Fadalko	2-0-5-5-0	12	0.60	-0.08	cp	3	gf
2000	Upgrade	9-1-10-2-0	22	2.14	0.77	cp	4	sft
1998	The Grey Monk	~~0-0-0-0-2~~	2	~~0.00~~	~~-2.00~~	cp	4	hvy
1997	Strong Promise	4-5-5-2-0	16	2.56	0.69	cp	4	gf
1996	Gales Cavalier	3-3-4-0-0	10	4.00	0.96	fr	3	gd
1994	Gale Again	3-3-6-0-0	12	3.00	0.75	hu	6	gf

DP

10/13 had 10 points or more in their Dosage Profile
8/13 had 12 points or more in their Dosage Profile

DI

10/10 had a DI of 0.54 and above
7/10 had a DI of 1.31 and above
6/10 had a DI of 2.08 and above
Majority Range : 1.31 to 3.00 - 60% of winners

CD

10/10 had a CD of -0.20 and above
7/10 had a CD of 0.40 and above
6/10 had a CD of 0.65 and above
Majority Range : 0.40 to 0.96 - 70% of winners

Average

DI 1.99 / CD 0.46

Running Style

fr-5 / cp-7 / hu-1 - If you start the race out the back you are likely to stay there. Setting the pace or sitting close to the pace is where the winner is most likely to come from.

Summary

A winners roll littered with speed based horses, helped by the fact the ground predominantly rides good or good to firm in this end of season chase. Only 3 winners had a CD on the minus side (none lower than-0.20) so stamina merchants should look to ply their trade elsewhere. 7/10 winners had a CD of 0.40 and above and 6/10 winners had a DI of 2.08 and above, again highlighting that speed is certainly the key at this time of year around the countries most gruelling and testing track. To further illustrate the speed bias all 10 Dosage strong winners had 0 points in the professional column of their Dosage Profile. Surprisingly, on 2 of the 3 occasions the ground was worse than good horses with less than 8 points in their DP won. The softer ground possibly blunting the speed horses advantage.

Notable Defeats

'08 Glenfinn Captain - 0-0-3-0-7 (10) / **0.18** / **-1.40** - sp 7/2
'04 Risk Accessor - 3-3-7-0-15 (28) / **0.51** / **-0.75** - sp 4/1
'96 Viking Flagship - 6-1-7-2-**2** (18) / 1.40 / **0.39** - sp 4/9

Future Champions Novices' Chase - Ayr

17th April - cl1 g2 - 2m4f - 5yo+

Dosage Strength

Year	Horse	DP	tot	DI	CD	Run sty	Field Size	Gng
2009	Deep Purple	5-1-7-2-1	16	1.46	0.44	fr	5	gd
2008	Starzaan	3-4-13-6-4	30	0.82	-0.13	cp	5	gd
2007	Yes Sir (dsq)	3-1-4-0-0	8	3.00	0.88	fr	6	gf
2006	Monets Garden	~~0-0-0-2-0~~	2	~~0.00~~	~~-1.00~~	fr	5	gd
2005	Locksmith	2-2-10-6-4	24	0.60	-0.33	fr	6	gd
2004	Keltic Bard	6-5-9-0-0	20	3.44	0.85	hu	7	gs
2003	Vol Solitaire	2-2-18-0-2	24	1.18	0.08	cp	5	gd
2002	Valley Henry	1-4-10-3-2	20	1.00	-0.05	cp	8	gd
2001	Grey Abbey	2-1-4-4-1	12	0.71	-0.08	fr	7	gf
2000	Gingembre	1-2-9-0-0	12	1.67	0.32	cp	5	gd
1999	Bouchasson	~~0-1-2-3-0~~	6	~~0.50~~	~~-0.33~~	fr	6	sft
1998	Eirespray	3-3-4-2-0	12	2.00	0.58	cp	8	gd
1997	Sparky Gayle	3-3-6-0-0	12	3.00	0.75	cp	8	gd
1996	Addington Boy	5-3-2-0-2	12	3.00	0.75	cp	5	sft
1995	Dancing Paddy	5-6-16-2-5	34	1.27	0.12	cp	3	gf

DP

13/15 had 8 points or more in their Dosage Profile
12/15 had 12 points or more in their Dosage Profile

DI

13/13 had a DI of 0.60 and above
10/13 had a DI of 1.00 and above
8/13 had a DI of 1.27 and above
Majority Range : 1.00 to 3.00 - 69% of winners

CD

13/13 had a CD of -0.33 and above
12/13 had a CD of -0.13 and above
9/13 had a CD of 0.08 and above
Majority Range : -0.13 to 0.88 - 92% of winners

Average

DI 1.78 / CD 0.32

Running Style

fr-6 / cp-8 / hu-1 - Ayr's Chase track suits horses that either front run or sit close to the pace. This is no better demonstrated than in this Grade 2 novices' chase which has been dominated by both running styles over the past 15 runnings.

Summary

This end of season novices' chase has not been a happy hunting ground for stamina heavy runners. The good ground on offer mixed with Ayr's relatively flat course allows horses with a speedier Dosage rating to control this race run over the intermediate distance of 2m4f. 13/13 winners had a DI of 0.60 and above and a CD of -0.33 and above. Both of these ranges can be reduced significantly with 8/13 winners having a DI of 1.27 and above and 9/13 having a CD of 0.08 and above. Only Bouchasson in 1999 and Monets Garden in 2006 had less than 8 points in their Dosage Profile with every other winner being classed as Dosage strong. The Dosage Profiles highlight the importance of speed in the Future Champions Novices' Chase with every winner having at least 1 point in the Brilliant section of their profile.

Notable Defeats

'09 I'msingingtheblues - **0-0-6-0-0 (6)** / 1.00 / 0.00 - sp 6/4
'05 My Will - **0-0-1-1-0 (2)** / 0.33 / -0.50 - sp 10/11
'03 farmer Jack - 3-1-10-3-5 (22) / **0.69** / **-0.27** - sp 15/8
'02 Spring Margot - **2-0-3-1-0 (6)** / 1.40 / 0.50 - sp 100/30
'98 Edelweis Du Moulin - 0-0-6-2-0 (8) / **0.60** / **-0.25** - sp evens

Scottish Champion Hurdle - Ayr

17th April - cl1 g2 Lmtd hcp - 2m - 4yo+

Dosage Strength

★★★★

Year	Horse	DP	tot	DI	CD	Run sty	Field Size	Gng
2009	Noble Alan	4-1-9-4-0	18	1.12	0.28	hu	14	gd
2008	Border Castle	7-9-12-6-4	38	1.38	0.24	cp	16	gd
2007	Emmpat	4-1-6-1-0	12	2.00	0.67	hu	8	gf
2006	Noble Request	1-4-3-0-0	8	4.33	0.75	hu	9	gd
2005	Genghis	5-3-2-4-0	14	1.80	0.64	cp	13	gd
2004	Copeland	3-0-9-4-0	16	0.88	0.13	cp	10	gs
2003	In Contrast	3-0-5-2-0	10	1.22	0.40	cp	5	gd
2002	Milligan	8-7-10-5-0	30	2.00	0.60	cp	5	gd
2001	Ulundi	13-1-24-10-4	52	1.00	0.17	cp	9	gf
2000	Mister Morose	~~2-0-0-4-0~~	6	~~0.50~~	~~0.00~~	fr	4	gd
1999	Fadalko	2-0-5-5-0	12	0.60	-0.08	cp	4	sft
1998	Blowing Wind	5-2-7-4-4	22	0.91	0.00	hu	4	gd
1997	Shadow Leader	2-1-16-4-1	24	0.85	-0.04	hu	11	gd
1996	Alderbrook	2-0-5-0-11	18	0.33	-1.00	hu	9	sft
1995	Home Counties	2-3-5-0-16	26	0.41	-0.96	hu	4	gf

DP

14/15 had 8 points or more in their Dosage Profile
12/15 had 12 points or more in their Dosage Profile

DI

13/14 had a DI of 2.00 and below
10/14 had a DI of 1.38 and below
0/14 had a DI below 0.33
Majority Range : 0.85 to 2.00 - 71% of winners

CD

12/14 had a CD of -0.08 and above
10/14 had a CD of 0.00 and above
9/14 had a CD of 0.13 and above
Majority Range : -0.08 to 0.75 - 86% of winners

Average

DI 1.35 / CD 0.13

Running Style

fr-1 / cp-7 / hu-7 - In contrast to the chase track, Ayr's hurdle track plays to the strengths of close to the pace and held up runners. Only Mister Mororse managed to make all but he did only have 3 opponents.

Summary

Horses with a Dosage Profile leaning on the speed side have dominated this race, especially in recent years. The last 9 winners have all has a CD of 0.13 and above and a DI of 0.88 and above. A possible reason for this may be the increase in field sizes producing races that are run at a more steady pace, allowing the speedier types to get into a better rhythm during the race. Ground conditions have also played a role in the prominence of speedier types with the ground only once riding worse than good in any of the past 9 runnings. DP totals point heavily in favour of the Dosage strong with only 2000 winner Mister Morose having less than 8 points in his profile. Once again the Brilliant column of the Dosage Profiles highlight the significance speed has in this grade 2 race, with 14/14 having at least 1 point in the Brilliant section and 13/14 having at least 2 points.

Notable Defeats

'08 Takeroc - **1-1-4-0-0 (6)** / 2.00 / 0.50 - sp 9/4
'04 Benbyas - 9-1-6-0-0 (16) / **4.33** / **1.19** - sp 7/2
'03 Westender - 2-0-17-13-2 (34) / **0.45** / **-0.38** - sp 11/8
'01 Auetaler - 2-0-17-5-12 (36) / **0.41** / **-0.69** - sp 4/1

Scottish Grand National - Ayr

17th April - cl1 g3 hcp - 4m 110yds - 5yo+

Dosage Strength

Year	Horse	DP	tot	DI	CD	Run sty	Field Size	Gng
2009	Hello Bud	2-2-5-0-1	10	1.86	0.40	fr	17	gd
2008	Iris De Balme	1-0-4-6-7	18	0.20	-1.00	hu	24	gd
2007	Hot Weld	4-1-3-0-0	8	4.33	1.13	fr	23	gf
2006	Run For Paddy	4-0-9-3-0	16	1.13	0.31	hu	30	gd
2005	Joes Edge	4-2-5-5-4	20	0.74	-0.15	hu	20	gd
2004	Grey Abbey	2-1-4-4-1	12	0.71	-0.08	fr	28	gs
2003	Ryalux	6-6-8-0-2	22	2.67	0.64	cp	19	gd
2002	Take Control	~~0-0-2-0-0~~	2	~~1.00~~	~~0.00~~	hu	18	gd
2001	Gingembre	1-2-9-0-0	12	1.67	0.33	hu	30	gf
2000	Paris Pike	6-0-2-0-0	8	7.00	1.50	cp	18	gd
1999	Young Kenny	1-0-8-0-11	20	0.33	-1.00	cp	15	sft
1998	Baronet	~~0-0-2-0-2~~	4	~~0.33~~	~~-1.00~~	cp	18	gd
1997	Belmont King	2-0-2-4-6	14	0.27	-0.86	fr	17	gd
1996	Moorcroft Boy	~~0-0-2-0-0~~	2	~~1.00~~	~~0.00~~	hu	20	sft
1995	Willsford	2-2-0-0-18	22	0.22	-1.36	cp	22	gf

DP

12/15 had 8 points or more in their Dosage Profile
10/15 had between 10 and 22 points in their Dosage Profile

DI

9/12 had a DI of 1.86 and below
7/12 had a DI of 1.13 and below
Majority Range : 0.20 to 1.13 - 58% of winners

CD

9/12 had a CD of 0.40 and below
0/12 had a CD between -0.85 and -0.16
Majority Range : N/A

Average

DI 1.76 / CD -0.01

Running Style

fr-4 / cp-5 / hu-6 - No major advantage to any running style in the Scottish National, hold up horses just take the honours however with 6 wins.

Summary

The Scottish Grand National is a minefield for Dosage analysis with 'gapping' stats appearing on more than one occasion. The best angle to attack this race from may be to strike a negative against heavily speed orientated runners. This may be a dangerous tactic however as 3 speedy types have won since the turn of the century and last years front running winner Hello Bud was not exactly short on pace. DP totals point towards the Dosage strong however there have been 3 Dosage weak winners, the last being Take Control in 2002. The strongest clue finder may actually come from the Dosage Profiles as even though this is a marathon chase every winner had at least 1 point in the Brilliant section of their profile.

Notable Defeats

'07 Nine De Sivola - **0**-0-6-2-0 (8) / 0.60 / **-0.25** - sp 5/1
'05 Cornish Rebel - 1-1-10-5-1 (18) / 0.64 / **-0.22** - sp 9/2
'96 Morgans Harbour - 1-0-7-14-2 (24) / 0.23 / **-0.67** - sp 11/2

Dosage Fact

1971 victor Young Ash Leaf was the last winner to have 0 points in the Brilliant section of their Dosage Profile.

Punchestown Novices' Hurdle - Punchestown

20th - 24th April - g1 - 2m - 5yo+

Dosage Strength

★★★

Year	Horse	DP	tot	DI	CD	Run sty	Field Size	Gng
2009	Hurricane Fly	2-1-9-4-0	16	0.88	0.06	cp	8	sft
2008	Jered	0-1-3-4-2	10	0.33	-0.70	cp	9	gd
2007	Clopf	5-1-8-6-0	20	1.00	0.25	cp	9	gd
2006	Iktitaf	12-4-10-0-0	26	4.20	1.08	hu	7	gd
2005	Wild Passion	2-0-0-1-5	8	0.33	-0.88	cp	8	sft
2004	Brave Inca	0-1-7-9-9	26	0.21	-1.00	cp	13	gs
2003	Back In Front	3-3-14-4-2	26	1.00	0.04	cp	9	gs
2002	Scottish Memories	3-0-3-4-2	12	0.60	-0.17	cp	8	gs
2000	Moscow Flyer	3-1-6-4-0	14	1.00	0.21	cp	7	gs
1999	Cardinal Hill	3-1-12-4-2	22	0.83	-0.05	hu	5	sft
1998	His Song	5-1-8-4-0	18	1.25	0.39	cp	5	hvy
1997	Midnight Legend	6-4-8-2-0	20	2.33	0.70	fr	9	gd
1996	Dance Beat	4-0-12-2-0	18	1.25	0.33	cp	7	sft
1995	Hotel Minella	4-3-9-0-2	18	1.77	0.39	hu	9	gs
1994	Klairon Davis	4-4-0-0-0	8	inf	1.50	hu	10	hvy

DP

15/15 had 8 points or more in their Dosage Profile
12/15 had 12 points or more in their Dosage Profile

DI

12/15 had a DI of 1.25 and below
9/15 had a DI of 1.00 and below
3/15 had a DI below 0.60
Majority Range : 0.21 to 1.25 - 73% of winners

CD

12/15 had a CD of 0.39 and below
19/15 had a CD of 0.25 and below
3/15 had a CD below -0.17
Majority Range : -0.17 to 0.39 - 60% of winners

Average

DI 1.21 / CD 0.14

Running Style

fr-1 / cp-10 / hu-4 - Close to pace runners dominate this race with 10 victories overall and 9 winners in the past 10 renewals. Front runners have had a poor time of it with only Midnight Legend winning it from the front back in 1997.

Summary

The strongest trend available in this Grade 1 novices' hurdle comes from the DP totals. All 15 winners had 8 points or more in their profile with 12/15 having 12 points or more. DI ratings cover a relatively large scale but it may be best to concentrate on well balanced individuals as 8/15 had a DI between 0.60 and 1.25. CD ratings cover a similarly large range and again concentrating on the well balanced horses may be the way forward. In recent years this race has started showing more of a bias towards less speedy types as 9 of the last 10 winners had a DI of 1.00 or below. Whether this trend will continue is open to debate but it is certainly something to keep in mind.

Notable Defeats

'09 Go Native - 0-0-2-4-10 (16) / **0.07** / **-1.50** - sp 100/30
'08 Fiveforthree - **0-0-3-1-2 (6)** / 0.33 / 0.83 - sp 9/4
'02 Adamant Approach - 8-6-2-4-2 (22) / **2.14** / **0.64** - sp 5/4
'97 Toast The Spree - 7-7-10-0-0 (24) / **3.80** / **0.88** - sp 4/1

Punchestown Gold Cup - Punchestown

20th - 24th April - g1 - 3m1f - 5yo+

Dosage Strength

Year	Horse	DP	tot	DI	CD	Run sty	Field Size	Gng
2009	Notre Pere	~~0-0-3-1-0~~	4	~~0.60~~	~~-0.25~~	cp	12	sft
2008	Neptune Collonges	~~0-0-0-2-0~~	2	~~0.00~~	~~-1.00~~	fr	9	gs
2007	Neptune Collonges	~~0-0-0-2-0~~	2	~~0.00~~	~~-1.00~~	cp	10	gd
2006	War Of Attrition	0-1-3-8-4	16	0.19	-0.94	fr	6	gd
2005	Kicking King	2-0-8-8-2	20	0.43	-0.40	cp	6	gs
2004	Beef Or Salmon	3-1-5-0-11	20	0.48	-0.75	hu	6	gd
2003	First Gold	2-0-0-4-2	8	0.33	-0.50	fr	7	gd
2002	Florida Pearl	0-0-4-8-6	18	0.13	-1.11	cp	7	gd
2000	Commanche Court	4-0-5-2-13	24	0.37	-0.83	hu	11	gd
1999	Imperial Call	3-3-4-0-2	12	2.00	0.42	fr	5	gs

DP

7/10 had 8 points or more in their Dosage Profile
6/10 had 12 points or more in their Dosage Profile

DI

6/7 had a DI of 0.48 and below
0/7 had a DI above 2.00
Majority Range : 0.13 to 0.48 - 86% of winners

CD

6/7 had a CD of -0.40 and below
0/7 had a CD above 0.42
Majority Range : -1.11 to -0.40 - 86% of winners

Average

DI 0.56 / CD -0.59

Running Style

fr-4 / cp-4 / hu-2 - Hold up horses come off worst in this Grade 1 championship race with only the 2 winners. Front runners and close to pace runners have hit the mark 4 times each.

Summary

The inclusion of Notre Pere and Neptune Collonges (twice) on the winners rostrum weakens the Dosage strength of this race slightly as both horses are classed as Dosage weak. Of the Dosage strong horses left for analysis 6 of the 7 winners had a DI of 0.48 and below and a CD of -0.40 and below, a definite pointer towards stamina heavy runners. The only horse to have a rating above this was the front running Imperial Call in 1999. Dosage Profiles also point in the direction of stamina heavy runners with every winner having at least 2 points in the Professional section of their profile.

Notable Defeats

'09 Imperial Commander - 3-2-4-2-1 (12) / **1.40** / **0.33** - sp 9/2
'08 Mossbank - 7-2-9-6-0 (24) / **1.29** / **0.42** - sp 7/2
'07 In Compliance - 3-1-6-4-2 (16) / **0.78** / **-0.06** - sp 6/4
'05 Kingscliff - 1-1-6-2-0 (10) / **1.00** / **0.10** - sp 7/2
'03 Native Upmanship - 5-0-9-0-0 (14) / **2.11** / **0.71** - sp 11/4

Dosage Fact

Before 1999 this race was run as a novice event. The last 5 winners of the 'old' race all had a CD above 0.00.

Champion Irish National Hunt Flat Race - Punchestown

20th - 24th April - g1 - 2m - 4-7yo

Dosage Strength

★★★★

Year	Horse	DP	tot	DI	CD	Run sty	Field Size	Gng
2009	Dunguib (dsq)	1-3-8-4-2	18	0.80	-0.17	hu	10	sft
2008	Cousin Vinny	1-2-16-1-0	20	1.22	0.15	cp	17	gd
2007	Mick The Man	2-0-11-5-0	18	0.71	-0.06	cp	19	gd
2006	Leading Run	6-1-3-4-4	18	0.89	0.06	hu	18	gd
2005	Refinement	4-2-6-8-2	22	0.69	-0.09	cp	19	sft
2004	Geill Sli	5-0-7-4-0	16	1.13	0.38	cp	13	gd
2003	Royal Rosa	4-5-14-7-0	30	1.14	0.20	cp	19	gd
2002	Supreme Developer	6-1-3-4-4	18	0.89	0.06	cp	17	gd
2000	Liss A Paoraigh	5-2-6-0-1	14	2.50	0.71	hu	13	gd
1999	Our Bid	~~0-0-1-0-1~~	2	~~0.33~~	~~-1.00~~	cp	19	gs
1998	Kings Road	~~2-0-0-4-0~~	6	~~0.50~~	~~0.00~~	cp	18	hvy
1997	Arctic Camper	3-3-2-0-0	8	7.00	1.13	hu	21	gd

DP

10/12 had 8 points or more in their Dosage Profile
9/12 had 14 points or more in their Dosage Profile

DI

8/10 had a DI of 1.22 and below
0/10 had a DI below 0.69
Majority Range : 0.69 to 1.22 - 80% of winners

CD

8/10 had a CD of 0.38 and below
0/10 had a CD below -0.17
Majority Range : -0.17 to 0.38 - 80% of winners

Average

DI 1.70 / CD 0.24

Running Style

fr-0 / cp-8 / hu-4 - Yet another bumper race where front runners are nowhere to be seen with 0/12 going the way of the pace setters. Close to pace runners have taken most renewals with 8 victories.

Summary

This Grade 1 bumper provides some very strong majority ranges that point firmly in the direction of well balanced individuals. With 80% of winners falling between DI 0.69 and 1.22 and 80% falling between CD -0.17 and 0.38 it is safe to assume Punchestown's 2 mile bumper course very much favours runners with a balanced Dosage Profile. Two speedily bred horses have taken this end of season contest, Artic Camper in 1997 and Liss A Paoraigh in 2000, but stamina heavy winners are nowhere to be seen. The lowest winning CD was last years disqualified winner Dunguib with a rating of -0.17 - any runner turning up with a CD below this in future renewals is likely find it difficult to get themselves into contention. DP totals point to the Dosage strong with 10/12 having 8 points or more in their profile, the last 9 winners all having 14 points or more.

Notable Defeats

'06 Hairy Molly - 0-0-5-9-6 (20) / **0.14** / **-1.05** - sp 11/2
'05 Missed That - 1-0-4-6-1 (12) / **0.33** / **-0.50** - sp 5/4
'04 Blazing Liss - 4-1-3-4-4 / **0.68** / **-0.19** - sp 6/4
'04 Knocknabooly - 3-0-1-14-2 (20) / **0.21** / **-0.60** - sp 4/1

Swordlestown Cup Novices' Chase - Punchestown

20th - 24th April - g1 - 2m - 5yo+

Dosage Strength

★★★

Year	Horse	DP	tot	DI	CD	Run sty	Field Size	Gng
2009	Barker	~~0-0-1-1-0~~	2	~~0.33~~	~~-0.50~~	cp	7	sft
2008	Big Zeb	4-0-8-8-2	22	0.57	-0.18	cp	7	gd
2007	Another Promise	0-2-2-4-2	10	0.43	-0.60	hu	7	gd
2006	Accordion Etoile	5-2-8-4-1	20	1.22	0.30	cp	6	gd
2005	War Of Attrition	0-1-3-8-4	16	0.19	-0.94	cp	7	sft
2004	Say Again	5-2-1-6-2	16	0.88	0.13	hu	5	gd
2003	Le Roi Miguel	3-1-4-2-0	10	1.50	0.50	fr	5	gs
2002	Moscow Flyer	3-1-6-4-0	14	1.00	0.21	cp	6	gd
2000	Tiutchev	2-0-16-0-2	20	1.00	0.00	cp	6	gd
1999	Sydneytwothousand	0-5-3-2-0	10	1.86	0.30	fr	6	gs
1998	Direct Route	3-3-4-2-0	12	2.00	0.58	cp	5	hvy
1997	Jeffell	~~2-3-1-0-0~~	6	~~11.00~~	~~1.17~~	fr	6	gd
1996	Ventana Canyon	1-1-13-5-4	24	0.55	-0.42	cp	7	sft
1995	Strong Promise	3-3-4-4-2	16	1.00	0.06	hu	5	gd
1994	Oh So Grumpy	5-7-2-0-2	16	4.33	0.81	hu	10	gd

DP

13/15 had 10 points or more in their Dosage Profile
11/15 had between 10 and 20 points in their Dosage Profile

DI

11/13 had a DI of 0.55 and above
9/13 had a DI of 0.88 and above
1/13 had a DI above 2.00
Majority Range : 0.43 to 1.50 - 69% of winners

CD

10/13 had a DI of -0.18 and above
9/13 had a DI of 0.00 and above
1/13 had a DI above 0.58
Majority Range : -0.42 to 0.30 - 62% of winners

Average

DI 1.27 / CD 0.06

Running Style

fr-3 / cp-8 / hu-4 - Close to pace runners have managed to get their heads in front on most occasions with 8 victories. Front runners have only won 1 of the last 9 renewals.

Summary

Although the Swordlestown Cup has gone to stamina heavy winners on 3 occasions the majority call is to side with more speed orientated individuals. 9/13 had a DI of 0.88 and above and 9/13 had a CD of 0.00 and above. Only 1 winner has had a DI above 2.00 and a CD above 0.58, '94 winner Oh So Grumpy, so extremely fast runners have also struggled around this undulating 2 miles. DP totals again point to the Dosage strong with only last years winner Barker and 1997 winner Jeffell failing to have 8 points or more in their Dosage Profile.

Notable Defeats

'08 J'y Vole - **0-0-6-0-0 (6)** / 1.00 / 0.00 - sp 3/1
'08 Thyne Again - 2-1-6-9-6 (24) / **0.33** / **-0.67** - sp 100/30
'06 Justified - 3-6-6-0-1 (16) / **3.00** / **0.63** - sp 13/8
'05 Watson lake - 4-1-5-0-0 (10) / **3.00** / **0.90** - sp 7/4

World Series Hurdle - Punchestown

20th - 24th April - g1 - 3m - 4yo+

Dosage Strength

★★★

Year	Horse	DP	tot	DI	CD	Run sty	Field Size	Gng
2009	Fiveforthree	~~0-0-3-2-1~~	6	~~0.33~~	~~-0.83~~	hu	10	sft
2008	Blazing Bailey	3-0-16-2-9	30	0.58	-0.47	cp	12	gd
2007	Refinement	4-2-6-8-2	22	0.69	-0.09	hu	9	gd
2006	Asian Maze	3-2-1-2-0	8	2.20	0.75	fr	12	gd
2005	Carlys Quest	4-3-5-2-0	14	2.11	0.64	hu	9	sft
2004	Rhinestone Cowboy	3-0-10-1-2	16	1.00	0.06	cp	8	gd
2003	Holy Orders	3-4-10-1-0	18	2.00	0.50	hu	6	gs
2002	Limestone Lad	3-3-2-2-2	12	1.40	0.25	fr	9	gd
2000	Rubhahunish	3-1-8-2-4	18	0.80	-0.17	fr	9	gd
1999	Anzum	0-1-6-0-13	20	0.25	-1.25	fr	6	gs
1998	Derrymoyle	5-3-2-0-2	12	3.00	0.75	hu	8	hvy
1997	Paddys Return	3-0-5-8-2	18	0.44	-0.33	cp	8	gd
1996	Derrymoyle	5-3-2-0-2	12	3.00	0.75	hu	10	sft

DP

12/13 had 8 points or more in their Dosage Profile
11/13 had 12 points or more in their Dosage Profile

DI

10/12 had a DI of 0.58 and above
8/12 had a DI of 0.80 and above
7/12 had a DI of 1.00 and above
Majority Range : 0.80 to 3.00 - 75% of winners

CD

11/12 had a CD of -0.47 and above
9/12 had a CD of -0.17 and above
0/13 had a CD above 0.75
Majority Range : -0.47 to 0.64 to 67% of winners

Average

DI 1.46 / CD 0.12

Running Style

fr-4 / cp-3 / hu-6 - No major advantage to any running style in this stayers hurdle, hold up runners holding a slight advantage with 6 winners.

Summary

The most striking trend that arises from the Dosage analysis is the distinct lack of stamina heavy winners over this 3 mile trip. In fact it is horses with a bias towards speed in their Dosage that have won the majority of runnings. Only 1999 winner Anzum can truly be classed as stamina heavy with his Dosage of DI 0.25 and CD -1.25. 10/12 winners had a DI of 0.58 and above and 11/12 winners had a CD of -0.47 and above. These ranges can be reduced further to highlight the lack of prowess shown by the stamina heavy as 8/12 winners had a DI of 0.80 and above and 9/12 winners had a CD of -0.17 and above. What perhaps is most surprising about this stayers race is the number of winners with a DI of 2.00 and above - 5/12 winners having such a rating. A final insult to the stamina heavy comes from the Dosage Profiles with every winner, apart from Anzum, having at least 3 Brilliant points in their profile. Last years winners Fiveforthree was the only winner to be classed as Dosage weak, every other winner had 8 points or more in their profile.

Notable Defeats

'08 Kazal - 1-0-5-2-2 (10) / **0.54** / **-0.40** - sp 4/1
'07 Brave Inca - 0-1-7-9-9 (26) / **0.21** / **-1.00** - sp 3/1
'99 Le Coudray - 1-0-8-4-5 (18) / **0.38** / **-0.67** - sp 1/2
'98 Le Coudray - 4-0-5-2-13 - 4-0-5-2-13 (24) / **0.37** / **-0.83** - sp 5/2

Kerrygold Championship Chase - Punchestown

20th - 24th April - g1 - 2m - 5yo+

Dosage Strength

★★★★

Year	Horse	DP	tot	DI	CD	Run sty	Field Size	Gng
2009	Master Minded	4-1-7-2-0	14	1.55	0.50	fr	6	sft
2008	Twist Magic	1-0-11-8-2	22	0.42	-0.45	cp	9	gd
2007	Mansony	~~1-1-4-0-0~~	6	~~2.00~~	~~0.50~~	hu	7	gd
2006	Newmill	~~0-0-4-2-0~~	6	~~0.50~~	~~-0.33~~	fr	6	gd
2005	Rathgar Beau	~~1-0-3-2-0~~	6	~~0.71~~	~~0.00~~	hu	7	sft
2004	Moscow Flyer	3-1-6-4-0	14	1.00	0.21	cp	7	gs
2003	Flagship Uberalles	6-1-7-4-0	18	1.40	0.50	hu	7	gs
2002	Strong Run	5-3-6-0-0	14	3.67	0.93	cp	7	gs
2000	Get Real	7-3-4-0-2	16	3.00	0.81	fr	7	gs
1999	Celibate	8-1-11-2-4	26	1.26	0.27	fr	6	gs
1998	Big Matt	~~2-0-2-0-0~~	4	~~3.00~~	~~1.00~~	cp	8	hvy
1997	Klairon Davis	4-4-0-0-0	8	inf	1.50	fr	7	gd
1996	Klairon Davis	4-4-0-0-0	8	inf	1.50	cp	8	sft
1995	Strong Platinum	3-3-4-4-2	16	1.00	0.06	hu	9	gs
1994	Saraemma	8-0-1-0-3	12	2.43	0.83	cp	9	hvy

DP

11/15 had 8 points or more in their Dosage Profile
9/15 had 12 points or more in their Dosage Profile

DI

10/11 had a DI of 1.00 and above
8/11 had a DI of 1.26 and above
0/11 had a DI below 0.42
Majority Range : 1.00 to 3.00 - 64% of winners

CD

10/11 had a CD of 0.06 and above
9/11 had a CD of 0.21 and above
7/11 had a CD of 0.50 and above
Majority Range : 0.21 to 0.93 - 64% of winners

Average

DI 1.75 / CD 0.61

Running Style

fr-5 / cp-6 / hu-4 - A fairly even spread of winners here, although close to pace runners just hold the advantage with 6 winners.

Summary

Very much a race dominated by speed with 10 of the last 11 winners having a DI of 1.00 and above and 10/11 having a CD of 0.06 and above. Both these ranges can be narrowed again to highlight the dominance of speed with 8/11 winners having a DI of 1.26 and above and 9/11 having a CD of 0.21 and above. Only the enigmatic Twist Magic has managed to win this Grade 1 chase with a stamina orientated Dosage rating. Dosage Profiles push the importance of speed once more with every winner having at least 1 point in the Brilliant section of their profile and 10/11 having at least 3 points. Four Dosage weak winners are a slight distraction from an otherwise strong Dosage race and with 3 of those Dosage weak winners successful in the past 5 years it would be foolish to eliminate any runner with less than 8 points in future renewals.

Notable Defeats

'09 Big Zeb - 4-0-8-8-2 (22) / **0.57** / **-0.18** - sp 9/2
'06 Fota Island - 4-1-1-4-4 (14) / **0.63** / **-0.21** - sp 9/4
'97 Arctic Kinsman - 1-4-7-10-0 (22) / **0.63** / **-0.18** - sp 7/2
'96 Sound Man - 4-0-2-4-4 (14) / **0.56** / **-0.29** - sp 5/2

Irish Champion Hurdle - Punchestown

20th - 24th April - g1 - 2m - 5yo+

Dosage Strength

★★★★

Year	Horse	DP	tot	DI	CD	Run sty	Field Size	Gng
2009	Solwhit	4-0-5-0-3	12	1.18	0.17	cp	9	sft
2008	Punjabi	2-5-16-1-2	26	1.36	0.15	cp	6	gd
2007	Silent Oscar	3-0-7-8-2	20	0.48	-0.30	cp	8	gd
2006	Macs Joy	4-4-3-3-2	16	1.46	0.31	cp	4	gd
2005	Brave Inca	0-1-7-9-9	26	0.21	-1.00	fr	5	sft
2004	Hardy Eustace	4-2-6-0-2	14	1.80	0.43	cp	9	gd
2003	Quazar	6-2-11-1-0	20	2.08	0.65	cp	6	gs
2002	Davenport Milenium	2-1-6-1-0	10	1.50	0.40	cp	6	gs
2000	Grimes	4-0-4-0-2	10	1.50	0.40	fr	9	gd
1999	Istabraq	11-9-26-10-0	56	1.43	0.38	cp	7	gd

DP

10/10 had 10 points or more in their Dosage Profile
8/10 had 12 points or more in their Dosage Profile

DI

8/10 had a DI of 1.18 and above
7/10 had a DI of 1.36 and above
0/10 had a DI above 2.08
Majority Range : 1.18 to 2.08 - 80% of winners

CD

8/10 had a CD of 0.15 and above
6/10 had a CD of 0.31 and above
0/10 had a CD above 0.65
Majority Range : 0.15 to 0.65 - 80% of winners

Average

DI 1.30 / CD 0.16

Running Style

fr-2 / cp-8 / hu-0 - A nightmare race for hold up runners with 0/10 renewals going the way of horses held up out the back. Close to pace runners have a strong hold on this race with 8 wins in the past 10.

Summary

As is to be expected the Irish Champion Hurdle plays into the hands of horses with a Dosage Profile that is leaning towards speed. 2007 winner Silent Oscar and 2005 winner Brave Inca (who can be classed as the 'champion' Dosage buster) are the only winners to have a DI below 1.18 and a CD below 0.15. 7/10 winners had a DI of 1.36 and above and 6/10 winners had a CD of 0.31 and above, highlighting the strength of runners with speed in their Dosage. This is not to suggest this Grade 1 is tailor made for extra speedy horses as no winner has had a DI above 2.08 or a CD above 0.65. DP totals point heavily in favour of Dosage strong runners with all 10 winners having 10 points or more in their profile.

Notable Defeats

'07 Iktitaf - 12-4-10-0-0 (26) / **4.20** / **1.08** - sp 9/4
'02 Ned Kelly - 5-0-7-0-0 (12) / **2.43** / **0.83** - sp 4/7
'02 Landing Light - 3-3-19-13-10 (48) / **0.48** / **-0.50** - sp 4/1
'00 Stage Affair - 3-2-18-7-4 (34) / **0.70** / **-0.21** - sp 3/1
'00 Blue Royal - 4-2-3-0-9 (18) / **0.71** / **-0.44** - sp 100/30

Dosage Fact

All 10 runners-up were classed as Dosage strong, all holding 8 points or more in their Dosage Profile.

Champion Novices' Hurdle - Punchestown

20th - 24th April - g1 - 2m4f - 4yo+

Dosage Strength

Year	Horse	DP	tot	DI	CD	Run sty	Field Size	Gng
2009	Mikael D'Haguenet	~~0-0-5-1-0~~	6	~~0.71~~	~~-0.17~~	hu	8	sft
2008	Tranquil Sea	2-0-8-4-0	14	0.75	0.00	cp	9	gd
2007	Glencove Marina	3-1-13-5-0	22	0.91	0.09	cp	10	gd
2006	Nicanor	4-3-10-9-0	26	0.86	0.08	fr	8	gd
2005	Asian Maze	3-2-1-2-0	8	2.20	0.75	fr	11	sft
2004	Sadlers Wings	4-1-20-13-2	40	0.60	-0.20	hu	8	gd
2003	Nobody Told Me	5-2-11-4-0	22	1.32	0.36	cp	13	gs
2002	Davenport Millenium	2-1-6-1-0	10	1.50	0.40	hu	8	gd
2000	Whats Up Boys	6-1-3-4-4	18	0.89	0.06	fr	7	gd
1999	Native Upmanship	5-0-9-0-0	14	2.11	0.71	hu	11	gs
1998	Ballygowan Beauty	0-0-2-0-12	14	0.08	-1.71	hu	9	hvy
1997	Istabraq	11-9-26-10-0	56	1.43	0.38	hu	8	gd
1996	Castlekellyleader	6-1-1-4-4	16	0.88	0.06	cp	13	sft
1995	Treble Bob	1-2-16-2-11	32	0.52	-0.63	cp	12	gd

DP

13/14 had 8 points or more in their Dosage Profile
11/14 had 14 points or more in their Dosage Profile

DI

12/13 had a DI of 0.52 and above
10/13 had a DI of 0.75 and above
2/13 had a DI above 1.50
Majority Range : **0.52 to 1.50 - 77% of winners**

CD

11/13 had a CD of -0.20 and above
10/13 had a CD of 0.00 and above
2/13 had a DI above 0.40
Majority Range : **-0.20 to 0.40 - 69% of winners**

Average

DI 1.08 / CD 0.03

Running Style

fr-3 / cp-5 / hu-6 - Hold up runners hold a slender advantage over close to pace runners with 6 victories to 5. Front runners come out worst with 3 wins.

Summary

The strongest trend available in this mid distance novice hurdle comes from DP totals, 13 of the 14 winners had 8 points or more in their profile with only last years winner Mikael D'Haguenet failing this stat. Stamina heavy horses have not shown up well here with only 2 winners having a CD below -0.20, Ballygowan Beauty being the last of these in 1998. The statistics suggest that well balanced runners perform best in this Grade 1 hurdle with the majority ranges highlighting their good record.

Notable Defeats

'08 Fiveforthree - **0-0-3-1-2 (6)** / 0.33 / -0.83 - sp 3/1
'07 Catch Me - 3-3-3-0-1 (10) / **3.00** / 0.70 - sp 11/4
'05 Sher Beau - **1-0-3-2-0 (6)** / 0.71 / 0.00 - sp 7/2
'04 Watson Lake - 4-1-5-0-0 (10) / **3.00** / **0.90** - sp 100/30
'03 Pizarro - 1-1-1-5-2 (10) / **0.33** / **-0.60** - sp 11/8

Champion 4yo Hurdle - Punchestown

20th - 24th April - g1 - 2m - 4yo

Dosage Strength

Year	Horse	DP	tot	DI	CD	Run sty	Field Size	Gng
2009	Jumbo Rio	1-0-8-3-4	16	0.45	-0.56	hu	8	sft
2008	Won In The Dark	7-1-13-5-0	26	1.26	0.38	hu	10	gs
2007	Punjabi	2-5-16-1-2	26	1.36	0.15	hu	10	gd
2006	Quatre Heures	0-1-11-2-0	14	0.87	-0.07	hu	8	gd
2005	United	3-3-10-0-0	16	2.20	0.56	hu	7	sft
2004	Cherub	1-2-12-7-2	24	0.60	-0.29	cp	13	gd
2003	Sporazene	6-7-18-3-4	38	1.38	0.21	hu	12	gs
2002	Quazar	6-2-11-1-0	20	2.08	0.65	hu	19	gd
2000	Topacio	2-1-9-4-0	16	0.88	0.06	cp	14	gd
1999	Katarino	0-0-7-1-0	8	0.78	-0.13	cp	9	gs
1998	Zafarabad	10-3-7-8-8	36	0.85	-0.03	hu	16	hvy
1997	Grimes	4-0-4-0-2	10	1.50	0.40	hu	13	gd
1996	Shaunies Lady	2-1-5-0-0	8	2.20	0.63	cp	20	sft
1995	Shaihar	5-1-12-12-0	30	0.67	-0.03	hu	20	gd
1994	Glenstal Flagship	6-4-10-0-0	20	3.00	0.80	cp	14	gd

DP

15/15 had 8 points or more in their Dosage Profile
11/15 had 16 points or more in their Dosage Profile

DI

13/15 had a DI of 0.67 and above
11/15 had a DI of 0.85 and above
1/15 had a DI above 2.20
Majority Range : 0.60 to 1.50 - 67% of winners

CD

14/15 had a CD of -0.29 and above
12/15 had a CD of -0.07 and above
9/15 had a CD of 0.06 and above
Majority Range : -0.29 to 0.40 - 67% of winners

Average

DI 1.34 / CD 0.18

Running Style

fr-0 / cp-5 / hu-10 - Not a race for a front running juvenile with 0/15 renewals heading the way of the pace setters. Hold up horses have an excellent record with 10 victories including 7 of the last 8 renewals.

Summary

This juvenile hurdle has seen ripe pickings for Dosage strong runners as all 15 winners had 8 points or more in their Dosage Profile. DI stats show that 13/15 winners had a rating of 0.67 and above but only 1 winner had a DI above 2.20. CD stats take a corresponding route with 14/15 having a rating of -0.29 and above but only 1 winner with a CD above 0.65. These statistics highlight the poor performance of stamina based runners with only last years victor, Jumbo Rio, having a DI below 0.60 and a CD below -0.29.

Notable Defeats

'03 Golden Cross - 8-2-12-0-0 (22) / **2.67** / **0.82** - sp 7/2
'00 Regal Exit - 5-4-7-0-0 (16) / **3.57** / **0.88** - sp 3/1
'98 Nomadic - 6-2-2-0-0 (10) / **9.00** / **1.40** - sp 9/2
'97 Quakers Field - **1-1-0-2-2 (6)** / 0.50 / -0.50 - sp 5/4

Celebration Chase - Sandown

24th April - cl1 g2 - 2m - 5yo+

Dosage Strength

Year	Horse	DP	tot	DI	CD	Run sty	Field Size	Gng
2009	Twist Magic	1-0-11-8-2	22	0.42	-0.45	cp	7	gd
2008	Andreas	4-0-8-2-0	14	1.33	0.43	cp	11	gd
2007	Dempsey	3-3-10-0-0	16	2.20	0.56	fr	8	gf
2006	River City	~~0-0-6-0-0~~	6	~~1.00~~	~~0.00~~	hu	4	gf
2005	Well Chief	6-1-9-2-0	18	1.77	0.61	hu	9	gd
2004	Cenkos	6-0-2-2-0	10	2.33	1.00	cp	11	gf
2003	Seebald	8-3-12-7-0	30	1.31	0.40	cp	5	gd
2002	Cenkos	6-0-2-2-0	10	2.33	1.00	fr	5	gd
2001	Edredon Bleu	~~0-0-0-2-0~~	2	~~0.00~~	~~-1.00~~	fr	6	gs

DP

7/9 had 10 pts or more in their Dosage Profile
5/9 had 14 pts or more in their Dosage Profile

DI

6/7 had a DI of 1.31 and above
0/7 had a DI above 2.33
0/7 had a DI below 0.42
Majority Range : **1.31 to 2.33 - 86% of winners**

CD

6/7 had a CD of 0.40 and above
0/7 had a CD above 1.00
0/7 had a CD below -0.45
Majority Range : **0.40 to 1.00 - 86% of winners**

Average

DI 1.67 / CD 0.51

Running Style

fr-3 / cp-4 / hu-2 - Not much advantage to any running style although front runners have only won 1 of the last 7 renewals.

Summary

With only last years winner Twist Magic flying the flag for stamina based horses it is safe to say the speedier types have thrived in this race. 6 of the 7 winners had a DI of 1.31 and above and a CD of 0.40 and above, highlighting the strength of the speed based animals. The 2 mile trip on generally good or better ground played right into the hands of the faster 2 mile chasers such as Cenkos and Dempsey but was a negative for stamina based runners such as Azertyuiop and Fadalko. Apart from the stamina influenced Twist Magic, who did have 1 point, every winner had at least 3 points in the Brilliant section of their Dosage Profile.

Notable Defeats

'05 Azertyuiop - 2-0-2-8-2 (14) / **0.27** / **-0.57** - sp 11/10
'02 Fadalko - 2-0-5-5-0 (12) / **0.00** / **-0.08** - sp 2/1
'01 Tiutchev - 2-0-16-0-2 (20) / **1.00** / **0.00** - sp 9/4

Betfred Gold Cup Handicap Chase - Sandown

24th April - cl1 g3 hcp - 3m5f - 5yo+

Dosage Strength

★★★

Year	Horse	DP	tot	DI	CD	Run sty	Field Size	Gng
2009	Hennessy	0-1-1-4-2	8	0.23	-0.88	cp	15	gd
2008	Monkerhostin	3-3-6-3-1	16	1.29	0.25	hu	19	gd
2007	Hot Weld	4-1-3-0-0	8	4.33	1.13	fr	10	gf
2006	Lacdoudal	2-1-8-5-0	16	0.78	0.00	cp	18	gf
2005	Jack High	2-1-3-8-0	14	0.47	-0.21	hu	19	gd
2004	Puntal	1-0-7-5-7	20	0.29	-0.85	cp	18	gf
2003	Ad Hoc	3-3-4-0-0	10	4.00	0.90	cp	16	gd
2002	Bounce Back	7-1-8-0-0	16	3.00	0.94	hu	20	gd
2001	Ad Hoc	3-3-4-0-0	10	4.00	0.90	hu	25	sft
2000	Beau	1-4-7-2-0	14	1.55	0.29	fr	20	sft
1999	Eulogy	3-0-3-6-2	14	0.47	-0.29	cp	19	gd
1998	Call It A Day	3-3-2-2-2	12	1.40	0.25	hu	19	gs
1997	Harwell Lad	2-1-9-0-0	12	1.67	0.42	hu	9	gf
1996	Life Of A Lord	3-3-6-4-2	18	1.00	0.06	hu	17	gf
1995	Cache Fleur	~~2-0-0-2-0~~	4	~~1.00~~	~~0.50~~	cp	14	gd

DP

14/15 had a 8 points or more in their Dosage Profile
11/15 had between 10 and 18 points in their Dosage Profile

DI

12/14 had a DI of 0.47 and above
9/14 had a DI of 1.00 and above
0/14 had a DI between 1.68 and 2.99
Majority Range : 0.23 to 1.67 - 71% of winners

CD

12/14 had a CD of -0.29 and above
10/14 had a CD of 0.00 and above
0/14 had a CD between 0.43 and 0.89
Majority Range : -0.29 to 0.42 - 57% of winners

Average

DI 1.75 / CD 0.21

Running Style

fr-2 / cp-6 / hu-7 - The Betfred Gold Cup has been a tricky race for front runners, with only 2 victorious in the past 15 renewals. Hold up runners are just favoured over close to pace runners with 7 winners to 6.

Summary

A tricky race for Dosage analysis with the appearance of a 'gapping' statistic muddying the waters slightly. This 'gapping' stat appears between 1.68 & 2.99 on the DI side and 0.43 & 0.89 on the CD side. What this appears to be highlighting is the good record of well balanced horses and the decent record of extremely fast horses. What is certain is the below average performance of stamina heavy horses in this season finale marathon chase. Although both '04 winner Puntal and last years winner Hennessey had ratings well on the stamina side they both only won their races by the smallest of margins, a short head in Puntal's case and a neck in Hennessy's, both almost losing out on the line to runners with more suitable Dosage ratings. DP totals point firmly in favour of Dosage strong winners with only 1995 winner Cache Fleur holding less than 8 points in his profile.

Notable Defeats

'09 Hoo La Baloo - 8-2-10-2-0 (22) / **2.14** / **0.73** - sp 6/1
'08 Iris De Balme - 1-0-4-6-7 (18) / **0.20** / **-1.00** - sp 9/2
'04 Scotmail Boy - 2-0-9-0-5 (16) / 0.68 / **-0.38** - sp 6/1
'03 Killusty - 3-0-5-0-0 (8) / **2.20** / **0.75** - sp 5/1
'02 Frenchmans Creek - **0-0-0-0-2 (2)** / 0.00 / -2.00 / sp 11/4

Swinton Hurdle - Haydock

8th May - cl1 g3 hcp - 2m - 4yo+

Dosage Strength

★★★

Year	Horse	DP	tot	DI	CD	Run sty	Field Size	Gng
2009	Joe Jo Star	2-0-6-2-0	10	1.00	0.20	hu	24	gd
2008	Blue Bajan	2-0-11-5-2	20	0.60	-0.25	hu	24	gd
2007	Leslingtaylor	4-4-16-3-5	32	1.00	-0.03	cp	23	gd
2006	Acambo	2-0-6-2-0	10	1.00	0.20	hu	21	gd
2005	Coat Of Honour	2-1-14-3-8	28	0.56	-0.50	cp	11	gs
2004	Macs Joy	4-4-3-3-2	16	1.46	0.31	hu	19	gd
2003	Altay	1-0-5-8-6	20	0.21	-0.90	hu	14	gs
2002	Intersky Falcon	5-1-16-0-0	22	1.75	0.50	hu	11	gd
2001	Milligan	8-7-10-5-0	30	2.00	0.60	hu	23	gd
2000	Mirjan	3-0-6-5-10	24	0.33	-0.79	cp	22	gd
1999	She's Our Mare	3-2-4-0-13	22	0.47	-0.82	hu	22	gd
1998	Rainbow Frontier	6-4-8-0-4	22	1.75	0.36	hu	16	gd
1997	Dreams End	9-0-15-10-4	38	0.77	0.00	hu	19	gf
1996	Tragic Hero	4-1-16-2-1	24	1.18	0.21	hu	19	gd
1995	Chief Minister	10-0-20-12-4	46	0.77	0.00	cp	13	gf

DP

15/15 had 10 points or more in their Dosage Profile
12/15 had 20 points or more in their Dosage Profile

DI

15/15 had a DI of 2.00 and below
12/15 had a DI of 1.46 and below
10/15 had a DI of 1.00 and below
Majority Range : 0.33 to 1.46 - 73% of winners

CD

13/15 had a CD of 0.36 and below
11/15 had a CD of 0.21 and below
3/15 had a CD below -0.50
Majority Range : -0.25 to 0.50 - 67% of winners

Average

DI 0.99 / CD -0.06

Running Style

fr-0 / cp-4 / hu-11 - Front runners have found it impossible to hold off the large fields in this handicap hurdle with 0 winners in the 15 renewals. Hold up horses on the other hand have thrived thanks the strong pace the large fields have generated, with 11 being successful.

Summary

Although the Swinton Hurdle is generally run on good or firmer ground and is run over the minimum trip on a flat track there has still been a generous amount of winners with a Dosage leaning on the stamina side. 10/15 winners had a DI of 1.00 and below and 11/15 had a CD of 0.21 and below, with the race averages also hinting at a slight stamina preference. The large fields and blistering pace this race is run at may be a contributing factor to these lower than expected averages. Once again the Dosage strong dominate this handicap with all 15 winners having 10 points or more in their profile.

Notable Defeats

'09 Caravel - 7-1-9-2-1 (20) / **1.67** / **0.55** - sp 5/1
'07 Emmpat - 4-1-6-1-0 (12) / **2.00** / **0.67** - sp 6/1
'05 Genghis - 5-3-2-4-0 (14) / **1.80** / **0.64** - sp 3/1
'02 Tucacas - 4-4-8-0-0 (16) / **3.00** / **0.75** - sp 3/1
'97 Northern Starlight - 5-1-8-0-0 (14) / **2.50** / **0.79** - sp 13/2

Appendix A

Current Chefs-de-Race list (correct as of September 2009).

Categories that the Chef's have been assigned to are in brackets after the horse's name.

Abernant (B)	Danzig (I/C)	Mill Reef (C/S)	Rough'n Tumble (B/C)
Ack Ack (I/C)	Dark Ronald (P)	Mossborough (C)	Round Table (S)
Admiral Drake (P)	Discovery (S)	Mr. Prospector (B/C)	Royal Charger (B)
Alcantara II (P)	Djebel (I)	My Babu (B)	Run the Gauntlet (P)
Alibhai (C)	Donatello II (P)	Nashua (I/C)	Sadler's Wells (C/S)
Alizier (P)	Double Jay (B)	Nasrullah (B)	Sardanapale (P)
Alycidon (P)	Dr. Fager (I)	Native Dancer (I/C)	Sea Bird II (S)
Alydar (C)	Eight Thirty (I)	Navarro (C)	Seattle Slew (B/C)
A.P. Indy (I/C)	Ela-Mana-Mou (P)	Nearco (B/C)	Secretariat (I/C)
Apalachee (B)	Equipoise (I/C)	Never Bend (B/I)	Sharpen Up (B/C)
Asterus (S)	Exclusive Native (C)	Never Say Die (C)	Shirley Heights (C/P)
Aureole (C)	Fair Play (S/P)	Nijinsky II (C/S)	Sicambre (C)
Bachelor's Double (S)	Fair Trial (B)	Niniski (C/P)	Sideral (C)
Bahram (C)	Fairway (B)	Noholme II (B/C)	Sir Cosmo (B)
Baldski (B/I)	Fappiano (I/C)	Northern Dancer (B/C)	Sir Gallahad III (C)
Ballymoss (S)	Forli (C)	Nureyev (C)	Sir Gaylord (I/C)
Bayardo (P)	Foxbridge (P)	Oleander (S)	Sir Ivor (I/C)
Ben Brush (I)	Full Sail (I)	Olympia (B)	Solario (P)
Best Turn (C)	Gainsborough (C)	Orby (B)	Son-In-Law (P)
Big Game (I)	Gallant Man (B/I)	Ortello (P)	Speak John (B/I)
Black Toney (B/I)	Graustark (C/S)	Panorama (B)	Spearmint (P)
Blandford (C)	Grey Dawn II (B/I)	Persian Gulf (C)	Spy Song (B)
Blenheim II (C/S)	Grey Sovereign (B)	Peter Pan (B)	Stage Door Johnny (S/P)
Blue Larkspur (C)	Gundomar (C)	Petition (I)	Star Kingdom (I/C)
Blushing Groom (B/C)	Habitat (B)	Phalaris (B)	Star Shoot (I)
Bois Roussel (S)	Hail To Reason (C)	Pharis II (B)	Sunny Boy (P)
Bold Bidder (I/C)	Halo (B/C)	Pharos (I)	Sunstar (S)
Bold Ruckus (I/C)	Havresac II (I)	Pia Star (S)	Sweep (I)
Bold Ruler (B/I)	Heliopolis (B)	Pilate (C)	Swynford (C)
Brantome (C)	Herbager (C/S)	Pleasant Colony (I)	T.V. Lark (I)
British Empire (B)	High Top (C)	Polynesian (I)	Tantieme (S)
Broad Brush (I/C)	His Majesty (C)	Pompey (B)	Teddy (S)
Broomstick (I)	Hoist The Flag (B/I)	Precipitation (P)	The Tetrarch (I)
Bruleur (P)	Hurry On (P)	Pretense (C)	Ticino (C/S)
Buckaroo (B/i)	Hyperion (B/C)	Prince Bio (C)	Tom Fool (I/C)
Buckpasser (C)	Icecapade (B/C)	Prince Chevalier (C)	Tom Rolfe (C/P)
Bull Dog (B)	Indian Ridge (I)	Prince John (C)	Tourbillon (C/P)
Bull Lea (C)	In Reality (B/C)	Princequillo (I/S)	Tracery (C)

Busted (S)	Intentionally (B/I)	Prince Rose (C)	Traghetto (I)
Caro (I/C)	In the Wings (C/S)	Promised Land (C)	Tudor Minstrel (B)
Carson City (B/I)	Key to the Mint (B/C)	Rabelais (P)	Turn-to (B/I)
Chateau Bouscaut (P)	Khaled (I)	Rainbow Quest (C/S)	Ultimus (B)
Chaucer (S)	King Salmon (I)	Raise A Native (B)	Unbridled (B/I)
Chief's Crown (I/S)	King's Bishop (B/I)	Reliance II (S/P)	Vaguely Noble (C/P)
Cicero (B)	La Farina (P)	Relko (S)	Vandale (P)
Clarissimus (C)	Le Fabuleux (P)	Reviewer (B/C)	Vatellor (P)
Colorado (I)	Luthier (C)	Ribot (C/P)	Vatout (S)
Congreve (I)	Lyphard (C)	Right Royal (S)	Vieux Manoir (C)
Count Fleet (C)	Mahmoud (I/C)	Riverman (I/C)	War Admiral (C)
Court Martial (B)	Man O' War (S)	Roberto (C)	What A Pleasure (B)
Creme dela Creme (C/S)	Massine (P)	Rock Sand (C/S)	Wild Risk (P)
Crepello (P)	Midstream (C)	Roman (B/I)	Worden (S)
Damascus (I/C)	Mieuxce (P)		

Sourced from: www.chef-de-race.com/dosage/chefs-de-race/chefs.htm

Appendix B

To explain how the Dosage Profile is calculated we will use Istabraq as our example.

Dosage Profile	Total	Dosage Index	Centre of Distribution
11-9-26-10-0	56	1.43	0.38

Istabraq

To calculate a horse's Dosage Profile (DP) we must first look at its four generation pedigree. Below is Istabraq's four generation pedigree. Chefs-de-Race sires are highlighted in bold and the categories they have been assigned to are in brackets.

<table>
<tr><th>1st Generation</th><th>2nd Generation</th><th>3rd Generation</th><th>4th Generation</th></tr>
<tr><td rowspan="8">**Sadlers Wells (CS)**</td><td rowspan="4">**Northern Dancer (BC)**</td><td rowspan="2">Nearctic</td><td>**Nearco (BC)**</td></tr>
<tr><td>Lady Angela</td></tr>
<tr><td rowspan="2">Natalma</td><td>**Native Dancer (IC)**</td></tr>
<tr><td>Almahmoud</td></tr>
<tr><td rowspan="4">Fairy Bridge</td><td rowspan="2">Bold Reason</td><td>**Hail To Reason (C)**</td></tr>
<tr><td>Lalun</td></tr>
<tr><td rowspan="2">Special</td><td>**Forli (C)**</td></tr>
<tr><td>Thong</td></tr>
<tr><td rowspan="8">Betty's Secret</td><td rowspan="4">**Secretariat(IC)**</td><td rowspan="2">**Bold Ruler (BI)**</td><td>**Nasrullah (B)**</td></tr>
<tr><td>Miss Disco</td></tr>
<tr><td rowspan="2">Somethingroyal</td><td>**Princequillo (IS)**</td></tr>
<tr><td>Imperatrice</td></tr>
<tr><td rowspan="4">Betty Loraine</td><td rowspan="2">**Prince John (C)**</td><td>**Princequillo (IS)**</td></tr>
<tr><td>Not Afraid</td></tr>
<tr><td rowspan="2">Gay Hostess</td><td>**Royal Charger (B)**</td></tr>
<tr><td>Your Hostess</td></tr>
</table>

With this information we can now work out Istabraq's Dosage Profile. To make it easier to visualize I have put the above information into the following table –

Generation	Pts	Stallion	Chefs?	B	I	C	S	P
1st Gen	16	**Sadler's Wells**	Yes	-	-	8	8	-
2nd Gen	8	**Northern Dancer**	Yes	4	-	4	-	-
2nd Gen	8	**Secretariat**	Yes	-	4	4	-	-
3rd Gen	4	**Nearctic**	No	-	-	-	-	-
3rd Gen	4	**Bold Reason**	No	-	-	-	-	-
3rd Gen	4	**Bold Ruler**	Yes	2	2	-	-	-
3rd Gen	4	**Prince John**	Yes	-	-	4	-	-
4th Gen	2	**Nearco**	Yes	1	-	1	-	-
4th Gen	2	**Native Dancer**	Yes	-	1	1	-	-
4th Gen	2	**Hail To Reason**	Yes	-	-	2	-	-
4th Gen	2	**Forli**	Yes	-	-	2	-	-
4th Gen	2	**Nasrullah**	Yes	2	-	-	-	-
4th Gen	2	**Princequillo**	Yes	-	1	-	1	-
4th Gen	2	**Princequillo**	Yes	-	1	-	1	-
4th Gen	2	**Royal Charger**	Yes	2	-	-	-	-
		Totals -		**11**	**9**	**26**	**10**	**0**

It is simply a case of adding up all the points that Istabraq has inherited throughout the four generations in each individual category. By doing this the Dosage Profile is created. From the above we can see that Istabraq's Dosage Profile is **11-9-26-10-0**.

Istabraq is a classic example of what I would call a 'Dosage Heavy' Horse; a horse that has a large number of points in its Dosage Profile. This indicates a horse that has been stoutly bred and comes from a strong line of sires that have a major influence with regards to the thoroughbred race horse.

To calculate a horse's Dosage Index the following equation is used.

(Speed)

$$\frac{\textbf{Brilliant + Intermediate + ½ Classic}}{\textbf{Solid + Professional + ½ Classic}}$$

(Stamina)

If we were to apply this to Istabraq then the equation would look like this –

$$\frac{11 + 9 + 13}{13 + 10 + 0}$$

This gives us Istabraq's Dosage Index of **1.43**.

To calculate a horse's Centre of Distribution the following equation is used.

$$\frac{\textbf{((2 X Brilliant) + Intermediate) – ((2 X Professional) + Solid)}}{\textbf{Total DP Points}}$$

If we were to apply this to Istabraq then the equation would look like this –

$$\frac{((2 \times 11) + 9) - ((2 \times 0) + 10)}{56}$$

This gives us Istabraq's Centre of Distribution rating of **0.38**.

The result of the formula will always be a number between +2 and -2.

Appendix C

Example of how to handicap a race using Dosage Ratings

Let's take a look at the following hypothetical race and narrow down the runners using Dosage.

Cheltenham Gold Cup – cl1 g1 - 3m 2f – Soft

Horse	DP	Total	DI	CD	Run Style
Denman	0-1-1-6-2	10	0.18	-0.90	cp
Tidal Bay	3-2-4-2-1	12	1.40	0.33	cp
Voy Por Ustedes	1-0-6-1-4	12	0.50	-0.58	cp
Cooldine	0-0-5-3-0	8	0.45	-0.38	cp
Air Force One	1-2-3-0-0	6	3.00	0.67	fr
Master minded	4-1-7-2-0	14	1.55	0.50	cp
Mon Mome	1-1-2-0-0	4	3.00	0.75	hu
Forpadydeplasterer	5-1-8-4-0	18	1.25	0.39	cp

As you can see I have included each horse's dosage rating and running style after the horse's name. The Dosage ratings can be found at www.pedigreequery.com and a horses running style can be found at www.racingpost.com. You will have to do a bit of your own research to determine a horses running style but this is not a lengthy process. I personally keep my own spreadsheets with lists of numerous horses Dosage ratings to save me having to go back to www.pedigreequery.com every time I want to study a race.

Once I have gathered the above information I would then turn to the Gold Cup Dosage trends page in this book and start narrowing the field -

- First stop is DP totals. From the analysis we can see that no winner in the past 15 renewals had less than 8 points. Mon Mome and Air Force One are struck of the list.
- Next is DI stats. 11/15 had a DI of 0.89 and below. Master Minded, Forpadydeplasterer and Tidal Bay all have negatives struck against their name.

- Next is CD stats. 11/15 had a CD of -0.06 and below. Once more Master Minded, Forpadydeplasterer and Tidal Bay gain negatives.
- Next I would look at the majority ranges and see if I can eliminate any of the runners that are left. Denman, Voy Por Ustedes and Cooldine all fit within the majority ranges.
- Lastly I would look at running style and see who is most suited to the race. As most winners of the Gold Cup run close to pace and the three left are close to pace runners, no negatives are given.

This leaves Denman, Voy Por Ustedes and Cooldine. From here I would then look to narrow down this group using other form analysis or other stats analysis.

This is a simple, but effective, example of how Dosage can be used to narrow the field; you may of course find other ways to use Dosage to enhance your form study.